Lodge of Saint Andrew

Lodge of Saint Andrew and the Massachusetts Grand Lodge

Anno lucis 5756-5769

Lodge of Saint Andrew

Lodge of Saint Andrew and the Massachusetts Grand Lodge
Anno lucis 5756-5769

ISBN/EAN: 9783337221522

Printed in Europe, USA, Canada, Australia, Japan

Cover: Foto ©Andreas Hilbeck / pixelio.de

More available books at **www.hansebooks.com**

PRESENTATION.

HE LODGE OF ST. ANDREW, at a Regular Quarterly Com
munication in December last, took formal notice of the fact, that a
century had elapsed since on petition of this Lodge, their own
Worshipful Master, General Joseph Warren, was made Grand
Master of Ancient Freemasons in Massachusetts. The occasion
was wholly devoted to that commemoration. By the exercises
of the evening the members of the Lodge were inspired to take action towards
presenting in permanent form, a narrative of the leading masonic events of the
past century and a quarter, which properly belong to the history of "St. Andrew's," and illustrate that of the Order in general. In this view, during the
winter of 1869-70, by official action of the Lodge, "the entire duty of collect
ing, arranging and editing selections from the records and archives of St.
Andrew's Lodge" was placed in committee, with instructions to report in a
"Centennial Memorial." That Committee, having the unanimous sanction of
the brethren of the Lodge, in giving in full the Centennial Celebrations by "St.
Andrew's," — and of putting the Celebration of the last December Quarterly
Communication first in order, inasmuch as the idea of publication originated on
that occasion, — have now the satisfaction of presenting this volume.

In taking leave of the responsibilities which were entrusted to them by the
Brethren of "St. Andrew's," the Committee would express their conviction,
that a perusal of this "Memorial," will quicken the love and veneration of its
members for their ancient Lodge, for the Most Worshipful Grand Lodge of
Massachusetts, and will also win enhanced devotion from the Fraternity in
general, for the ANCIENT SOCIETY OF FREE AND ACCEPTED MASONS.

Memorial Committee.

EZRA PALMER, *Master.*
HAMILTON WILLIS,
THOMAS RESTIEAUX,
WM. F. DAVIS,
S. H. GREGORY,
A. A. WELLINGTON.

BOSTON, JUNE, A. D., 1870.

NEW MASONIC TEMPLE, BOSTON, ERECTED 1864.

THE

LODGE OF SAINT ANDREW,

AND THE

MASSACHUSETTS

GRAND LODGE.

Conditi et Ducati, Anno Lucis

5756 — 5769.

BOSTON:

PRINTED BY VOTE OF THE LODGE OF ST. ANDREW

1870.

CONTENTS.

LODGE OF ST. ANDREW.

1756

AUDI VIDE TACE

CHARTER of the LODGE

NOV. 30. 1756.

To all and sundry to whose knowledge these presents shall come,

GREETING :

SHOLTO CHARLES DOUGLAS, Lord Aberdour, Grand Master of the Free and Accepted Masons of Scotland, with consent of the Brethren of the Grand Lodge of Scotland, hereunto subscribing —

WHEREAS, a petition hath been presented to the Grand Lodge, in name of Isaac DeCoster, David Flagg, George Graham, George Lowder, George Bray, George Hodge, Henry Ammes, William Burbeck, and James Tourner, Free and Accepted Masons, residing at Boston, in New England, praying that they and such other Brethren as they should find to be duly qualified, should be constituted and erected into a Mason Lodge, under the name, title and designation of the LODGE OF ST. ANDREW, to be held in Boston, at New England : which petition having been openly read in presence of the Grand Lodge assembled, it was unanimously Resolved and Ordered, that the desire of the same should be granted.

KNOW YE, THEREFORE, That We, by and with the advice and consent of the Grand Lodge of Scotland, have constituted, erected and appointed, and hereby constitute, erect and appoint the Worshipful Brethren above named, and their successors in all time coming, a true and regular Lodge of Free and Accepted Masons, under the name, title and designation of the Lodge of St. Andrew, to be held at Boston, in New England, and ordain all regular Lodges within Scotland or elsewhere, holding of the Grand Lodge of Scotland, to hold and respect them as such for the future. And We, with advice and consent foresaid, give

and grant to them and their successors, full and ample power to meet, convene
and assemble as a regular Lodge ; to enter and receive Apprentices, pass Fellow-Crafts, and raise Master Masons, upon payment of such regular and reasonable compensations as they shall think proper for supporting their poor decayed
Brethren, widows and orphans, agreeable to their stations, and to elect and
make choice of a Master, Wardens and other Office Bearers, annually or otherwise, as they may have occasion. And we hereby recommend to our foresaid
Brethren so constituted, to obey their superiors in all things lawful and honest,
as becometh the honour and harmonie of Masonry. And that they faithfully
become bound and engaged not to desert said Lodge, and that none of them
presume, upon any pretence whatever, to make separate meetings among themselves, without the consent, approbation, or presence of their Master and Wardens for the time ; nor collect money or other funds separate from the common
stock of their Lodge, to the hurt or prejudice of the poor thereof. The said
Worshipful Brethren being always bound and obliged, as by their acceptance
hereof they faithfully bind and oblige themselves and their successors, in all
time coming, to obey the whole Acts, Statutes, and Regulations of the Grand
Lodge of Scotland, as well these already made, as those hereafter to be made, for
the utility, welfare and prosperity of Masonry in general, and to pay and perform whatever is stipulated or demanded from them for supporting the dignity
of the Grand Lodge, and to record in their Lodge book, which they are hereby
enjoyned to keep, this present Charter of Erection and Constitution, with the
Regulations or By-Laws already made, or hereafter to be made by them from
time to time, with their other proceedings and Annual Elections, as they happen,
to the end the same may be the more readily seen and observed by their Brethren ; subject, nevertheless, to the review of the Grand Lodge aforesaid. And
in like manner the said Brethren and their successors are hereby required to
attend the whole General Meetings and Quarterly Communications of the said
Grand Lodge by their Representatives, being their Master and Wardens for
the time, or by Proxie in their name duly authorized by commission from their
Lodge, such Proxies being Master Masons or Fellow-Crafts, belonging to some
established Lodge, to the end the said Brethren may be duly certified and informed of the proceedings of the Grand Lodge, to whom they may represent
their grievances or any other matters concerning Masonrie, as they shall see
cause. And We hereby declare the precidencie of the foresaid Brethren in the

Grand Lodge to commence from the date of these presents, and appoint this our Charter to be recorded in the book of the Grand Lodge, in terms of the regulations in that behalf.

Given under our hand and seal, in the Grand Lodge, held in St. Mary's Chapel, in the city of Edinburgh, and the Seal of the Grand Lodge is hereunto appended this thirtieth day of November, one thousand seven hundred and fifty-six years.

Apud Edinburgum trigesimo	ABERDOUR, G. M.
Novembris, 1756. Recorded	GEO. FRAZER, D. Grand Mr.
in the Book of the G. Lodge.	RCH'D TOD, Sub G. M.
Pr. ALEX'R DOUGALL, G. Secty.	HENRY CUNINGHAME, S. G. W.
GEO. BEAM, G. Clerk.	WILL. BUDGE, J. G. W.

Composition of two Guineas to this Grand Lodge for the Charter, paid unto

JAMES HUNTER, G. Tr.

Charter of Constitution and New Erection, in favor of the Lodge of Saint Andrew, to be held at Boston, New England, 1756.

[ENDORSEMENT BY THE GRAND LODGE OF MASSACHUSETTS.]

To all the Fraternity of Free and Accepted Masons in the State of Massachusetts, the Most Worshipful ISAIAH THOMAS, Esq., Grand Master of the State aforesaid, sends GREETING:

KNOW YE, that by virtue of the power vested in me as Grand Master, and in conformity to a vote of the Grand Lodge of Massachusetts at their Quarterly Communication, on the 11th day of September, A. L. 5809, I do hereby authorize and empower St. Andrew's Lodge, of Boston, formerly under the jurisdiction of the Grand Lodge of Scotland, but lately admitted under our jurisdiction, to take rank in Grand Lodge, at all their Quarterly Communications, Festivals, and Funerals, and all other regular and constitutional meetings, agreeably to the date of their ancient Charter.

Given under my hand this eleventh day of December, A. L. 5809.

Attest, ISAIAH THOMAS,

JOHN PROCTOR, Gd. Secretary. Grand Master.

Aberdour G M
Geo: Frazer D Grand m.

Rich Tod Sub G M
Henry Cuninghame S. G: W:
Will: Budge J. G. W:

Apud Edinburgum trigesimo Novembris 1756
Recorded in the Books of the Grand Lodge
Alex: Dougall G: Sec.y
Geo: Beam. G. Clerk
James Hunter G. Tr

A

HISTORICAL SKETCH

OF

FREEMASONRY IN SCOTLAND,

WITH

A MEMOIR OF ST. ANDREW.

BY R. W. CHAS. W. MOORE.

THE exact period of the introduction of Freemasonry into Scotland is uncertain. That it existed there at a very early date is generally admitted; though there are no authentic data respecting it, prior to the beginning of the twelfth century.

During what are usually termed the mediaeval, or "dark ages," there appeared in Europe, those travelling associations of architects, which, under the authority and patronage of the See of Rome, were employed almost exclusively by the Papal Church, in the erection of those splendid monasteries and magnificent cathedrals, the remains of which are even now the admiration of the scholar, and the wonder of the popular world. And it is worthy of remark, as an interesting historical reminiscence, that at that period of the history of the Romish hierarchy, "wherever the Catholic religion was taught, the meetings of Freemasons were sanctioned and patronized," through these semi-religious travelling companies of practical builders. This fact is now so generally admitted by the learned, whether friendly or otherwise to our Institution, that it is not deemed necessary here to cite authorities in its support.

When King David I., in the early part of the twelfth century, contemplated the introduction into Scotland, of the Bernardine Monks, and the Abbeys of Melrose, Kelso, and Kilwinning had been projected, one or more of these travelling Lodges, or Guilds, was summoned from the Continent and employed in their erection.

This is the earliest authentic record we have of the appearance of Freemasonry in the kingdom ; unless, indeed, we adopt the theory that the Culdees, as the conjectural successors of the Essenes, were a fraternity of Freemasons. On this hypothesis, the existence of the Order in Scotland may, without difficulty, be traced to a much earlier date. But such an inquiry would be foreign to our present purpose.

It may be remarked, in this connection, that there is extant, in the Hay's MSS. in the Advocates' library at Edinburgh, the record of an ancient Charter of the Craft, which recites that, " for sa meikle as from adge to adge it has been observed amongst us that the Lairds of Roslyn has ever been patrons and protectors of us and our privileges ; " and then proceeds to authorize the Lord of Roslyn to purchase a new recognition and confirmation of that right from the King. This Charter is without date ; but it is doubtless very ancient, being referred to as an old deed in the subsequent Charter of renewal, about the year 1628. In this document we are told that the former Lords of Roslyn had from time to time obtained Charters from several of the kings of Scotland, confirming their jurisdiction over the Masonic Fraternity ; but that these muniments and records were " consumed in ane flame of fire within the Castle of Roslyn," which conflagration occurred in the year 1554, through the depredations of the troops of Henry VIII. King of England.   " These facts," says a distinguished Scotch authority, " confirm the accounts of those historians who relate that the original grant, or Charter of jurisdiction over the Lodges in Scotland, was made by King James II. of that kingdom, to St. Clair, the great Earl of Caithness and Orkney, who founded the chapel of Roslyn Castle about the year 1441." The Order must have flourished in Scotland, continues the writer just quoted, a long time before this ; for otherwise we cannot imagine how its numbers and its consequence should have attracted the notice of the king, nor why the Grand Mastership of the institution should be deemed a gift worthy the acceptance of so distinguished a nobleman. And hence also there is derived additional credit to the assertion of old writers on Masonry, who affirm that King James I. of Scotland, who died A. D. 1437, settled a yearly revenue of four pounds Scots, to be paid by every Master Mason to a Grand Master, to be chosen by the Grand Lodge and approved by the crown. If an institution so worthy of royal patronage and so dignified as to excite the ambition of nobles to preside over its mysteries, had been of recent origin, its foundation, or at least its introduction into Scotland, would have been noted by the historians and annalists of that kingdom. But as no such record is to be found, the conclusion is irresistible that the Order there was of early and uncertain date, and that it was originally venerable and august, or had acquired its elevated and imposing character by imperceptible degrees, in long progression of time.

The foregoing particulars are believed to be sufficient to show, first, that Masonry in Scotland is of great antiquity; and, secondly, that it was originally derived from a pure and legitimate source, — that those companies or Lodges, which were invited into the kingdom by David I. were identical with those "travelling associations of architects" which appeared in Europe during the Middle Ages, under the patronage of the See of Rome. The Masonry of Scotland and the Masonry of England are but different streams flowing from a common fountain.

One of the first Lodges in Scotland, under the present system of organization, of which we have any reliable account, was held at Kilwinning, in Ayrshire, about the close of the fifteenth century. How long it had been in operation before that period, cannot now be ascertained. It is worthy of remark, however, in this connection, that it has always been understood among our Brethren in Scotland, that until the beginning of that century, the "annual assemblies" of the Fraternity, or meetings of the Grand Lodge, were held at Kilwinning, and that this practice continued until their removal to Edinburgh, shortly before the appointment of the St. Clairs as hereditary Grand Masters.

For the period of more than a century and a half subsequent to the granting of the first of the Charters before mentioned, the office of Grand Master of Scotland was filled, without interruption, by the St. Clairs of Roslyn. In the year 1736, William St. Clair, "the last Roslyn," being "under the necessity of alienating his estate, and having no children, was anxious that the office of Grand Master should not become vacant at his death." He accordingly assembled together the Lodges in and about Edinburgh, and having represented to them the advantage that would accrue to the Order by having a nobleman or gentleman *of their own choice* as Grand Master, he graciously intimated his intention of resigning into the hands of the Brethren, every title to that office which he then possessed, or which his successors might claim, either under the grants of the

Scottish Kings, or from the kindness of the Fraternity. In furtherance of this generous and voluntary surrender of his hereditary authority, circular letters were dispatched in the name of "the four Lodges in and about Edinburgh," to all the Lodges in Scotland, inviting them to appear in the metropolis, either personally or by proxies, on the next St. Andrew's day, to concur in the election of a Grand Master for Scotland. Thirty-three Lodges were represented at the meeting held in pursuance of this invitation. The Deed of Resignation was read and accepted. To the great honor of the Brethren present, the first use they made of their newly acquired power was, by their free suffrages, then for the first time exercised, to elect and constitute for their Grand Master, him who had so munificently resigned into their hands his official dignity and prerogatives. He held the office until the 30th November, 1737, when he resigned it, and George, Earl of Cromarty, was elected Grand Master. He was succeeded in 1738, by John, Earl of Kintore: and he, in 1739, by James, Earl of Morton; and he, again, in 1740, by Thomas, Earl of Strathmore. His successors were, in 1741, Alexander, Earl of Leven; 1742, William, Earl of Kilmarnock; 1743, James, Earl of Wemyss; 1744, James, Earl of Moray; 1745, Henry David, Earl of Buchan; 1746, William Nisbet of Dirleton, Esq.; 1747, Francis Charteris of Amisfield, Esq.; 1748, Hugh Seton of Touch, Esq.; 1749, Thomas, Lord Erskine; 1750, Alexander, Earl of Eglintoun; 1751, James, Lord Boyd; 1752, Rt. Hon. Geo. Drummond, Lord Provost of Edinburgh; 1753, Charles Hamilton Gordon, Esq.; 1754, the Hon. James, Master of Forbes; and, in 1755-6, SHOLTO CHARLES, LORD ABERDOUR, under whose authority ST. ANDREW'S LODGE was constituted, and whose name is affixed to its Charter. He was the first Grand Master who had been honored with a re-election. This probably did not arise from any disinclination on the part of his predecessors to serve the Grand Lodge for a longer term than one year, or, on the part of their Brethren to re-elect them; but at that early period of the Grand Lodge, it was doubtless deemed expedient, independently of any necessity which may have been felt to exist on the subject, to strengthen the Body, by interesting in its administration as many of the nobility and gentlemen of the kingdom, as could conveniently be induced to assume the responsibility of its management. This having been accomplished, to the desired extent, the one-term rule was discarded, and the Grand Masters, from that to the present time have, with few exceptions, been honored by at least a second election.

MEMOIR OF ST. ANDREW.

ST. ANDREW, in whose name our Lodge was chartered by the Grand Lodge of Scotland on the 30th of November, 1756, was born at Bethsaida, a city of Galilee, situated on the shores of the Lake Tiberias, in Palestine. As the name imports, it was a place for fishing and hunting, the adjacent country abounding with deer and the sea with fish. It is said that Philip the Tetrarch formed it into a magnificent city and called it Julias, after the daughter of the Emperor Augustus. And it was here that Jesus performed many of his miracles.

Andrew was the brother of Simon Peter, and both were the sons of John, or Jonas, a fisherman of the place of their nativity. The former, before the advent of Jesus as a public teacher, had been a Disciple of John the Baptist, and was probably a member of the Essenian Sect, to which John belonged. If so, this will, in some measure at least, account for the learning and ability which he subsequently exhibited in his public ministry. He was the first person whom Jesus received as a Disciple, and who afterwards, with his brother Simon Peter, became one of his Apostles. He followed Christ until his crucifixion; when, with the other Apostles, he entered upon his public ministry. Departing from Jerusalem, he first travelled through Cappadocia, Galatia, and Bithynia, instructing the inhabitants in the new faith; and then continued his journey along the Euxine Sea, into the desert of Scythia. An ancient author tells us that he first came to Amynsus, where he preached in one of the Jewish Synagogues, converted many of the people, and ordained priests. He next went to Trapezium, a maritime city on the Euxine Sea; from whence, after visiting many other places, he came to Nice, in Northern Italy, where he stayed two years, preaching and working miracles with great success. Leaving here he passed to Nicomedia, and from thence to Chalcedon, whence he sailed through the Propontis to the Euxine again, and from thence went to Heraclea, and afterwards to Amastris ; in all of which places he encountered many difficulties, but overcame them by his invincible patience and resolution. He next proceeded to Synope (a city on the same sea, and famous as the birth and burial place of King Mithridates), where he met his brother Peter and united with him in the work of the ministry. The inhabitants were mostly Jews, who, "partly from a zeal for their religion and partly from their barbarous manners, were exasperated against him, and entered into a confederacy to burn the house in which he lodged. But being disappointed in their design, they treated him with the most savage cruelty, throwing him on the ground, stamping upon him with their feet, pulling and dragging him from place to place ; some beating him with clubs, some pelting him with stones, and others, to satisfy their brutal revenge, biting off his flesh with their teeth ; until, apprehending that they had entirely deprived him of life, they cast him out into the fields. But he miraculously recovered, and returned publicly into the city ; by which, and other miracles that he wrought among them, he converted many from the error of their ways and induced them to become Disciples of Jesus." He afterwards returned to Jerusalem, and from thence travelled over Thrace, Macedonia, Thessera, Achaia, and Epirus, "propagating and confirming the doctrine he taught, with signs and miracles." At last he came to Patræ, a city of Achaia, in Greece, where, after converting large numbers of the inhabitants, he finally sealed his faith with his blood. He was here arrested by order of Agenas, pro-consul of Achaia, and having resisted every temptation to renounce his mission and sacrifice to the gods of the heathen, he was treated with the utmost severity, and finally crucified on the 30th of November, A. D. 69. The Cross used on this occasion, was of the form called *Crux decussata*, and commonly known as St. Andrew's Cross. It was made of two pieces of timber, crossing each other in the centre, in the form of the letter X. Contrary to the usual custom, he was fastened to the cross with *cords* instead of *nails*, that his death might be the more lingering and tedious. In this condition, says one authority, "he hung two whole days, teaching and instructing the people in the best manner his wretched situation would admit of, being sometimes so weak and faint as scarce to have the power of utterance. In the meantime, great interest was made to the pro-consul to spare his life ; but the Apostle earnestly begged of the Almighty that he might now depart, and seal the truth of his religion with his blood." His prayers were heard, and he expired, as before stated, on the last day of November. His body is said to have been decently and honorably interred by Maximillia, a lady of quality and estate, who Niceporus tells us, was the wife of the pro-consul. Constantine the Great afterwards removed it to Constantinople, and buried it in the great Church he had erected in honor of the Apostles. Here it remained until the year A. D. 369, when, it is said, a Scottish Abbot of the name of Regulus, caused it to be again removed from Constantinople to Scotland, and buried in a church, with a monastery, which he had erected to the Saint at Abernethy.

The festival of St. Andrew was instituted in Scotland in the year A. D. 359, and from that time to the present has been generally observed as the great national religious festival and gala-day of Scotchmen, wherever dispersed.

The Saint was admitted into the Masonic Calendar, and his " anniversary " adopted as a Masonic Festival, on the 30th of November, 1737. Previously to this time, the " Festival Days " of the Order in Scotland (as in every other country in Christendom), had been, from the early days of Christianity, the 24th of June, and the 27th of December. But the peculiar condition of the Order there at the date above given, and the important changes which then took place in its organization and government, led to a corresponding change in its anniversary festivals.

Such are the more prominent points, historical and legendary, in the life of this distinguished Apostle, as they have come down to us from the early days of Christianity. A more elaborate narrative was not deemed necessary for the purpose of the present sketch.

CELEBRATION

OF THE

CENTENNIAL ANNIVERSARY

OF THE

MASSACHUSETTS GRAND LODGE

BY THE

LODGE OF ST. ANDREW,

DEC. 23, 1869.

ALLEGORY. — SCOTLAND and AMERICA united in MASONRY under the
Patronage of ST. ANDREW.

Introduction

~-.-~

Having been precluded by the action of the Grand Lodge of the State, from a more formal celebration of the *One Hundredth Anniversary* of the establishment in Boston, of the "Grand Lodge of *Ancient* Masons," St. Andrew's Lodge availed itself of its Quarterly Meeting, on the 23d of December, 1869, to take such notice of an occasion, historically and personally so interesting to its Members, as the peculiar circumstances under which they were assembled would allow.

The Lodge was opened at an early hour in the afternoon, at the house of Bro. J. B. SMITH, in Bulfinch Street, and having transacted its ordinary business, the Brethren, in commemoration of an ancient masonic custom, were "called from labor to refreshment," and sat down to an entertainment provided for the occasion by the celebrated caterer at whose house they were convened.

On the removal of the cloth, the Worshipful Master, EZRA PALMER M. D., addressed the Lodge, on the auspicious circumstances under which they were met, in the following congratulatory address:

BRETHREN OF THE LODGE OF ST. ANDREW :

I bid you a cordial welcome to these tables so liberally provided with the luxuries of the season.

The large number of members assembled to-night is a subject of congratulation, as it denotes an interest not only in our time-honored regular quarterly communications, but also in the fact that at this meeting we commemorate the Centennial Anniversary of the establishment of the "Massachusetts Grand Lodge," in which our Lodge so largely participated, and whose first Grand Master was at the time of his appointment, Worshipful Master of this Lodge.

A retrospect of one hundred years! What interesting suggestions does it awaken! From the date of one hundred years ago we readily recede to the middle of the last century, when our beloved Lodge was duly constituted. We recall the source and history of its Charter. We read its early records, and find that it was one of the few masonic institutions which regularly held their communications, not only through the distracting period preceding the Revolution, but also through the turbulence of the War itself. All this and more flashes to the memory, and questions like the following present themselves : Ought not much of our old history to be revived ? Ought not a committee be appointed to open our many long-closed volumes of records of this early date and furnish us some of their valuable contents ?

I am happy to say that something will be done to-night in that direction.

My right hand neighbor at the table has delved into the past and will give you what preceded and constituted the organization of the Grand Lodge of Massachusetts. And now, Brethren, I call upon R. W. Bro. CHARLES W. MOORE to respond to the sentiment.

"THE MASSACHUSETTS GRAND LODGE, AND ITS RELATIONS WITH ST. ANDREW'S LODGE."

R. W. BRO. MOORE then delivered an interesting address on the early history of the Grand Lodge of "*Ancient* Masons" (as it was originally denominated); tracing the manner of its organization, referring in terms of eulogy to the distinguished brethren who formed its first Board of Officers, and comprehensively sketching, with clearness and precision, the important part sustained in its establishment by SAINT ANDREW'S LODGE; illustrating this point of his address by historical data from the records of the two bodies, and other reliable and official sources.

The committee have the pleasure to lay this address before the brethren of the Lodge in the following pages. Bro. Moore has, since its delivery, elaborated it by the addition of such further documents as seemed to be necessary to illustrate the early history and struggles of the Lodge, more fully and satisfactorily than a general course of remark would admit of.

ADDRESS

W. Master and Brethren:

It may not be an extravagant assumption nor yet an improbable one, to suppose that ONE HUNDRED YEARS ago this night, more or less of the members of St. Andrew's Lodge, either in their associate or individual capacity, were assembled together at their Hall, in the old Green Dragon Tavern, and were there engaged in maturing the necessary measures for the successful organization, on the following Wednesday (being the 27th day of December), of a second Grand Lodge in the then town of Boston, to be thereafter known as the "Grand Lodge of *Ancient Masons*," with their beloved and distinguished Brother Dr. JOSEPH WARREN, for its Grand Master. To the organization of this body, and the connection of St. Andrew's Lodge with it, I propose to limit the remarks I am about to submit in answer to the call with which you have been pleased to honor me.

The history of Freemasonry in Massachusetts is marked by three distinct and notable epochs. The first of these was the organization of the "St. John's Grand Lodge" in 1733, with the R. W. HENRY PRICE for its Grand Master: The second, the establishment of the Grand Lodge of "*Ancient Masons*," (subsequently styled, and more generally known in masonic history as "The Massachusetts Grand Lodge,") on the 27th of December 1769, with the R. W. JOSEPH WARREN, for its Grand Master: And the third, the consolidation and union in 1792, of these two Grand

Lodges into one body, to be thereafter known as the " Grand Lodge of the Commonwealth of Massachusetts," with the R. W. JOHN CUTLER, for its Grand Master. It is with the second of these leading events that we, as a Lodge, are at this time more particularly concerned.

On the 30th of July, 1733, there was organized and opened at the Bunch of Grapes Tavern, on the corner of King (now State) and Kilby Streets, in the town of Boston, the first Grand Lodge of Freemasons ever erected on the American Continent. The authority under which the Brethren on that occasion acted, was a commission, or in the language of that day, a " deputation," from the Grand Master of Masons in England, to R. W. HENRY PRICE of Boston, constituting and appointing him Provincial Grand Master for New England. The body so formed was denominated, and continued to be known until nearly the close of the century, as " The St. John's Grand Lodge." It went into immediate active operation by constituting on the evening of its own erection, " The First Lodge in Boston." This was the beginning of the existence of Freemasonry in America, on its present and modern plan of organization.

On the 30th of November, 1756, a Charter was granted by the Grand Lodge of Scotland, for the erection of a Lodge in Boston, under the name and title of the " LODGE OF ST. ANDREW ; " but was not received by the petitioners until the following year, when the Lodge was regularly organized under it. It had, however, previously been in operation, as will hereafter appear. The issuing of this Charter was objected to and resisted by the St. John's Grand Lodge, which had then been in existence twenty-three years, as an infringement of its lawful jurisdiction. It was claimed by that body that the commission of Grand Master Price gave him and his successors, exclusive masonic authority in the Province. This claim was not well founded. Massachusetts, like all the other colonies and dependencies of the British Crown, was open and free to the joint occupancy of the three Grand Lodges of that kingdom : namely, of England, Ireland and Scotland. The right, therefore, of the Grand Lodge of Scotland, or of the Grand Lodge of Ireland, or both together, to establish Lodges within the Province, was as clear and undoubted as that of the Grand Lodge of England to authorize the establishment of English Lodges within the same territory. This right of common jurisdiction in the Provinces was not, however, so clearly understood by the Brethren composing the St. John's Grand Lodge, as by the parent Grand Lodges of Great Britain (which alone had control over it), as will be seen by the letter, hereafter cited, from the Grand Master of Scotland. The result was a long and exciting controversy, which was not always particularly distinguished for its amiability or fraternal courtesy. To such an extent indeed had this feeling of unkindness and spirit of exclusiveness obtained, that the St. John's Grand Lodge, by a formal vote, forbade all masonic intercourse with the members of St. Andrew's Lodge, declaring their organization to be irregular and without lawful authority. This vote was in the following terms, and was adopted April 8, 1761 :

" Voted, That it be, and it is hereby recommended and ordered by the Grand Master, that no Member of a regularly constituted Lodge in Boston, do appear at the meeting (or the Lodge so called) of Scotts Masons in Boston, not being regularly constituted in the opinion of this (Grand) Lodge. The Master and Wardens of the several Lodges, are desired to take notice of this Order at their next meeting."

This was a declaration of outlawry to which the proscribed Brethren could not passively submit, without a dishonorable abnegation of their masonic character and prerogatives. On the receipt of a copy of it, the members of the Lodge laid their grievances before their parent Grand Lodge of Scotland, and sought the interposition of that body to relieve them from the embarrassments and humiliation to which they were so unjustly subjected, and received from the Earl of Elgin and Kincardin, its Grand Master, an answer, under date Edinburgh June 4, 1762, from which the following is an extract :

" The last reason assigned by the Lodges in Boston for their unkind behavior to you is, that the Right Worshipful Jeremiah (Jeremy) Gridley, Esq., looks upon your Charter as an infringement of his Province as Grand Master of North America ; it is my opinion there may be some mistake in this ; you say he saw, read and approved of your Charter ; if he had any objections, he certainly would have signified them to you when you showed him your Charter. I am confident my R. W. Brother Jeremiah Gridley, Esq., knows and observes the principles of Masonry better, than to take offence where there is not the smallest reason given for it. I do not doubt nor dispute his authority as Grand Master of all the Lodges in North America, *who acknowledge the authority, and hold of the Grand Lodge of England*, as he certainly has a warrant and commission from the Grand Master of England to that effect. The Grand Master and Grand Lodge of Scotland have also granted a warrant and commission to our R. W. Bro. Col. John Young, Esq., constituting and appointing him Provincial Grand Master of all the Lodges in North America, who acknowledge the authority and hold of the Grand Lodge of Scotland. These Commissions, when rightly understood, can never clash or interfere with each other."

It will be seen by this answer that the right of the Grand Lodge of Scotland to an equal and common jurisdiction with the Grand Lodge of England in the Province, is asserted and insisted on by the Grand Master of the former ; and I am not aware that it was then, or ever, subsequently or anterior to the Revolution, questioned or denied by the latter body. So far as I am able to ascertain from the record, the objection to the recognition of St. Andrew's Lodge on this ground, was here permitted to subside, or was not urged with its former pertinacity.

Of the appointment of Col. John Young as " Provincial Grand Master of all the Lodges in North America," we have no other record than that here given. It is evident, however, that if that Brother had, at any time subsequent to his appointment, entered upon the active duties of his office, the effect would have been to supersede the authority of Dr. Warren ; but as this did not occur, the only inference to be drawn from it is, that his commission was suffered to lie in abeyance. It is certain that Warren was never removed or molested in his authority by it.

It would occupy too much of our time to follow this unpleasant controversy in detail, through all its intricate and various windings to its final result ; nor is this necessary, my only object being to illustrate the trials and embarrassments to which the Lodge was subjected in the early days of its history, its successful triumph over them, and final attainment to the elevated position it now holds among its sister Lodges. Passing over the intervening years, we find that in January, 1766, the Lodge passed the following vote, and directed the committee whose names are attached to it, to lay the same before the St. John's Grand Lodge : —

Right Worshipful Grand Master, Right Worshipful Deputy Grand Master, and Worshipful Wardens and other Grand Officers of the Grand Lodge of St. John in Grand Lodge assembled :

As harmony and sincere friendship are ornaments which add the greatest lustre to Masonry, the Lodge of St. Andrew being assembled for the purpose of promoting brotherly love and unity, have unanimously voted, That the compliments of this Lodge should be presented to the Right Worshipful Grand Master of North America, the Right Worshipful Deputy Grand Master, Grand Wardens and all the Brethren holding under them, desiring their company at the Lodge of St. Andrew, whenever it may be agreeable to them, and that there may be a happy coalition.

SAMUEL BARRETT,
EZRA COLLINS,
WILLIAM PALFREY,   } Committee.
SAML. DANFORTH, JR.,
JOSEPH WARREN.

This communication was presented to the Grand Lodge on the 24th of January, accompanied by a letter from the Grand Secretary of the Grand Lodge of Scotland, which, the record says, "highly reflected on the Right Worshipful Grand Master." The action on it by that body was deferred until the 27th, and then resulted in the adoption of the following remarkable answer :

Voted, That Isaac Decoster, David Flagg, George Graham, George Lowditt, George Bray, George Hodge, Henry Ammes, William Burbeck and James Tourner, the persons named as Free and Accepted Masons in the Constitution of a Lodge called St. Andrew's Lodge in Boston in New England, by the Grand Master of Scotland, were not at the time of their application for it, or at the date of said Constitution, free and accepted Masons.

4

Voted, That the aforesaid application as free and accepted Masons was an imposition on the Grand Lodge of Scotland.

Voted, That the aforesaid persons who petitioned for the said Constitutions and all persons who have since been added to them in their Fraternity are irregular Masons.

Voted, That it appears from the Records of the Grand Lodge, that several of the members of said irregular Lodge have at different times applied to this Grand Lodge for liberty to visit the Lodges under our jurisdiction, and have, for said irregularity, been refused this liberty, and further that all the Members of our Lodges have been prohibited by vote of this Grand Lodge to visit said irregular Lodge. Voted, therefore, that the Free and Accepted Masons under this jurisdiction cannot visit said Fraternity according to a request of their Committee in writing, dated the 24th of January, inst.

Voted, that the aforesaid votes be recorded in the Grand Lodge Books, and that a copy of the same be given to the Committee of the Fraternity above mentioned, when demanded.

Voted, that the Grand Master be desired by the first opportunity to transmit to the Grand Master of England a copy of the above votes.

The bad spirit in which these votes were written, is not their most objectionable feature. The Brethren who composed the Committee of the Lodge, with the exception of Ezra Collins, were all made Masons in St. Andrew's Lodge, under the authority of its Charter from the Grand Lodge of Scotland, and were, therefore, as lawfully made, and entitled to as much consideration and respect, as the Grand Master who presided over these deliberations. The validity of the Charter of the Lodge, and the lawful making of the petitioners for it, were matters in which the Grand Lodge had no control or right to interfere. Both subjects had passed beyond its reach. Whatever may have been irregular in the proceedings of the Lodge in the earlier days of its organization, had been masonically regularized and confirmed by the Grand Lodge of Scotland, under whose authority it existed, and to which body it was alone amenable. If the St. John's Grand Lodge had any grievances to complain of, it was to that body its complaints should have been preferred.

The Lodge could not, consistently with its own self-respect, pass over in silence an assault so unfraternal and derogatory to its character. We accordingly find that at a meeting held on the following 10th of April, the votes adopted by the Grand Lodge on the 27th of January, were ordered to be read, and that in answer to them, "the following votes were unanimously passed by thirty-four Brethren then present," viz :

1st. Voted, That the first vote of the Grand Lodge, which asserts that " Isaac Decoster, David Flagg, George Graham, George Lowditt, George Bray, George Hodge, Henry Ammes, and James Tourner, the persons named in the Constitution of a Lodge, called St. Andrew's Lodge in Boston, were not at the time of their application, or at the date of said Constitution, Free and Accepted Masons," is erroneous and contains its own refutation.

2d. Voted, That the second vote of the said Grand Lodge which asserts that the aforesaid application was " an imposition on the Grand Lodge of Scotland," is at least a mistake ; the truth being as follows : Our Worshipful Brother James Logan, who had been Master of a Lodge in Scotland, and a member of the Grand Lodge there, was, when in Boston, A. D. 5754, perfectly informed of the manner and circumstances by which the persons aforesaid became acquainted with the mysteries of Masonry, and was desired upon his return to Scotland, truly to represent their difficulties to the Grand Lodge of Scotland, and to endeavor to procure for them a Charter : The Grand Lodge of Scotland finding from the relation given by our Brother Logan, that a number of persons in Boston, intrusted with the secrets of Masonry, were, notwithstanding their repeated application, refused admittance into the regular Lodges in said Boston ; the said Grand Lodge in their great wisdom, thought fit to grant them a Charter of new erection, with ample privileges, thereby manifesting their approbation of them as Free and Accepted Masons.

3d. Voted, That it appears from the fourth and fifth votes of the Grand Lodge, that the members of St. Andrew's Lodge, have acted consistently with their character as Masons, in their application to the Grand Lodge for liberty to visit the Lodges under their jurisdiction, and that the conduct of said Grand Lodge in refusing them, and prohibiting their members from visiting the Lodge of St. Andrew, was directly subversive of the principles of Masonry.

4th. Voted, That the Lodge of St. Andrew have in time past, shown all due respect and regard to the members of the Grand Lodge in Boston, and to the Brethren under their jurisdiction, and that their future behavior shall ever demonstrate their affection for them, and their determined resolution to embrace every method, consistent with the good of Masonry and their own honor, to promote a social intercourse with persons whom they so highly esteem as Brethren and friends.

5th. Voted, That the aforesaid votes of the Grand Lodge, and the above votes of this Lodge, be recorded in the Books of this Lodge.

6th. Voted, That a copy of the complimentary address, from this Lodge to the Grand Lodge in Boston, together with the votes of said Grand Lodge in consequence of said address, and the above votes, be transmitted to the Grand Lodge in Scotland, by the first opportunity.

7th. Voted, That Bros. William Burbeck, Samuel Barrett, Moses Deshon, Ezra Collins, William Palfrey, Samuel Danforth, jr., and Joseph Warren, be a committee to present the aforesaid votes to the Grand Master and Grand Lodge in their next meeting.

A true copy from the original.

MOSES DESHON,
WILLIAM BURBECK,
SAMUEL BARRETT,
EZRA COLLINS,   } Committee.
WILLIAM PALFREY,
SAML. DANFORTH, JR.,
JOSEPH WARREN.

It cannot escape notice that the tone of these votes is in beautiful contrast with the temper of those to which they are in answer. They were communicated to the Grand Lodge as directed in the seventh vote, on the 25th of April ; when a committee of the Lodge being announced as in attendance, it was by that body

Voted, That Bro. Richard Gridley, Bro. Joseph Gardner, Bro. A. C. Savage, Bro. Edmund Quincy, G. S., Bro. Thomas Walley, Bro. John Joy, Bro. John Cutler, be a committee from this Lodge to meet said committee of said St. Andrew's Lodge, to hear what they have further to offer, on Monday next, at this House, at 6 o'clock, P. M.

The two committees met, in accordance with this vote, at the Royal Exchange Tavern in King Street, where the existing differences seem to have been fully and frankly discussed. The character of their discussions and the results to which they had arrived were communicated to the Grand Lodge by its Committee, on the 2d of May, in the following report :

To the Right Worshipful Grand Master, Deputy Grand Master, Grand Wardens and members of the Grand Lodge of Free and Accepted Masons, held at Boston, for all North America, where no other Grand Master is appointed :

Whereas, on Friday, the 25th of April, 5766 (being Grand Lodge night), a committee from the Lodge (commonly called St. Andrew's Lodge), sent up to said Grand Lodge a number of votes, passed in their said Lodge, the 10th of April last, and at the same time requested to be admitted to communicate something further, *viva voce*, to the said Grand Lodge : whereupon the said votes were read, and were found to be couched in very disrespectful terms, in several parts of them, to a Grand Lodge, and some of their assertions, wholly ambiguous. It was then moved, whether the said committee should be admitted into the Grand Lodge, to explain those doubtful parts of their votes, and to deliver what they had further to offer to the Grand Lodge. Upon the question being put, it passed in the negative, as being inconsistent with the votes of the Grand Lodge of January 27th last passed. A motion was then made, that a committee be appointed, out of the members of the Grand Lodge, to confer with said committee, relating to the premises, and to inquire into the state of the difference subsisting between the said Grand Lodge, the Lodges subordinate to it, and the said St. Andrew's Lodge, which motion being seconded, the Grand Lodge were pleased to make choice of us, the subscribers, to be their Committee for the purposes aforesaid, who agreed to meet the other committee at the Royal Exchange Tavern, on Monday the 28th of April last ; and the Grand Lodge adjourned to Friday, the 2d of May instant, to receive their report.

The two committees having met accordingly, the Chairman of the Grand Lodge committee having opened the business for which they had met, the first question was, what the St. Andrew's Lodge committee had to communicate to the Grand Lodge, that they desired admittance, as before mentioned ? To which one of them replied, that they as a committee, thought that there were some expressions in the votes of St. Andrew's Lodge, which they thought too harsh, and that they were willing *viva voce*, to soften those terms, to show they did not fail in the respect that was due to the Grand Lodge. Then they reiterated their former address to the Grand Lodge, of January 24th last, which brought on a long argument, wherein all the Grand Lodge's objections to them for the irregularity of their beginning and subsequent proceedings were fully urged, and their vindication of themselves was as strongly opposed to those objections. At last this question was put to them, what they had to propose to the Grand Lodge, to bring about the accommodation they so much desired? for the language of the Constitutions for irregularities, was submission ! To which they replied as follows, and desired it to be minuted, viz : —

1st. The Committee from St. Andrew's Lodge moving to be admitted into the Grand Lodge, held last Friday night, was to explain and soften the terms of their votes of April 10th, 5766.

2d. They also acknowledge in behalf of said Lodge, that all the proceedings of those persons before their application for a constitution from the Grand Master of Scotland, were irregular and wrong ; but are fully of opinion, that the proceedings of said St. Andrew's Lodge, after their Constitution, have been regular and just ; and that, although they, before their Constitution, were irregular, yet the Grand Master of Scotland has a power of dispensation, and can make irregular Masons, regular. Therefore they think themselves regular.

3d. They also propose and desire to be admitted to visit our Lodges and that our Lodges visit them, and that there may be a union of love and friendship, between the several Lodges.

Upon which your Committee, after mature deliberation of their votes presented last Grand Lodge night, and the minutes which they desired us to make of their Concessions, etc., at their meeting with us ; and after largely discoursing upon the affair with said Committee, came to the following determination :

1st. That their explanation of the first vote of the Grand Lodge, viz : "that it is erroneous, and contains its own refutation," is not satisfactory to us, although they think the day their Constitution bore date, their power commenced. Our opinion is, their power could not commence before the receipt and possession of said Constitution.

2d. Their answer to our second vote, wherein they say, "it is at least a mistake," we would observe, they produce no copy of any application, but declare the Grand Master of Scotland was duly informed of their being irregular Masons, and that Decoster had applied to us for admittance into the Lodge, but was refused, only by two votes, upon which the rest despaired of gaining admittance among us ; therefore, it appears to us not improbable, but the Grand Master of Scotland might know their circumstances.

3d. Their third vote, which says, "that it appears from the fourth and fifth votes of the Grand Lodge, that the members of St. Andrew's Lodge have acted consistent with their character as Masons, in their application to the Grand Lodge, for liberty to visit the Lodges under this jurisdiction,"——"and that the conduct of said Grand Lodge in refusing them, and prohibiting their members from visiting the Lodge of St. Andrew, was directly subversive of the principles of Masonry : " it is our opinion the first part of the above vote is premature ; they not considering the Laws of Masons require irregular Masons to make a proper submission, before they can be received.—The last part is disrespectful and injurious to this Grand Lodge, and discovers they were unacquainted with the laws and principles of Masonry.

4th. We are glad to find by their fourth vote, that "it is their determined resolution to embrace every method, consistent with the good of Masonry and their own honor, to promote a social intercourse with persons whom they so highly esteem as brethren and friends." And we doubt not the Lodges under this jurisdiction will ever show as great a zeal to promote love and friendship, and the principles of Masonry, as any Lodge whatever.

RICHARD GRIDLEY,
EDMUND QUINCY, JR.,
JOHN CUTLER,
JOSEPH GARDNER,   } Committee.
THOMAS WALLEY,
JOHN JOY.

BOSTON, May 2d, 1766.

N. B. Bro. Abram Savage was absent at giving in the above report, he being another of the Committee.

The asperity of the controversy was softened. The storm was broken. Still, dark and threatening clouds obscured the prospect. The future was uncertain. Nothing definite had been reached. And having unsuccessfully exhausted its powers of endurance in efforts to establish more amicable relations, and to effect a fraternal reconciliation of its difficulties with the Brethren of the St. John's Grand Lodge, the Lodge sought the aid of the three Military Lodges attached to foreign regiments then stationed in Boston, in a petition to the Grand Lodge of Scotland for the appointment, in virtue of its own inherent and undoubted right, of a Grand Master for the Province, clothed with the ample powers of an officer of that distinguished rank. The co-operation of the officers of these Lodges was probably the more readily obtained by reason of the favorable consideration in which the young and popular Warren was held by the military men of that day. One of the reasons urged by the petitioners in support of their petition, was the necessity for a less precarious and uncertain protection than they then enjoyed, of the rights of Brethren who had enrolled themselves and were in sympathy with the so-called *Ancient* Masons : to which relation I shall hereafter have occasion to refer more in detail. The prayer of the petitioners was granted, and the R. W. Joseph

Warren, at the time Master of St. Andrew's Lodge, was commissioned on the 30th of May, 1769, by the Rt. Hon. GEORGE, Earl of Dalhousie, Grand Master of Masons in Scotland, "to be Grand Master of Masons in Boston, New England, and within one hundred miles of the same." Under this authority the Grand Lodge of *Ancient* Masons, better known as the "Massachusetts Grand Lodge," was organized at Mason's Hall, in the Green Dragon Tavern (the property of St. Andrew's Lodge), on the 27th of December, 1769, with the following officers : —

JOSEPH WARREN,   .   .   .   Grand Master.
JEREMIAH FRENCH, Esq., Capt. in 29th Reg. Senior Grand Warden.
PONSONBY MOLESWORTH, Esq., "   "   "   Junior Grand Warden.
WILLIAM PALFREY, (by proxy),   Grand Secretary.
THOMAS CRAFTS,   .   Grand Treasurer.
JOSEPH WEBB,   Grand Marshal.
PAUL REVERE,   .   Senior Grand Deacon.
SAMUEL DANFORTH,   .   .   .   Junior Grand Deacon.
THOMAS URANN, CALEB HOPKINS,   Grand Stewards.
EDWARD PROCTOR,   Grand Sword-Bearer.

Of the above officers, Bros. Warren, Crafts, Webb, Revere, Danforth, Urann, Hopkins, and Proctor, were active members of St. Andrew's Lodge. The Wardens, Bros. French and Molesworth, were members of Military Lodges, then temporarily in the Province, and were obviously appointed to the offices named, for the purpose of completing the organization, and in compliment to the military Brethren on the station, who had taken an active interest in the success of the new enterprise. They, however, occupied their places but for a single session of the Grand Lodge. At the second meeting of that body on the 12th of January, these offices were filled *pro tem.* by Bros. Joseph Webb and Moses Deshon. The regular Wardens, it is believed, soon after left the Province ; and it is certain that they never subsequently took any active part in the affairs of the Grand Lodge. The two military Lodges, namely, No. 58 of the Registry of England, and No. 322 of the Registry of

Ireland, which had united in the petition to the Grand Lodge of Scotland, were present by their Masters and Wardens, at the organization on the 27th of December, 1769, and also at the succeeding meetings Jan. 12, and March 2, 1770; but were never present afterwards. — The withdrawal of these two Lodges was supplied March 2, 1770, by a Charter to Tyrian Lodge, Gloucester, and to Massachusetts Lodge, Boston, May 13th. The latter was a branch of St. Andrew's Lodge, the petitioners, without an exception, being members of it. The Brethren to whom the Charter was granted were Joseph Tyler, James Jackson, Isaac Rand, William Palfrey, John Hill, Nathaniel Cudworth, Joshua Loring, and John Jeffries. Tyler was the first Master. A Charter was also granted to St. Peter's Lodge, Newburyport, March 6, 1772. These were the only Charters which bore the name of Gen. Warren, as Grand Master. — The third of the military Lodges was not present at the formation of the Grand Lodge, nor subsequently. Thus within about two months after its establishment it became, practically, little more than a *duplication* of St. Andrew's Lodge, which was now in a condition where it could successfully assert its own integrity, and protect its own rights. The Grand Lodge so formed and constituted, was a child of its own. It had watched its incipiency and subsequent advancement with the solicitude natural to the relation it sustained to it ; and it anxiously looked forward to the day when it should attain to full manhood and take its place as an independent masonic power within the Province, as the day which was to mark the recognition of its own rightful prerogatives, and relieve it of the embarrassments and unjust imputations to which it had been subjected for more than a decade of its legal existence. It was an anxious and momentous day to its members, and was destined to signalize one of the most interesting and important epochs in the early history of Freemasonry on the American continent.

The new body was erected as an *Ancient* Grand Lodge, in sympathy with the seceding Grand Lodge established in London, about 1738, — producing a schism in the Fraternity in England that was not healed until 1813. But this statement is too general for a clear understanding of the precise relation which the Grand Lodge of Scotland primarily, and the Massachusetts Grand Lodge subsequently, sustained to that unwarrantable act of recusancy. The schismatic body originated with some restless Brethren in London, who, in 1738, becoming dissatisfied with certain measures of the established Grand Lodge of England, seceded from that body and organized themselves into independent Lodges, under what they, without authority, claimed to be the York Constitutions. They were originally few in number and of little influence in the fraternity ; and had they been left to themselves, would probably have soon abandoned their unlawful proceedings, and relapsed into the insignificance from which they sprung. But unfortunately, and as the event proved, unwisely, the Grand Lodge at London publicly denounced them, and then undertook to exclude them from its Lodges, by an unauthorized alteration of the ritual. This gave to the recalcitrant Brethren an advantage of which they were but too ready to avail themselves ; and calling to their aid the assistance of an Irish masonic adventurer, of some tact and ability, and increasing the number of their Lodges, they in turn denounced their mother Grand Lodge as having violated the established landmarks and corrupted the ancient ritual of the Order ; thereby resolving itself into a Grand Lodge of *Modern* Masons. This denunciation was followed by the erection in London, of the irregular and clandestine body which long filled a prominent and important place in masonic history, as the Grand Lodge of *Ancient* Masons.

In order to place this factitious distinction of *Ancient* and *Modern* Masons in its true light, it may be proper to say that these terms are not to be received in their common and ordinary acceptation. All legitimate Masonry, wherever practiced in the Lodges, at that or the present time, is equally *Ancient*, by whatever name it may be called. It all has a common origin, and is derived from a common source, whether that source be the valley of the Nile, or Eleusis, or Tyre, or Jerusalem — a pre-historic or a modern age. The Masonry of England, of Scotland, of Ireland, and of America, and wherever else it is to be found in its purity, is identical. The only difference in the antiquity of either, is in the comparative date of its introduction and organization in their respective territories.

But to return. The Grand Lodge of Scotland never officially endorsed or fully sympathized with the disturbing elements in England ; nor did it approve of or sanction the changes introduced into the ritual by the Grand Lodge of that kingdom. Neither did it justify or uphold the recusant Brethren in their irregular proceedings. On the contrary, it occupied neutral ground, and recognized both parties, irrespective of their local dissensions. Lawrie, in his History of Masonry in Scotland, elucidates this point in the following words : —

" In the general History of Free Masonry, we have already given an account of the schism which took place in the Grand Lodge of England, by the secession of a number of men, who, calling themselves Ancient Masons, invidiously bestowed upon the Grand Lodge the appellation of Moderns. These Ancient Masons, who certainly merit blame, as the active promoters of the schism, chose for their Grand Master, in the year 1772, his Grace the Duke of Athol, who was then Grand Master elect for Scotland." (It is believed that anterior to this date, this Grand Lodge had been without an actual Grand Master, that place having been filled by Laurence Dermott, under the assumed title of Deputy Grand Master.) " From this circumstance, more than from any particular predilection, on the part of the Grand Lodge of Scotland for the Ancient Masons, the most friendly intercourse has always subsisted between the two Grand Lodges ; and the Scottish Masons, from their union with the Ancients, imbibed the same prejudices against the Grand Lodge of England, under the Prince of Wales and Lord Moira, arising merely from some trifling innovations in ceremonial observances, which the Grand Lodge of England had inconsiderately authorized. From these causes the Grand Lodges of Scotland and England, though the brethren of both were admitted into each others' Lodges, never cherished that mutual and friendly intercourse which, by the principles of Freemasonry, they were bound to institute and preserve."

And this indicates the relation which the Massachusetts Grand Lodge held to the so-called Ancient Masons of London. While it did not absolutely endorse the change, slight as it was, in the ritual, by the *modern* Grand Lodge, it did not sympathize with the schismatics in their extreme radical measures for its correction.

General Warren continued to preside over the Massachusetts Grand Lodge as its Grand Master, until his premature death on Bunker Hill, on the 17th of June, 1775. He left the body firmly established, in an eminently prosperous condition, and with a high and honorable reputation in the community. The records show that he was absent but on three occasions during his Grandmastership, and that he was then engaged in important business of "public interest." The last record in which his name appears, is dated March 3, 1775, at the conclusion of which is appended the following memorandum : —

"19th April, 1775. Hostility commenced between the troops of G. Britain and America, in Lexington Battle.

" In consequence of which the Town was blockaded and no Lodge held until Dec. 1776.

It appears from this, that the Grand Lodge failed to hold its annual meeting in December, 1775, only. This was during the " siege of Boston," and when the town was occupied by British troops. Its officers were among the leading and most active patriots of the day, and to them a residence in the town was neither safe nor prudent. They did, however, assemble on the 8th of April, 1776, for the purpose of burying the remains of their late lamented Grand Master, which had then just been recovered from their rude resting-place on Bunker Hill. The hiatus in the meetings of the body, therefore, covered but about one year, including one annual meeting. The reasons for this omission were such as to render it not merely wholly unavoidable, but expedient and proper. This fact is both interesting and important, as it furnishes the connecting link in the chain, — the bridge over which the Masonry of the *Colony* passed into the *State*, preserving the continuity and succession unbroken. Organization is the breath of a Grand Lodge, and improvement the condition on which it holds its jurisdiction. The elder Grand Lodge was not so fortunate in this respect as its younger sister, but it was happily relieved of its embarrassments by the union of 1792.

In 1773, General Warren received a new commission from the Rt. Hon. Patrick, Earl of Dumfries, Grand Master of Masons in Scotland, dated March 3, 1772, appointing him Grand Master of Masons for the Continent of America. This commission being read in Grand Lodge, the record says, " The M. W. Grand Master, *by virtue of the authority granted him in the foregoing commission,* ordered the Grand Secretary to read a commission dated at Boston, New England, 1773, appointing Joseph Webb, Esq., Deputy Grand Master under him." The appointment of a Deputy, by written commission, was, it is believed, an unusual proceeding ; but for which, in the present case, the terms of the record would seem to indicate that the Grand Master had received special authority. Be this as it may, the fact is an interesting one, and if the character of the commission was a matter of personal preference, it may not be too great a draft upon the imagination to suppose that he had a special object in it, — a foreshadowing of coming events, when the use of it might be important to the welfare of his beloved Grand Lodge. At the present time such a document would not be considered of any moment, inasmuch as the Deputy, by appointment, would succeed his principal by virtue of Masonic usage, and in self-preservation, — on the same principle that the Senior Warden succeeds to the chair on the death or absence of the Master of the Lodge. But the rule of succession appears not then to have been very clearly understood by the Brethren, and the question, whether the death of the Grand Master did not dissolve the Grand Lodge, was discussed, *pro* and *con.* with much zeal and ability. And this is the more remarkable in view of the fact, that the chair of the sister Grand Lodge had, on several previous occasions, been occupied by the Deputy Grand Master, or a Past Grand Master, when made vacant by death or otherwise. The 21st of the " Old Regulations," established by the Grand Lodge of England 1721, met this case in the following words : " If the Grand Master die during his Mastership, or by sickness, or by being beyond sea, or any other way, should be render'd uncapable of discharging his office, the Deputy, or in his absence the Senior

Grand Warden, or in his absence the Junior Grand Warden, or in
his absence any three present Masters shall assemble the Grand
Lodge immediately ; in order to advise together upon that emergency, and to send two of their number to invite the last Grand
Master to resume his office, which now of course reverts to him :
And if he refuse to act, then the next last, and so backward. But
if no former Grand Master be found, the present *Deputy* shall act
as principal, till a new Grand Master is chosen." The brethren
appear not to have been acquainted with this regulation ; and hence
their embarrassment. The succession of Deputy Grand Master
Webb to the vacant seat, was finally concurred in by both parties,
and he continued to preside over the Grand Lodge until 1777,
when he was formally elected Grand Master ; which place he occupied until 1782, when he was succeeded by Dr. John Warren, the
younger brother of General Warren.

At this time, the Grand Lodge assumed the distinctive title by
which it was subsequently known, in the adoption of the following
resolution : —

— " *Resolved.* That this Grand Lodge be forever hereafter known and called by the
name of The Massachusetts Grand Lodge of Ancient Masons, and that it is free and
independent in its government and official authority, of any other Grand Lodge, or
Grand Master in the universe."

This resolution, which was the first formal "declaration of independence" by any Grand Lodge on this continent, was adopted on
the 6th of December, 1782, and was a full, unequivocal and irrevo-
cable severance of its connection with the Grand Lodge of Scotland. But a majority of the members of St. Andrew's Lodge,
did not see their way clear to accept a measure so radical in its
consequences, without the consent and concurrence of that body.
The matter was viewed as a question of conscience and loyalty ; and
the decision to which the Lodge arrived, after a full and earnest
consideration of the subject, and a careful weighing of its duties
and obligations to its Scottish parent, was communicated to the
body which had thus declared its independence, — and with which

it had acted in harmony and cordiality from the beginning,—in the following courteous and brotherly letter, in answer to an invitation to unite with the Lodges acknowledging the independent jurisdiction, in celebrating the approaching Festival of St. John :

Boston, December 21, 1782.

BRETHREN —

We, the subscribers, being chosen a committee in behalf of St. Andrew's Lodge, to answer a letter received the 12th inst., by the hands of the Grand Secretary, in which letter we are informed of your intention of celebrating the Feast of St. John, and the installing your Grand Officers, likewise a declaration in which it appears you have assumed an independency of all Lodges in the universe :

With all due respect, we would observe to you, that an evening was appointed to take said letter and declaration into consideration, and after debating upon them, the following question was put, "Whether this Lodge acknowledge the Massachusetts Grand Lodge, independent of the Grand Lodge of Scotland, and all other Grand Lodges in the universe." The Lodge could not consent to the declaration, supposing it to be inconsistent with the principles of Masonry, necessary to be observed for the good of the craft, amidst all the variety of circumstances incident to human affairs.

There were present at this meeting of the Lodge forty-nine members who voted as follows — yeas 19, nays 30, — 49.

By the aforegoing vote, Brethren, you have the sense of St. Andrew's Lodge.

From your affectionate
and loving Brothers,

JAMES CARTER,
SAMUEL GORE,
ALEXANDER THOMAS, } Committee.
JOHN SPRAGUE, JR.,
WM. BURBECK.

To the Most Worshipful Master and Wardens of the Grand Lodge.

February 25, 1782.

This terminated the connection of St. Andrew's Lodge with the Massachusetts Grand Lodge ; which body it was instrumental in bringing into existence, and with which it had lived and worked in fraternal love and sympathy from the day of its foundation. The separation was the result of an honest conviction of duty, and can be regarded only as a beautiful illustration of its enduring fidelity to the beloved parent under whose immediate care and protection it had decided again to enrol itself.

It is evident from the vote given in the above letter, that there was a wide difference of opinion among the members of the Lodge on the subject ; which difference subsequently led to most serious consequences. So dissatisfied indeed were the minority of the members with the decision to which the majority had come, and to such an extent were their personal feelings interested, that, having failed to possess themselves of the Charter of the Lodge, they withdrew and applied to the Grand Lodge and obtained authority for the establishment of a new Lodge ; or, as they claimed, a continuance of their old Lodge, under the name of "The Rising States Lodge," with Bro. Paul Revere for its Master, to take rank and precedence in Grand Lodge from the date of the Charter of St. Andrew's Lodge ; or in the words of the Record of that day, "to hold rank as the oldest Lodge under the jurisdiction." This new Lodge was organized on the 4th of September, 1784, and continued a precarious existence until 1811, when it was dissolved. St. Andrew's Lodge had, in the meantime, re-affiliated itself and renewed its obedience to the Grand Lodge of Scotland.

The present Grand Lodge of the Commonwealth, was the result of a union in 1792, of the St. John's and the Massachusetts Grand Lodges. A brief reference to the conditions on which St. Andrew's Lodge consented to dissolve its connection with its parent Grand Lodge of Scotland, and to enrol itself under the jurisdiction of the united body, may, therefore, neither be inappropriate nor uninteresting.

The union took place, and the organization of the body was consummated, under the distinctive title of "The Most Ancient and Honorable Society of Free and Accepted Masons, for the Commonwealth of Massachusetts," "in union with the Most Ancient and Honorable Grand Lodges in Europe and America, *according to the old Constitutions*," with the stipulation that "all distinctions between *Ancient* and *Modern* Masons, shall, as far as possible, be abolished."

The result of this action was the establishment of a Grand Lodge of *Ancient* Free and Accepted Masons, and the invidious appellation of *Modern* Masons was happily and forever erased from the masonic vocabulary of Massachusetts. This opened the way for a union of St. Andrew's Lodge with it, and though the subject was agitated, and some preliminary measures were adopted by the Lodge at an earlier date, no decisive progress in the premises was made until 1807, when the following letter was addressed to the Grand Lodge, and read before that body on the 14th of December in that year :

M. W. AND RESPECTABLE BRETHREN : —

St. Andrew's Lodge, having ascertained by a committee appointed for the purpose, what is due from them to their Parent, the G. L. of Scotland, have determined to remit to the said G. L., the balance due, and request of them an honorable dismission, and if obtained, to unite themselves under your jurisdiction, provided they can be received in such manner and placed in such situation as will comport with the honor and dignity of both Lodges—and as it is necessary they should know whether this object can be obtained, previous to their writing the Grand Lodge of Scotland, the manner and form of which will depend on the arrangement which is made with your respectable Lodges, as they will not, by any means, solicit dismission from the Lodge which gave them birth, and whom they hold in the highest veneration and esteem, without the fullest assurances of being received and placed in such a station in your Lodge, as beseems their antiquity ; and that they may with pleasure, render to you that respect which is due to the Head of the Grand Mason Family of this Commonwealth. They have for the purposes above alluded to, appointed Bros. Elisha Sigourney, Andrew Sigourney, Benj. Hurd, Jr., David Bradlee, James Green, Henry Purkitt, and James Farrar, a committee to wait upon and confer with any committee your respectable Lodge may please to appoint, on the business herein mentioned.

You will, therefore, please to take this subject into your wise consideration, and the above committee will meet your committee, at any time and place they may appoint to discuss this business. That it may terminate in such manner as will tend to promote the honor, harmony and prosperity, of the whole masonic family of this Commonwealth, is ardent wish of St. Andrew's Lodge, by whom I am directed to give you the above information, and in whose behalf I have the honor to subscribe myself,

with respect and esteem, your fraternal

and obedient servant,

JOSEPH SMITH, *Secretary.*

M. W. G. L. of Mass.

On the receipt of this letter, the Grand Lodge appointed a committee to confer with the committee of St. Andrew's Lodge on the subject, consisting of R. W. Bros. Josiah Bartlett, Timothy Whitney, John Warren, James Laughton, Isaiah Thomas, Allen Crocker, and Daniel Davis. The joint committees met at the Green Dragon Tavern, on the 5th of December, when the committee of the Grand Lodge called the attention of the committee of St. Andrew's Lodge to the following article in the Constitutions of the former body :

"All Lodges heretofore established may retain their original Charters (the dates and Grand Lodges from whence they were respectively issued, being recorded by the G. Sec.) ; and a due representation, with the payment of equal quarterly payments, or assessments, shall entitle such Lodges to take precedency according to seniority."

It is the unanimous opinion of the committee that by this article, the Lodge you so honorably represent, may connect itself with the Grand Lodge of this Commonwealth, and that a compliance with the requisition there specified, will entitle it to all the privileges of such a connection.

I am with paternal esteem, &c.,

JOSIAH BARTLETT, *Chairman.*

To the above the committee of St. Andrew's Lodge made the following respectful reply :

WORSHIPFUL BRETHREN, —

The committee of St. Andrew's Lodge have the pleasure to inform you that they are perfectly satisfied with the propositions this day made them, on the part of the Grand Lodge, and which, they have no doubt, will meet the approbation of their Lodge, and which they will take the earliest opportunity of laying before them ; necessary steps will be immediately taken to procure an honorable discharge from their parent Lodge, which, when received, shall be immediately communicated to your Grand Lodge.

| December 15th, 1807. | ELISHA SIGOURNEY, Chairman of the Committee of St. Andrew's Lodge. |

The committee of the Grand Lodge of Massachusetts.

The subject was allowed to remain in abeyance at this point, to enable St. Andrew's Lodge to communicate with the Grand Lodge of Scotland, until September 11, 1809; at which date, a satisfactory answer having been received from Scotland, the Lodge directed its committee to communicate the result to the Grand Lodge, then in session. The committee were courteously received and seated at the right of the Grand Master in the East. Its chairman, R. W. Bro. Elisha Sigourney, then arose and read the following document : —

"At a special meeting of St. Andrew's Lodge, held at Masons' Hall, on Thursday evening, September 7, 1809, Voted, That Bros. Elisha Sigourney, Benj. Hurd, David Bradlee, James Green, Andrew Sigourney, Henry Purkitt, and Benjamin Hurd, be a committee to wait upon and inform the G. L. of this Commonwealth, at the Quarterly Communication, to be held the 11th, inst. ; that St. Andrew's Lodge will, at the next annual Communication of the G. Lodge, become one of its members, agreeably to the Communications made in December, 1807.

A copy from the Records.

Attest,   JOSEPH SMITH, Sec.

The committee of St. Andrew's having retired, it was, on motion,

Voted, That a committee of this Grand Lodge be chosen, consisting of the following R. W. Brethren, viz: — R. W. Josiah Bartlett, John Chadwick, Ephraim Bremen, and the two G. Wardens, to wait on the R. W. committee of St. Andrew's Lodge, and inform them that the W. Grand Lodge, had most cordially received their affectionate and brotherly communication ; that they with heartfelt satisfaction, anticipate the happy consequences of this Union, and promise a parental regard to the interests of the Lodge they represent, and invite them to a seat this evening, and a participation of the pleasures and intercourse of the same."

The committee from St. Andrew's Lodge then returned again to the Grand Lodge, escorted by the Grand Marshal and the committee of the Grand Lodge, and were replaced at the right hand of the M. W. Grand Master.

And here the subject rested until the annual communication of the Grand Lodge in the following December, when the W. Master of St. Andrew's Lodge, JAMES GREEN, Esq., being present, rose and addressed the M. W. G. Master, in terms expressive of the high satisfaction his Lodge had realized, in the candid and honorable proceedings of the M. W. G. Lodge in completing and confirming the admission of it under its jurisdiction, and declarative of their resolution strictly to conform to all its rules and regulations. He then delivered the Charter of St. Andrew's Lodge, for record and endorsement (says the record). "All which was cordially and affectionately reciprocated by the G. Master in behalf of the Lodge."

This may properly be regarded as the conclusion of the subject ; but these proceedings are too interesting, and too essential to a full and clear appreciation of this important point in the history of the Lodge, to be passed over so summarily. I therefore offer no apology for transferring from our own records, the following more complete and perfect narration of the transactions, in the order of their occurrence. At a meeting of the Lodge held at the Green Dragon Tavern, on the 14th of December 1809, Bro. ELISHA SIGOURNEY inquired of the R. W. Master if he and his Wardens attended the Grand Lodge at its communication on the 11th inst., and if so, to inform the Lodge of their reception, and the proceedings of the Grand Lodge. To this request the W. Master Green, made the following reply :

"That he and the Wardens did attend the Grand Lodge, and after the same was duly organized (St. Andrew's Lodge being placed in their proper station, the first on the left of the Grand Master), the Grand Marshal informed the Most W. Grand Master that St. Andrew's Lodge had taken their seats for the first time as a member of the Grand Lodge, and it was probable the W. Master had some communication to make. I then arose and addressed the Most W. G. Master in the following manner :

Most Worshipful Grand Master,—The friendship of my respected Brethren of St. Andrew's Lodge (far more than my merits), having induced them to elect me their Master the ensuing year, it devolves upon myself in union with my R. W. Bro. Purkitt, Senior Warden and my Bro. Zeph. Sampson, Junior Warden, in obedience to their commands, to present ourselves before you as their representative, and to inform you that St. Andrew's Lodge having *honorably* exonerated itself from its parent Grand Lodge, do now with pride and pleasure recognize the Grand Lodge of the Commonwealth of Massachusetts, as the only rightful and lawful authority by which it will in future be governed, agreeable to the votes passed unanimously in Grand Lodge, December 5807, September 5809. I am also directed to present you its original and ancient Charter, to be countersigned and recorded in the Grand Lodge Books ; also a list of the names of its officers and members. Although this auspicious hour has been long protracted, the members of St. Andrew's Lodge flatter themselves, that being now united with, and aided by the *Wisdom* of the Grand Lodge ; cemented by the *Strength* of her sister Lodges, they shall not only partake of the *Beauty* of the Masonic superstructure, but in some measure add thereto, by such conduct as shall designate correct citizens, promote the honor of the craft, and be conducive to the felicity of man."

After which the Grand Master approached and presented me with his right hand and bid us a hearty welcome in behalf of the Lodge we had the honor to represent, and most cordially congratulated the Grand Lodge upon the acquisition of what he was pleased to term the ancient and respectable Lodge of St. Andrew's as one of its members, which bright link, he observed, now completed the Masonic Chain of Massachusetts.

The Grand Lodge then proceeded in the business of the elections for the year ensuing, and the Honorable and Most Worshipful Josiah Bartlett, Esq., was elected Grand Master ; R. W. Bro. Francis J. Oliver, Grand Senior Warden ; and R. W. Bro. Oliver Prescott, Esq., Grand Junior Warden ; R. W. Bro. Andrew Sigourney, Grand Treasurer ; and R. W. Bro. John Proctor, Grand Secretary (the two last officers chosen unanimously).

The selection of a Brother of St. Andrew's Lodge to the high and responsible office of Grand Treasurer, from among the numerous Lodges under their jurisdiction, and at the first moment of its connection, must, I think, be received not only as a mark of honor and confidence conferred on Bro. Andrew Sigourney, but also of high respect paid St. Andrew's Lodge, and as such I trust it will be duly appreciated.

The R. W. Master then delivered the Charter regularly endorsed by the Grand Lodge, and which he had received from Bro. Elisha Sigourney, in whose care it was for that purpose. Bro. Elisha Sigourney then addressed the W. Master and informed him that having received the Charter of St. Andrew's Lodge from the R. W. Bro. Burbeck, "on his death bed" (to whose care it was intrusted), under a solemn injunction never to give it up until the difficulties which then existed between the Grand and St. Andrew's Lodge should be settled (and which charge having been approved of by the Lodge), that happy time having now arrived, he with pleasure divested himself of the trust reposed in him, and in presence of the Lodge committed the Charter to the R. W. Master, whose rightful privilege it was to take charge thereof.

The transactions of the Lodge at this meeting closed here. But at its regular communication on the ensuing 12th of April, they were consummated and confirmed by an official visit from the executive officers of the Grand Lodge; when the following highly interesting and gratifying proceedings took place :

The Lodge was opened in due form on the first degree of Masonry, at 8 o'clock, when the Grand Marshal entered and informed the R. W. Master, that the Most W. Grand Master, with his Grand Officers, were ready to visit St. Andrew's Lodge.

The R. W. Master having appointed the R. W. Brethren, Benj. Hurd, James Farrar, David Bradlee, Benj. Smith and Joab Hunt, a committee to wait upon the Grand Lodge to the Lodge Room, directed them to proceed. The committee, attended by the Marshal and Stewards, proceeded to the room where the Grand Officers were assembled, and escorted them to the door of the Lodge-room; then opening to the right and left, the Grand Officers preceded by the Marshal, entered and were introduced to the R. W. Master by the Grand Marshal; they then severally took their seats on the right of the Officers of St. Andrew's Lodge.

The Right Worshipful Master then arose and welcomed the Grand Officers in the following appropriate address :

Most Worshipful: "The long wished-for period having arrived, that St. Andrew's Lodge have anticipated with pleasure, the various obstacles being removed, which have kept asunder those who ought to have been allied by the tenderest ties ; in the name and behalf of St. Andrew's Lodge I bid you a cordial welcome. While the records of St. Andrew's Lodge furnish evidence of the rectitude of its conduct, they will fully evince the respect it has ever borne the Grand Lodge of the Commonwealth of Massachusetts and its pleasure, Most

Worshipful, is in no small degree enhanced by acknowledging the authority and becoming a member of the Grand Masonic Family under your administration, who have been so repeatedly elected to preside at its head with honor to yourself and satisfaction to your brethren. Permit me, Sir, to return the thanks of St. Andrew's Lodge for the honor of this visit, and to yourself, your officers, and the members of the Grand Lodge, its ardent wishes for your and their peace and prosperity."

The Grand Officers then took the stations of St. Andrew's officers, and the Grand Lodge was opened in ample form, and the Rev. Bro. Josiah Bartlett, as Grand Chaplain, invoked the blessings of the Deity on the assembly. The Charter and By-Laws of the Lodge were read by the Grand Secretary, and the records were examined by the Most Worshipful Grand Master. The members of the Lodge then recited a lecture on the First Degree of Masonry, after which the Most Worshipful Grand Master addressed the Lodge in the following elegant and truly fraternal discourse :

" *My Respected Brethren,* —

When I recollect that within these walls were displayed the early specimens of Masonic eloquence in our country; that beneath this venerable arch, the *distinguished badge* I so unworthily wear, was *first* suspended on our illustrious WARREN, whose life and death were instructive lessons of benevolence and patriotism ; that around this ancient altar commenced the labors of the late Massachusetts Grand Lodge, the influence of which, in connection with a similar institution, has extended from the limits of this metropolis to every section of our territory ; and especially when I indulge a pleasing fancy that your respected predecessors are viewing with complacency an official visit from your adopted patron, while at the same time they bestow a grateful remembrance on your distant parent, I feel sensations easier for you to conceive than for me to describe, and which you can best reciprocate by expressive silence.

" In the appropriate duties of this occasion, I shall only remark on the masonic history, that its doctrines and precepts may be readily traced from the luxuriant garden of paradise to the magnificent city of Jerusalem, when the capacious mind of the illustrious Solomon, comprehending the traditions of the most remote antiquity, applied the instruments of operative masons to illustrate the principles of our Order, and establish a system, which for six thousand years, has resisted the influence of ignorance, superstition, and political combi-

nation ; whilst its genial power in every age has softened the calamities of war
and alleviated the miseries of man.

" Reverence to the Supreme Architect of the Universe, a dignified obedience
to the civil authority, an affectionate regard to the characters and interests of
our brethren, justice to our neighbors, and unfeigned benevolence, are its avowed
objects.   To preserve and cherish these as far as we are able, is the duty of
all who are united by its solemn obligations.

" The erection of Lodges, the adoption of general regulations, and an uni-
formity in practice, so far as the habits and customs of different countries will
allow, have been always inculcated, and the formation and support of Grand
Lodges, whose authority should comprehend a convenient territory, have been
found by long experience to promote the prosperity of the fraternity.   No
arguments are necessary to confirm this fact in the United States.   A regular
intercourse among the brethren has extensively diffused the benefits, and the
flourishing state of eighty-six Lodges within this jurisdiction, evince, at least
an equal progress with other establishments for the promotion of public and
private happiness ! "

The Grand Master then dwelt upon the duties of the Grand
Lodge and its subordinates respectively, and closed as follows :

" We now, my respected brethren, congratulate you on the present situation
of St. Andrew's Lodge, and from the results of this auspicious interview, we
are bound to remark, that the wisdom of your by-laws, the accuracy of your
records, the regularity of your proceedings, and the respectful address of
your R. W. Master, discover a continuance of that laudable zeal, which, for
nearly sixty years, has been successfully exerted for its respectable support.
The cradle of its infancy was rocked with anxious solicitude, its blooming youth
was defended with vigilance and assiduity ; and its revered manhood, cherished
by industry and perseverance, will conduct it to an honorable old age, which is
not confined, like the fleeting days of man, to a single generation.   Your knowledge of the nature and design of our institution ; your experience in its ceremonies, and a strict observance of the precepts which, from a pressure of other
avocations, I have barely hinted at, will best preserve and extend its usefulness.
Erected on the Rock of Charity, and cemented by beneficence, it will remain
unshaken, when you and your successors are numbered with its venerable

founders ; whom, we humbly hope, are participating the pleasures of that exalted Grand Lodge, tiled with impenetrable secrecy, and from whence no traveler returns."

Thus was happily consummated a union between the two bodies, which has continued uninterrupted by any jarring interests to the present day, and which it is earnestly hoped may be continued in brotherly love and harmony through many succeeding ages. The felicitous period in the history of the Lodge had now been reached, when, in the language of a poet contemporaneous with its own birth, its members could reverently unite and say —

> "Now let us thank the Eternal power : convinced
> That Heaven but tries our virtue by affliction,
> That oft the cloud which wraps the present hour,
> Serves but to brighten all our future days."

Before leaving the subject entirely, a few words explanatory of the original organization of the Lodge, to which references have already been incidentally made, may not be out of place here, inasmuch as after the question of jurisdiction had been virtually disposed of, this was the principal objection urged against its recognition by the St. John's Grand Lodge. It was early assumed, and as late as January 27, 1766, officially voted by the latter body, that the petitioners for the Charter "were not at the time of their application for it, or at the date of said constitution, free and accepted Masons ;" and that their petition, as such, "was an imposition on the Grand Lodge of Scotland." This was said ten years after the Lodge had been in operation under its Charter, and when the authenticity of that instrument had ceased to be denied. That there were irregularities in the incipient stages of its formation, the committee of the Lodge, in consultation with a similar committee of the Grand Lodge, are said to have conceded, but denied the allegation that any imposition had been practiced on the Grand Lodge of Scotland. It would seem to us of the present day, that if the committee had cited to their doubting

brethren, the unusual and significant endorsement placed on the
back of their Charter by its parent Grand Lodge, simultaneously
with its issuance in 1756, this branch of the objection would have
been irrefutably, if not satisfactorily answered. This endorsement
is in the following words:

"CHARTER OF CONSTITUTION *and* NEW ERECTION, *in favor of the* LODGE
OF ST. ANDREW, *to be held at Boston, New England,* 1756."

No other logical construction can be given to the words "NEW
ERECTION," than that they imply a pre-erection, and consequent
pre-existence of the Lodge; and that whatever irregularities were
committed in its earlier proceedings were, by this endorsement,
intended to be regularized and confirmed by the Grand Lodge
making it. That body must, therefore, have been, — as the Lodge
and its committees had on all proper occasions maintained, — fully
informed of all its acts and doings antecedent to its application for
the Charter. Hence the charge of imposition would have been
easily disposed of.

And now a word in reference to the irregularities complained
of, and which constituted the second objection urged against
the recognition. The Lodge was composed of *Ancient* Masons,
who, in consequence of the difficulties in England, did not recognize the *Modern* Grand Lodge, so called, at London, or its laws, as
of any authority beyond its own immediate jurisdiction. The regulation enacted by it in 1721, requiring that all Lodges thereafter to
be established should, previously to going into operation, obtain a
warrant or charter from the Grand Lodge, or be deemed irregular,
they rejected as not applicable to them. Taking this view of
the subject, which, if not positively erroneous, was liable to objection, they organized themselves into a Lodge, relying on what
was then better known than now, as the law of "immemorial
usage," or inherent right, for their justification; and commenced
"work" in or about the year 1752. The question of regularity,
however, having arisen, they appealed to the Grand Lodge of
Scotland for advice, and in due time, as we have seen, received

from that distinguished body, a Charter of "Constitution and NEW-ERECTION," as a regular Lodge under its jurisdiction.

Such cases were not uncommon at that early day of masonic organizations; nor was this an isolated one in the Colonies. We find in the proceedings of the Grand Lodge of Scotland, under date November 30, 1759, that "several Scotch brethren, *having erected a Lodge* at Charleston, South Carolina, transmitted five guineas to the Grand Lodge for the use of the masonic poor. Grateful for this unexpected instance of benevolence," continues the record, "the Grand Lodge ordered a Charter to be made out and transmitted to them; they having signified a wish to hold their meetings under the Scottish Banner, by the name of The Union Kilwinning Lodge." This was a parallel case, and corresponds literally with the proceedings of the brethren who, in 1752, first organized St. Andrew's Lodge.

Such cases were also common at that day, on the Continent; and in other parts of the old and new world, at a much later period. They were known as "isolated Lodges," or Lodges not under warrant of any Grand Lodge. As recently as 1774, there were three Lodges of this description in India, two in Holland, five in Dutch Guiana, and others elsewhere. We are not aware that there are any of this class of Lodges now in existence, they having been superseded by a safer and more systematic rule of masonic government; except in the case of the "Lodge of Antiquity" at London. That being one of the "four old Lodges" by which the Grand Lodge of 1717 was organized, it was stipulated, as one of the conditions of the new order of things, that it and its associate Lodges, should continue to hold under the ancient law of "inherent right"; and it is, therefore, at this time, without a warrant from any Grand Lodge, though amenable to the laws of the Grand Lodge of England.

I have referred to these cases merely for the purpose of showing that the brethren who laid the corner-stone of St. Andrew's Lodge, about the year 1752, were not wholly without authority and justification for the manner of their proceeding.

The endorsement of the Charter by the Grand Lodge of Massachusetts in 1809, is signed by ISAIAH THOMAS, Grand Master, and is in the following words : —

"I do hereby authorize and empower St. Andrew's Lodge of Boston, formerly under the jurisdiction of the Grand Lodge of Scotland, but lately admitted under our jurisdiction, to take rank in Grand Lodge, at all their Quarterly Communications, festivals, and funerals, and all other regular and constitutional meetings, *agreeably to the date of their ancient Charter.*"

The question of rank or precedence has never been pressed by the Lodge, nor is it practically of any importance ; but viewed in the light of history, it may be proper, and perhaps of interest to the members of the Lodge, to state the facts bearing on this point, as they appear on the record.

In 1733, the St. John's Grand Lodge constituted "The First Lodge in Boston ;" in 1750, it erected "The Second Lodge in Boston ;" and in the same year, it granted authority for "The Third Lodge in Boston." This last Lodge ceased to exist about the year 1753, and no other was established in the town, except St. Andrew's, until 1772. The "First" and "Second" Lodges continued, with varied success, until interrupted and scattered by the events of the revolutionary war. The last never recovered itself, and its name does not appear on the records of the Grand Lodge later than 1775. In 1783, the members of both these Lodges had become so much reduced, and their meetings had been so long suspended, that it was deemed advisable by their few surviving members, to abandon them altogether, and out of the wreck to form a new Lodge. It will be seen however from what follows, that the material remaining was scarcely sufficient for this purpose ; but by the aid of members of St. Andrew's Lodge, a Charter was obtained by them, of which the following is an authentic copy :

To all the Fraternity of Free and Accepted Masons to whom these presents shall come.

The Most Worshipful John Rowe, Esq., Grand Master of Ancient, Free and Accepted Masons, duly authorized and appointed, and in ample form installed, together with his Grand Wardens, send   Greeting :

Whereas, a petition has been presented to us by John Cutler, Nathaniel Patten, Job Prince, Wm. Burbeck, and Mungo Mackay, a committee in behalf of the *first* and *second* Lodges of St. John, showing that it has been inconvenient for them to meet in their separate capacities, and that it will be for the benefit of Masonry that they be united in one Lodge, and that they will resign all powers by which they acted in those separate capacities, being desirous to form a complete and independent union. They, therefore, pray that they with such others as may think proper to join them, may be erected and constituted a regular Lodge of Free and Accepted Masons, under the name, title and desig-. nation of St. John's Lodge, with full power to enter Apprentices, pass Fellow-crafts, and raise Master Masons : which petition, appearing to us as tending to the advancement of Ancient Masonry, and the general good of the Craft, have unanimously agreed that the prayer of the petition be granted.

Know ye, therefore, that we the Grand Master and Wardens, by virtue of the power and authority aforesaid, and reposing special trust and confidence in the prudence, fidelity and skill in Masonry of our beloved brethren above named, have constituted and appointed, and by these presents, Do constitute and appoint the said John Cutler, Nathaniel Patten, Job Prince, Wm. Burbeck, Mungo Mackay, and others, all Ancient, Free and Accepted Masons, resident in Boston, in the County of Suffolk, and Commonwealth of Massachusetts, a regular Lodge of Free and Accepted Masons, under the name, title and designation of St. John's Lodge, hereby giving and granting unto them and their successors, full power and authority to meet and convene as Masons, within the town of Boston aforesaid, to receive and enter Apprentices, pass Fellow-crafts, and raise Master Masons, upon the payment of such moderate compositions for the same, as may hereafter be determined by said Lodge. Also to make choice of Master, Wardens and other Office bearers annually, or otherwise as they shall see cause. To receive and collect funds for the relief of poor and decayed brethren, their widows or children, and in general to transact all matters relating to Masonry, which may, to them, appear for the good of the Craft, according to the ancient usages and customs of Masons. — And we do hereby require the said constituted brethren, to attend at the Grand Lodge, or Quarterly communication, by themselves or proxies (which are their Master and Wardens for the time being). And also to keep a fair and regular record of all their proceedings, and lay the same before the Grand Lodge when required. — And we do hereby enjoin upon our said brethren, to behave themselves respectfully and obediently to their superiors in office, and not desert said Lodge, without the leave of their said Master and Wardens.

And we do hereby declare the precedence of the said Lodge, in the Grand Lodge and elsewhere, *to commence from the date of these presents*, and require all Ancient Masons to govern themselves accordingly, and to acknowledge and receive them and their successors.

Given under our hands and the seal of the Grand Lodge affixed at Boston, New England, February 7th, 1783, of Masonry 5783.

JOHN ROWE, G. M.
RICHARD GRIDLEY, D. G. M.
JOHN CUTLER, S. G. W.
JOB COMEE, J. G. W.

And that Brother Nathaniel Patten be appointed their Master.

NATHANIEL BARBER, JR. *G. Sec.*

William Burbeck and Mungo Mackay, named in the Charter, were at the time, members of St. Andrew's Lodge, and seem to have courteously lent their names for the occasion. Nathaniel Patten was a member of the "First Lodge," and Junior Grand Warden of the St. John's Grand Lodge, in 1787. John Cutler was a member of the second Lodge, and the first Grand Master after the union in 1792. Job Prince was Junior Grand Warden in the same year, and may have been a member of the "Second Lodge." It is possible, and perhaps not altogether improbable, that some of these brethren held membership in more than one of the Lodges in the town; for the present law, in this respect, was either not then recognized, or was frequently disregarded.

And now, W. Master, having, as concisely as the nature and importance of the subject would allow, noticed some of the more salient points in the history of our own beloved Lodge, — its trials, its struggles, its final success, — and having also indicated the close and intimate relations which, in its earlier days, it held to the Grand Lodge, on the eve of whose CENTENNIAL ANNIVERSARY we are now assembled, and the memory of which we still cherish with the veneration and ardor of youth, I ask permission to submit the following preamble and vote for your consideration :

WHEREAS, the Grand Lodge of this Commonwealth has voted to celebrate the approaching Centennial Anniversary of the establishment in this city of the " Massachusetts Grand Lodge," in anticipation of what would have been the pleasure, and in view of the early close and intimate relations of the two Bodies, perhaps the especial duty, of this Lodge to commemorate : And whereas, it is manifestly right and proper that the proposed fraternal recognition of the occasion by our adopted and venerated mother, should not be allowed to pass by without the cordial co-operation of her eldest daughter : Therefore,

Voted, That St. Andrew's Lodge will unite with the Grand Lodge of Massachusetts, in celebrating, on Tuesday next, the Centennial Anniversary of the establishment of the Massachusetts Grand Lodge, and the inauguration of her own distinguished son, General Joseph Warren, as its first Grand Master.

Worshipful Bros. Parkman, Willis, Sherman, Stearns, and others, followed in remarks approving the Resolutions, and they were unanimously adopted.

The subject of opening the records and archives of the Lodge was next formally considered with the view of collecting material for a Centennial Memorial.

CELEBRATION

OF THE

CENTENNIAL ANNIVERSARY

OF

THE LODGE OF ST. ANDREW,

NOVEMBER 29, 1856.

FIRST MASONIC TEMPLE IN BOSTON, ERECTED A. D. 1830.

Introduction

A determination to celebrate the Centennial Anniversary of the Lodge of St. Andrew, in a distinguished manner, had long been a cherished purpose of its members. The eventful series of the first one hundred years of the Lodge's history, together with the preservation of the most ancient Masonic charter in the State of Massachusetts, which had been granted to "St. Andrew's" A. D. 1756, by the Most Worshipful Grand Lodge of Scotland, would be completed on the thirtieth day of November A. D. 1856. During the year previous, on several occasions, this proposed celebration was informally considered, but nothing of an official character took place, until at a communication of the Lodge, July 24, 1855, when, on the announcement that the Right Worshipful Charles W. Moore, Grand Secretary of the Grand Lodge of Massachusetts, a member of "St. Andrew's" and a noted Brother of the order, was about to visit Europe, the Lodge voted, on motion of Brother Charles Allen Browne,

That R. W. Bro. C. W. Moore, be authorized and requested to invite the M. W. Grand Lodge of Scotland, to attend by delegation, the Centennial Anniversary of St. Andrew's Lodge to be celebrated in Boston, on St. Andrew's day, in the year of our Lord 1856.

At the ensuing quarterly communication of the Lodge, held September 27, 1855, on motion of W. Bro. John R. Bradford, it was voted,

That a committee be appointed with full powers to make all necessary arrangements for celebrating the Centennial Anniversary of the sealing of the Charter of the Lodge of St. Andrew, by Sholto Charles Douglas, Lord Aberdour, Grand Master of the Free and Accepted Masons of Scotland, at Edinburgh, 30th of November, A. D. 1756.

Under the above vote, the following named members of the Lodge were appointed a Committee :

Brothers JOHN R. BRADFORD,	CHAS. W. MOORE,
THOMAS RESTIEAUX,	SAMUEL P. OLIVER,
WILLIAM PARKMAN,	CHAS. ALLEN BROWNE,
THOMAS W. PHILLIPS,	C. J. F. SHERMAN.

At a subsequent Communication, the Lodge voted to have prepared, in honor of the approaching Centennial celebration, and to be worn first on that occasion, a superb gold jewel, emblazoned with the cross of Saint Andrew, as a Member's Badge.

On the eighth of November, 1855, in regular Lodge communication, R. W. Bro. Chas. W. Moore, made a report by address, as follows :

Worshipful Master and Brethren :

On leaving for Europe in August last, you were pleased to make me the bearer of an invitation to the M. W. Grand Lodge of Scotland, to attend by delegation, or otherwise, the celebration of the Centennial Anniversary of our Lodge, November 30th, 1856. And I have to report thereon, Sir, That the Grand Lodge of Scotland, not being in session at the time when I was in Edinburgh, I could not, as I had desired, communicate the invitation in person to that distinguished body. I accordingly placed it in the hands of the respected Grand Secretary of Scotland, and received his assurance that he would submit it to the Grand Lodge at its next Quarterly meeting, and inform me of the deliverance thereon. When the result of the action of the Grand Lodge of Scotland is received, I shall take pleasure in communicating it to the Lodge.

I availed myself of the opportunity of my visit to Edinburgh to consult the records of the Grand Lodge in relation to the origin of our beloved "St. Andrew's," and have the pleasure herewith to transmit as matters of interest and future reference, extracts from them. I also hand you for the same purpose a letter from the R. W. Grand Secretary of Scotland, in answer to one from me of the day before, in particular reference to our Charter.

The action of the Scotch Grand Lodge in response to the above invitation, was the appointment by commission of two delegates, who were present and participated in the services on the occasion of the celebration, as representatives of the Grand Lodge of Scotland.

PROCEEDINGS IN COMMITTEE.

Agreeably to the wish of the Lodge, and with ample powers, the "Centennial Committee" now took upon itself all the arrangements for the great celebration. The Hon. Nathaniel B. Shurtleff, a member of "St. Andrew's," was made Secretary of Committee, and the 29th day of November, at 5 P. M., was fixed for the time of celebration, on account of St. Andrew's day, which is the thirtieth, falling in 1856 on the Sabbath. It was decided that the principal features of the occasion should be an Oration, with odes and original music, the services to take place in the Grand Hall of the Masonic Temple, to be succeeded by a banquet in the lower hall, and the following were

INVITED GUESTS.

M. W. GRAND LODGE OF SCOTLAND,
All GRAND MASTERS in the United States and the Canadas,
M. W. GRAND MASTER of GRAND LODGE OF MASSACHUSETTS,
R. W. DEPUTY GRAND MASTER and G. WARDENS,
W. MASTERS of all BOSTON LODGES,
M. EX. GRAND HIGH PRIEST of GRAND CHAPTER,
HIGH PRIESTS of SUBORDINATE CHAPTERS,
M. EM. GRAND COMMANDER of GRAND ENCAMPMENT of
MASSACHUSETTS and RHODE ISLAND,
E. COMMANDERS of SUBORDINATE ENCAMPMENTS.

Tickets of invitation were given to the LADIES of the above named distinguished guests, and to two ladies for each member of the Lodge of St. Andrew.

The further proceedings of the Committee will appear in the subjoined correspondence :

2 BEACON ST., BOSTON,
16th May, 1856.

Dear Brother : —

At a meeting of the Centennial Committee of the Lodge of St. Andrew in Boston, held this evening for the purpose of making arrangements for the Centennial Celebration of the constitution of the Lodge by the Grand Lodge of Scotland, on the thirtieth day of November, A. D. 1756, it was unanimously voted: — That Worshipful Brother Hamilton Willis be requested to prepare an Oration for that occasion.

In compliance with the directions of the committee, I have the honor to transmit to you the above vote, with an earnest hope that you will find it in your power to comply with the wishes of the Lodge.

With much respect
I am fraternally yours,
NATHANIEL B. SHURTLEFF, *Sec. of the Com.*

To Hamilton Willis, Esq., Past Master of the Lodge of St. Andrew.

BOSTON, June 26, 1856.

MY DEAR SIR: —

Your note of the 16th ulto., conveying to me the wish of the Lodge, that I would prepare an Oration for the Centennial Anniversary to be celebrated next St. Andrew's day, is at hand.

The peculiarly eventful, nay extraordinary history of the Lodge of St. Andrew, together with the resources at its command, I know must prompt the gentlemen of the committee to amply meet on that occasion, the laudable desire of the brethren, by a complete Celebration, and one of no ordinary character. In this view, as well as for other considerations, my own opinion has pointed to another member of St. Andrew's for the fulfilment of the distinguished part in the Festival, which they have now assigned to me. I need not mention the name of this Right Worshipful brother, so conspicuous in Freemasonry, so exceedingly endowed with skill and acquirement "in the art," for response to the needs of this anniversary. But I must presume, that our most accomplished "workman" has begun to feel that it is high time for younger "craftsmen" to explore the ancient fields of Masonic lore, narrative, Lodge history, and incident, which he has gleaned with so much honor to himself, and usefulness to "the Order." I therefore, — with I trust becoming sensibility, — shall undertake this duty in the earnest hope that, by fidelity at least to the bright record of the Lodge of St. Andrew, I may, in some satisfactory measure, respond to the generous confidence reposed in me, and to the sentiments of the Fraternity.

Sincerely yours,
HAMILTON WILLIS.

To Hon. Nathaniel B. Shurtleff, Secretary of "St. Andrew's" Centennial Committee.

It will be shown in making up the full account of this memorable occasion, that Brethren both within and without the roll of "St. Andrew's," did volunteer their graceful muse, to swell the intellectual feast of the day and occasion.

The Committee's arrangements being perfected in the most admirable manner, with that thoroughness of excellent detail which received unqualified encomium, the

RECORD OF THE CELEBRATION

is given in the Lodge Books in the following language :

A special communication of the Lodge of St. Andrew was held at the Masonic Temple, on Saturday, November 29, A. L. 5856, at five o'clock, P. M. for the purpose of celebrating its one hundredth anniversary. The Lodge assembled in the ante-room promptly at the hour appointed, all the members being present, with exception of the venerable brother Baldwin, brother G. C. Stearns, and brother H. W. Suter.

The Worshipful Master opened a Lodge of Master Masons "in form," and at once proceeded to the Grand Hall, where the invited guests, with their ladies, had already assembled to the number in all, of some four hundred.

ORDER OF CELEBRATION.

VOLUNTARY ON THE ORGAN.

BY J. H. WILCOX, ESQ.

PRAYER.

BY THE CHAPLAIN OF THE LODGE.

BRO. PETER WAINWRIGHT.

ORIGINAL HYMN.

BY BRO. NATHANIEL B. SHURTLEFF.

Almighty Archi - tect, di - vine, O'er these assembled brothers shine With mild, benignant ray;

Almighty Archi - tect, di - vine, O'er these assembled brothers shine With mild, benignant ray;

Vouchsafe a happy gath'ring here, With nought t'alloy fraternal cheer On this centennial day.

Vouchsafe a happy gath'ring here, With nought t'alloy fraternal cheer On this centennial day.

May all who meet within this hall,	And may the pastime of this night
To grace St. Andrew's Festival	Contentment add to pure delight
This rare event employ !	To consecrate the scene !
And friends who join us on this eve,	And when these hours of love have pass'd,
May they thy bounteous gifts receive,	May life, made brighter while they last,
And share with us the joy !	Be holier that they 've been !

ORATION

BY

W. BRO. HAMILTON WILLIS,

PAST MASTER

OF

THE LODGE OF ST. ANDREW.

On account of the length of this Oration, several passages were not spoken in the delivery, and the historical portion, relating to the Lodge of St. Andrew, was condensed. It is now given in full, as originally furnished to that body for the press, in response to their vote in March, 1857. This Oration contains the only history, in print or manuscript, of " St. Andrew's " which has ever been prepared.

THE ORATION

Worshipful Master,

      and Brethren of the Lodge of St. Andrew : —

In a Republic, whose natal day has not reached its centennial era by a score of years, the celebration of the one-hundredth anniversary of a Masonic Institution within its border, is a distinguished event. The contemplation of such an epoch brings the mind irresistibly to pause and linger upon the thought of what a century has brought forth ! It inspires us to draw thence, reflections which shall brighten the veneration for Free Masonry, of those within, and win the increased respect of those without its portal.

Brethren of St. Andrew's, on this, the centennial of our Lodge, with all its eventful record fulfilled, it is befitting to celebrate it with fraternal congratulations. It behooves us moreover, to remember that this occasion is imposing, and instructive ;—that it is good for us to dwell on the retrospection ; and, above all, to approach the commemorative duty its presence enjoins, in a spirit of reverence becoming the votaries of an Institution which hails from the Great Architect, through whose unwavering beneficence to the long roll of " workmen," the glory of Masonic principles, our own birth-right, have been preserved in bright memorial from a great antiquity.

In contemplating the history of Free Masonry, we are led to recognize, in the luster of its progress, a Divine protection; that its Constitution, founded upon the Holy Scriptures, became a steadfast guide, and that its cardinal principles have been faithfully adhered to. It is this well-tried basis, that has given our Order an existence almost co-eval with the Year of Light. To the Brethren of this, and succeeding generations of Masons, working with fervency and zeal, will remain the duty of handing Masonry down in perpetuity, free from the rust of neglect or innovation, with all its ancient land marks firmly established.

The scroll of centuries, which have been numbered since this Order caught its inspiration from the noblest instincts of the heart, and assumed form and identity, exhibits no period when Masonry made so decided an impression on the times, receiving itself quickening impulses,—certainly in all the modes of growth and establishment in the eye of the world,—as in the first century period of our own " St. Andrew's." The two signal events of this period, whence the greatest consequences to Masonry have sprung, are, First,—the reformation in matters essentially of jurisdiction, together with the revival thereupon experienced in England A. D. 1717; when instead of the illimitable privilege of assemblage hitherto allowed, without warrant of constitution. it was determined by general consent, that thereafter, Lodges or assemblages of Masons should work only by legally authorized grants, in the form of Charters, or Warrants, emanating from Grand Lodge. Secondly,—and co-eval with the first,—the introduction of Masonry into North America.

Let us consider them in this order:—

The immense results flowing from the comparatively simple steps adopted by the Brethren of Great Britain, A. D. 1717, regarding the details of Masonic Government, can scarcely be over-estimated, and they are to be attributed to the inherent force of the great principles underlying the Order, rather than to any exalted merit of origination. The germ of prosperity was already in the Institution ;. it remained for these trusting Brethren to give opportunity for its expansion. These wise steps imparted stability, a point of concentration, unity and effect. Their tendency was to promote regular intercourse, thus better preserving intact those ancient land marks, which, hallowed by antiquity, had gathered their ties around the vitals of the Institution. The watchful eye of universally recognized authority was necessary to guard the great heart of Masonry alike from the dogmatism of zealous devotees, and from the attack of fanatical foes. The general acquiescence, no less than admiration, with which the new regulations were welcomed, filled the Brethren with enthusiasm, and secured a wholesome impulse throughout Europe. In place of irregular meetings of individuals without Charters, or an admitted head, regular and duly constituted Lodges were established all over Great Britain. The new regulation became a success.

Scotland! — What memories arise with the mention of old Scotia's name! Among thy hills, thy dells, thy wild heaths, thy bleak domains, held fast in the breasts of thy faithful sons, the " Mystic Tie " has been a precious boon, charming, cheering, alike the lonely Cotter and the Chief of Clan ! " St. Andrew's " names thee reverently :— Scotland ! where ever since the first Lodge met in the Abbey of Kilwinning A. D. 1437, the beneficent tenets of Masonry had flourished, here they now took fresh start. At Edinburgh, A. D. 1736 the new principle of election to the office of Grand Master, was sustained. The Grand Lodge of Scotland, in its present constituted form, as distinguished from the ancient form of " annual assemblages," dates from this year. Sir William St. Clair called the convocation, November 30, thirty-three leading Lodges being represented, and having no male heir, he then formally surrendered the hereditary right of his family to the office of Grand Master, which had been granted to his ancestor, William St. Clair, Earl of Orkney and Caithness, Baron of Roslin, by the Second James of Scotland, in 1437, and afterwards made hereditary. He was however thereupon unanimously elected to the office, in token of his relinquishment of the honorable heritage, and from that time annual elections have been held. Lord Aberdour, whose

name is borne upon our own Charter, was the first Scottish Grand
Master, who has been honored by re-election to that high office.
This noble-born Brother, subsequently held a similar position in the
Grand Lodge of England.   In all, two Grand Lodges and five sub-
ordinate Lodges in the United States, were chartered by the Scotch
Grand Lodge.

Previous to 1737 the Scotch "annual assemblies" were held on
St. John's Day. It was this year changed to " St. Andrew's
Day," 30th of November ; and all Lodges of Scottish descent do so
observe it.   This day commemorates therefore the entire independence of the Grand Lodge of Scotland, as well as being the anniversary of the crucifixion of the Patron Saint of that Kingdom.

The Grand Lodge of Ireland was formed A. D. 1729. The inauguration of reform was not confined to Great Britain, but extended with Anglo-Saxon social or commercial influence, among the
nations everywhere.   The possession of the Secrets of Masonry became, to the merchant, ship-master or traveller, a passport for introduction and safe conduct in foreign ports ; to be a " bright " Mason
was to own an accomplishment of more value to the enterprising,
adventurous gentleman, than many acquirements ; at home or
abroad the Fraternity saw their account in a knowledge of the
" Mystic Tie."

In France, where since the second century, the Masonic art had
been cultivated, a surprising impulse was imparted by the new organization of A. D. 1743.   It very soon partook of the national char-
acteristic ; appearing with a pomp and ceremony elsewhere unknown ; new grades, together with civil and religious orders were
added.   This state of prosperity lasted until the breaking out of the
French Revolution ; a temporary check was then experienced. It
recovered itself, continuing to bear upon the rolls, names illustrious
in the literary, civil and military history of that nation.   The Emperor Napoleon was a Mason.

In Germany, the order was reorganized under royal patronage,
and the Prince Royal of Prussia was initiated in 1738 :—this per-
sonage subsequently instituted a Lodge at Berlin.

It is painful to remember, that our gallant Order encountered serious opposition at one period in Germany, from the ladies of the Emperor Joseph's Court. What unmasonic discourtesy could the Brethren have committed to incur the enmity of that always powerful sex! It is pleasing to record, however, that this opposition graciously yielded to representations made by the distressed Brotherhood, in behalf of the character of Free Masonry, just as that gentle sex have ever since done, without a murmur, and with intuitive perception of right, evincing that delicate courtesy and good sense, for which, surely they will ever be distinguished.

In Holland, the Institution flourished after its establishment in due form, A. D. 1734. Nearly every town had its Lodge. So popular was it to be a Mason, that aristocratic Dutchmen set up Lodges, composed exclusively of one or another of their Social Circles. A Magisterial Lodge was also held, where none but Magistrates were admitted. These were innovations upon well settled usage, but Masonry has met many such, without lasting prejudice. Francis I, of Germany, when he was Duke of Tuscany was made a Mason in the Low Countries, by Lord Chesterfield, who opened a Lodge of "emergency" for the purpose. The following forcible testimony to the character of Dutch Masons, was given before their "States General:"—

"Free Masons are the most faithful subjects, uniformly obedient to their government, and true to their country. The greatest union prevails among them. They are utter strangers to hypocrisy or deceit; they cheerfully discharge every reciprocal office, and the institution is truly venerable."

Such was the eloquent tribute, spoken under oath in truly the highest official presence, more than a century ago, to the character of Masonry.

In Denmark and in Sweden, Free Masonry stands very high. It is, too, of great antiquity in both countries. The frequent maritime intercourse with Great Britain, afforded the Danes and Swedes the most favorable opportunity of copying the best Masonic organization. Their Charters, also, are derived from the Grand

Lodge of Scotland. It is stated that the "Halls of the Society of Masons are superb. They are among the finest edifices of the great towns."

Russia, twenty years after the organization referred to at London, A. D. 1717, established her first Lodges. All classes in this Empire became patrons ; but politics have now and then interrupted their harmonious working, and at one period the Lodges were held only in private. There is better order now.

In Spain and Portugal, the Inquisition nearly paralyzed our Order. For ages, " the tenets " moved with vitality only in the secret repositories of the steadfast. But in 1727 there was a revival ; at Madrid, Lisbon, Oporto, and elsewhere in Portugal, Masonry was planted anew. Subsequently, in the larger cities of Italy, through Church and State it began to embrace the humble and the exalted. Still the Pope of Rome issued his Bull against the Order, A. D. 1738 ; bitter persecution was endured until Foreign Princes, mainly at the prompting of their Masonic faith, interfered successfully to mitigate the wrath of jealous Rulers. The edicts, however, are still in force.

During the violence of the French Revolution — from 1790 onward,— the meetings of Free Masons were interfered with, and sometimes stopped by the European Powers : — this fact however, is worthy of record, namely, that in England, our Lodges were expressly exempted in Acts of Parliament for the suppression of secret meetings.

Switzerland, Hungary and Poland, had each received Speculative Masonry by the middle of the eighteenth century. In Bohemia, also, "it was fashionable to be a Free Mason."

Thus much for results in Europe, which are fairly claimed to have come to pass, from the transactions of the year 1717 : when a few enlightened British Brethren, in conjunction with several venerable Lodges, animated by a desire to strengthen, and promote the usefulness of their beloved Institution, took Masonic counsel together at the " Apple Tree " Tavern, in London, and established the Most Worshipful Grand Lodge of England.

It will be pertinent, for a fuller understanding of this most important measure in the annals of Free Masonry, to state, that from the era of the earliest recorded Grand Master in Great Britain, A. D. 924, up to the times here treated of, the rule was as follows:

Any sufficient number of Masons, assembled, were empowered to practise the Rites of Free Masonry, without warrant of Constitution. The privilege was in the aggregated individual Brethren. But at the organization of the Grand Lodge of England the following regulation was adopted, under date A. D. 1721.

To wit: —

"The privilege of assembling as Masons, which has hitherto been unlimited, shall be vested in certain Lodges, or assemblies of Masons, convened in certain places; and that every Lodge to be hereafter convened, excepting the four old Lodges, at this time existing, shall be legally authorized to act, by warrant from the Grand Master for the time being, granted to certain individuals by petition with the consent and approbation of the Grand Lodge in communication; and without such warrant no Lodge shall be hereafter deemed regular or constitutional."

"The Grand Lodge of England" here, and thus far, mentioned, must not be confounded with the Grand Lodge of York, where the first General Assembly of Masons was held in modern times in the tenth century—otherwise styled The Grand Lodge of All England. The former was also styled The Grand Lodge of "The South," and the latter The Grand Lodge of "The North."

By A. D. 1780, a competent authority states the number of "Regular" Lodges in Europe, to have been twelve hundred and forty-seven. Of these, over four hundred were in Great Britain and Ireland, and four hundred and eighty-four in France.

It is not assumed, that the above regulation, which was simply instrumental, was the sole cause of the regeneration of Free Masonry all over Europe, as has thus far been narrated. No; it is not enough to declare that this ancient Order was touched by the magic wand of modern organization to accomplish this. The time had come, — the march of mind, material advances, the invention

of gun-powder, of the Mariners compass and the art of printing —
they need not be enumerated, — the political advance, the Revolution of 1689, progress in the condition of society, etc. ; suffice to say
the age had gone forward, morally and materially, whilst Masonry,
which had been equal to the emergency in every age, respectively,
from the remotest antiquity, till the dawn of the eighteenth century,
was now to meet the test of that, — the test of the age upon and
before it.   There was a crisis, a turning point ; and the question
before our British Brother Masons of 1717 was, must the Order
remain in the back-ground? I will not say succumb ; must it rust
out or become only a splendid, it may be a weird, a mythical tradition? No! no! the vital Masonic principle, as old, as new, as sure
as the instinct of manhood, possessed inherently the germ of advance to meet that crisis of A. D. 1717, as it will to meet the requirements of future ages by still other, newer organizations, if need
be.   Ay, already we have an example in point, presently, in due
course to be recorded here.   I allude to the organization of Speculative upon Operative Masonry.   But let us first trace the beneficent pathway of the Order around the world, and next proceed to
the second signal event of the past century, before we touch our
emblems of inspiration.

    We resume, then, the progress of Masonry beyond Europe. —
Evidence of undeniable data shows that the spread of Masonry
which followed these transactions, was not confined to one continent.   The refreshing fountain, from the well-springs of Free
Masonry, sent its pure stream everywhere.   In Asia, whence, following the sun light in its track, "the Art," with its sister Arts,
have travelled to the West ; the " craft " were again set at work, and
the " Mystic Word " was sought.   At Aleppo, A. D. 1740, an
English official gathered together a Lodge.   In Bengal, Madras,
Calcutta, at several points in the East Indies, in China, Batavia,
Ceylon, and even at still more remote places, Masonic Lodges were
constituted.   The native nobility, with the so styled upper classes,
were attracted to the Order, and extraordinary success attended the
" work " of the Brethren.   The M. W. Grand Lodge of England,

availing of the opportunity afforded by the preponderating commercial intercourse of Great Britain, engaged itself in planting Lodges within and beyond her Provinces. This parent body sent letters of compliment, accompanied by suitable gifts, to prominent natives of distant lands, in token of their patronage of "the Art," oftentimes receiving in return, grateful assurances of the deep hold it had secured.

In Africa, about the year 1736, a Lodge was erected on the banks of the River Gambia, another at the Cape of Good Hope in 1773 ; also at St. Helena, Tunis, Morocco and Madagascar, and at the Sandwich Islands. In 1796 Mohammedan Brethren visited the Grand Lodge of Massachusetts.

The French and Dutch, in their respective colonies, favored the introduction of Masonry. Doubtless, the interests of civilization, peace and good-will, perhaps even the dictates of ordinary prudence, helped thus to enlarge the sphere of our Order, at this comparatively early period, in communities situated far away from the centre of power in Europe. Motives of policy, convenience or sociality, may have been involved in this rapid extension. But from whatever aspect, or by whomsoever the subject is reviewed, it is gratifying to know that the ancient renown of the Brotherhood was again recognized, and fully appreciated for its manifold beneficent abilities as well as for its precious power over the sensibilities of the untutored.

Such are some of the fruits of the Order's "new steps," or " modern organization," and they were but a development as has been already considered of the latent force, always present in the bosom of Free Masonry, in embryo, wonderfully traced by the hand of the Supreme Artificer, to give potentiality to the " Mystic Art," towards winning its eternal way, strewing flowers, unobtrusively, over the checkered life-route of man, no matter under what circumstances, how benighted ; how illumined be his condition, spiritual or physical, even to lands where christianity has not yet been taught.

We come now to the second signal epoch of the eighteenth century in Masonry, namely, its introduction "in due form" into North America. This epoch, the most marked and consequential in all its history, was inaugurated by three important events, as follows : —

First, by the erection of the " Saint John's Grand Lodge of Free and Accepted Masons for New England," under seal of Grand Master, Lord Viscount Montague, 30th July, A. D. 1733, at the " Bunch of Grapes Tavern," State street, Boston, with Right Worshipful Henry Price as Grand Master. This commission bore date 30th of April, that year, from the Grand Lodge of England. The next year the Grand Master was invested with power to establish Masonry in all North America. The celebrated Dr. Franklin was in this same year commissioned by St. John's Grand Lodge to establish the first Lodge in Pennsylvania.

Second, by the erection of " The Lodge of St. Andrew," in Boston, under a Charter dated, 30th of November, A. D. 1756, granted by the Grand Lodge of Scotland.

Third, by the appointment, under seal of the Grand Master, the Right Honorable George, Earl of Dalhousie, on the 30th of May, A. D. 1769, of the Master of " The Lodge of St. Andrew," the Worshipful Joseph Warren, to be " Grand Master of the Masons in Boston, New England, and within one hundred miles of the same," — a grant of power which was, under date March 3d, 1772, by Grand Master, the Right Honorable Patrick, Earl of Dumfries, extended over the " Continent of America." Both of these authorizations were also made by the Grand Lodge of Scotland.

The consummation of this last grant of Masonic jurisdiction, came to be best known in history as " The Most Worshipful Massachusetts Grand Lodge." But before " it " strictly became entitled to that designation, " it " passed through a record peculiarly interesting as well as altogether unprecedented in Masonic annals.

Inasmuch as " This Grand Lodge " begun at the instance of, and was inseparably associated for fifteen years with St. Andrew's Lodge, — whose history will be detailed, in course, further on in this address, — the following succinct statement, touching both, will be in point here.

At the beginning, then, in 1769, the style of Massachusetts Grand Lodge was the "Provincial Grand Body." In June, 1775, "its" Grand Master fell on Bunker Hill, and a new appointment from Scotland was solicited. None was legally needed — none came. On the 8th of March, 1777, "to soften the rigor of the war," and from the exigency of the situation, a Grand Master was duly elected. On the 6th of December, 1782, a "declaration of independence" speaks for itself, as follows : —

" Resolved, That this Grand Lodge be forever hereafter known and called by the name of The Massachusetts Grand Lodge of Ancient Masons, and that it is free and independent in its government and official authority, of any other Grand Lodge or Grand Master in the universe."

The two Grand Bodies, namely, "The Massachusetts" and "St. John's Grand Lodge," continued, all along from their respective commencements, to exercise authority in a common jurisdiction, until March, A. D. 1792, when the former, having alone tided Grand Lodge organization uninterruptedly through the distractions caused by the American Revolution, they made a union, forming the present "Most Worshipful Grand Lodge of Massachusetts," under the official title of "The Grand Lodge of the Society of Ancient Free and Accepted Masons, for the Commonwealth of Massachusetts."

St. Andrew's Lodge, originally founded under the ancient mode of assemblage, up to A. D. 1769, acknowledged allegiance solely to the parent body in Scotland ; from that date until January, 1784, the Lodge in part, acknowledged the authority of "The Massachusetts Grand Lodge of Ancient Masons." After 1784, St. Andrew's ceased to be represented in that Grand Body ; but having always retained its original Charter, this Lodge continued to work under it, owning allegiance to Scotland alone up to the 11th of September, 1809, at which date St. Andrew's placed itself, with the consent of The Grand Lodge of Scotland, under the jurisdiction of the Grand Lodge of Massachusetts, where in honorable affiliation, this Lodge now is, still holding its original Scotch Charter, with the endorsement of its adopted parent.

From 1769, the time of its election, till 1792, the time of its
"consolidation," this "Massachusetts Grand Lodge of Ancient
Masons" chartered twenty-nine Lodges in New England and one
in New York. Nineteen of these are now alive. Tyrian Lodge of
Gloucester, Massachusetts, was the first one, and Massachusetts
of Boston, was the second ; the former under date of March 2d,
and the latter, of May 12th, A. D. 1770.

I have thus sketched an outline of the leading incidents which
ushered the benign "'Mystic Art' in due and approved form,"
upon the new scene of this Western Continent ; an epoch that we
have called the second signal one of the eighteenth century in
Free Masonry, reserving much filling up — as above stated — for
the more detailed history of "St. Andrew's." And now from the
foundation of these Institutions, at what was at that time the
Metropolis of this hemisphere, from the devotion, ability, skill and
sterling character of the Brethren, who laid in perfect work the
corner-stones of the Masonic edifice in New England, from the zealous rivalry which prevailed between the two "Grand Bodies," and
from the strength, position, and special influence of " St. Andrew's,"
by reason of these causes, I say, may be traced the rapid, and general diffusion of the glorious principles of Masonic Faith, in ample
form, with purity, intelligence and "skill of craft," over a thriving
continent, at a period co-eval with their invigorated diffusion
through the people of the " Old World."

Before passing this division of the topic it is necessary to remark, upon what under the present established political and
Masonic government of the United States, seems an anomaly : —
Namely, the existence of two "Grand Bodies" in one and the
same territory and common jurisdiction ; and it is also to be stated
that, during the time of the transactions in the colony, the St.
John's and Massachusetts Grand Lodges did not agree in the
courtesy or legality of such common jurisdiction, etc. This aforesaid state of things, however, under the circumstances, was nevertheless in proper accord with Masonic law and usage, to wit : —
Either of the regularly constituted Grand Masonic Bodies of Great

Britain or Ireland, the parent country, had the indisputable right to grant jurisdiction in any of its colonies. These New England colonies were joint possessions of the same crown, and being subject to the same Power, were equally at the Masonic disposal of each of the Grand Bodies of the British Empire. Under precisely similar circumstances, the same practice exists at this moment in the Canadas, where Lodges work with Charters respectively granted by the Grand Lodges of England, Ireland and Scotland ; moreover it is true that Masonic jurisdiction is not in all cases restrained by the limits of political sovereignty any more than, as a matter of course, must such jurisdiction be confined to geographical lines, or ordinary social distinctions. In the archives of the Lodge of St. Andrew, — whose members were prominent actors in the age, and among the transactions of which we are here speaking, — is preserved the following document. It will be seen that it not only bears directly on this point, but it also lights up another Masonically important historical issue, pregnant in its day with great consequences. The document is as follows : —

"The right of commission, by the Grand Lodge has been exercised before the erection of your Lodge, as instance the appointment of Colonel John Young to be Provincial Grand Master of all the Lodges of North America, who acknowledge the jurisdiction of Scotland. The exception which is now taken to your Charter by the St. John's Grand Lodge on account of the so styled infringement by the Scotch Grand Lodge is gratuitous."

(Letter of the Earl of Elgin and Kincardine, Grand Master, Grand Lodge of Scotland, A. D., 1762).

But historical justice requires the additional remark here, because bearing upon and largely qualifying opinions on that old question of jurisdiction, to this effect : — during the whole progress, it lasted scores of years — of this memorable contest at Boston, in our Order, what is known as "Ancient and Modern Masonry," a really absurd issue, — certainly a gratuitous one in America, — deeply pervaded several wide spread important portions of the Masonic Family. It prevailed severely in New England : — but here again, for the sake of the continuity of my subject matter, I must reserve all consideration of it, for its proper place, in the narrative of our own " St. Andrew's."

Having now rapidly surveyed the successive steps of the Order, in setting foot on this continent, let us — in happy imitation of the plan of the " Ancient Ritual," in " all regular and well governed " circumstances, — pause for contemplation, summon in review the Grand Institution, its causes of success, and repeat its admonitions.

The unknown origin of Free Masonry ought not longer to attract the astute research of the learned. Let us cling to the more valuable and significant fact of its mysterious, nay its almost miraculous preservation from so remote an antiquity. We know that Lodges, or assemblages of Masons, in some form, existed ages anterior to the necessity which called " the Order " so conspicuously into notice, under the Wise Grand Master, King Solomon, at the building of the Temple. It was given to the attentive mind and cunning hand, who planned and executed that marvellous structure, so to mould the physical and mechanical material at his disposal, that each should be admirably economized for the purposes designed. " Labor and Refreshment " were harmoniously proportioned. From the " designs " drawn on that " Trestle Board," sprang anew the " Temple " of Masonry, in later times curiously tesselated by the handiwork of the craft. King Solomon's work was finished ; but the work of the Mason had only begun. The skilful teachings, taught by the " Master," were held fast in " faithful breasts ; " through them the " secrets " have been handed down to us. The world would not hold its own records ; but Age upon Age bears evidence, in admired monuments, the labor of brethren, to vouch with unerring accuracy, and in superb memento, for the perfect work of the " operative " Freemason.

As we follow on in the current of centuries, to periods within reach of modern records, abundant evidence is shown to prove that agreeably to ancient usages of the craftsmen, they continued to assemble; Charters, together with powers of special privilege from sovereign rulers, are extant, confirming such right. Here and there in prominent mention among national archives, the duties, objects and dispensations for these "societies" are found. The Charter granted by James II. to the Earl of Orkney, A. D. 1441, is kept in the archives of the Order. The Charter of our own "St. Andrew's" is in terms a duplication, with all the landmarks duly set, of the one erecting the Grand Lodge of Scotland by the Fourth James of the kingdom. The chronicles, as well as ordinary tradition, for more than two thousand years, testify to the presence of Masonry in important transactions of those ages.

But in the early part of the eighteenth century, as we have seen, the force of concentrated effort came to be better understood; Freemasonry, wrapped in the folds of a renowned antiquity, bearing within itself almost the absolute heritage of command, was, nevertheless, fully awake to the spirit of the times which it encountered. Renewed zeal discovered itself in its concerns; the time-hallowed "ancient landmarks" were re-set; the usages, ceremonies and due observances of the Fraternity were more exactly inculcated; that division of labor, together with precision in government, which contributed to those material pillars of strength and beauty under our ancient Grand Masters, — when the Temple workmen were operating, — became more and more recognized; so that, before the noon of the century, Freemasonry had re-appeared, in its pristine glory, in new fields of usefulness, under due control. Verily, the "Mystic Tie" grandly stood forth a beacon light to the world, heralding faith, hope and charity, from pillars of "Wisdom, Strength and Beauty."

Europe, and generally the "old world," on to near the middle epoch of our colonial dependence saw Freemasonry illustrated almost wholly by the "operative kind." During this period, which embraced all those ages that have come down to us in anything like historic annals, the precious tenets of the Order served as a panoply and ark of safety for the protection of the brotherhood, and the integrity of their faith. But, as gradually mankind grew

11

more and more elevated in the standard of intelligence, as knowledge was diffused, as the benefit of useful discoveries was imparted,
and an acquaintance with the arts and sciences was more generally
sought, the "craftsmen," keenly alive to the interests of their
fellow-men, and in response to the genius of the age, generously
relinquished the tenacity of their hold upon the inestimably valuable secrets of "operative Masonry." The cherished secrets, the
wonderfully drawn Trestle Boards, the designs of the Master
Mason, — all priceless jewels of the Order held, as it were, from time
immemorial, in trust for the benefit of mankind, whether within or
without the "Inner door of the temple," — were made known, given
up freely at the behests of an improved and advancing people. A
thoroughly trained chosen acquaintance with those manifold arts
which made up the proud distinctive accomplishments of the Operative Mason, ceased thereupon to be "with good report and recommendation," the sole condition of admission into the Lodges. The
sphere of the Masonic Institution was hereby to be heightened
immeasurably in moral grandeur, while it was not longer to go on
enlarging its practical daily usefulness to the human race as an art.
A different field at once opened, new relations came to pass, fresh
connections presented themselves, and the latent strength, the
intellectual and moral capacity of Masonry, was now really to be
tested. A principle, which had hitherto illustrated itself to the eye
of the learned, and been commended to the gazing wonder of the
masses, only by means of superb edifices, costly intricate struct-
ures, and the noblest monuments; now straightway appeared
solely in the sublime, but simple attributes of a charitable association; bound together by immutable links, as inscrutable as before,
to the uninitiated. It is then, since this cardinal feature of Freemasonry, always inherent in its bosom, has been brought prominently forward into the view of the world; in other words, it is
since the Institution was re-organized in its "speculative" kind exclusively, that it has come to meet the issue, to stand trial with
society, in this Western Hemisphere. In fact, the introduction of
Masonry into America, was co-eval with the great feature exhibited
in its triumphal progress, which we have thus sketched.

And now in reflecting upon the leading causes, that have power-
fully conspired to place "speculative Freemasonry" in the prized
situation it holds in all communities ; in reflecting upon the causes
of its marvellous universality ; we are forced to assert its admirable
fitness to the wants of men in every station of life ; together with
the harmony which its beneficent tenets invoke towards reconcil-
ing man to his fellow-man, by bringing in sympathetic contact,
under the working of perfect system those tender sentiments which
lay in the breasts of all mankind, ready to be moved when the right
chord is touched. The Masonic secrets cannot be described to the
uninitiated ; but the faithful brother knows them all as the spirit of
Masonry. The grand secret is, its five points are, again and again
the "Spirit of Masonry," and they may be patent to every one,
who is duly and fully prepared to recognize their power, and to
suffer his heart to beat in unison with the hearts of those, who have
earlier felt, and sooner embraced their renewing vitality. Every
human being, no matter what his strength, or capacity of gifts
vouchsafed, does, at moments here and there in life's pilgrimage,
feel the need of that gentle regard, that friendly grasp, that delicate
courtesy, which they alone, who worship at the same shrine, do fully
bestow, — can fully reciprocate. The charity which only gives, is
secondary, — oh ! how far less worthy indeed, — to that charity, which
kindling with emotion at the tale of distress, opens with whole
heart to the sufferer and forever more, in weal or woe is friend and
brother. Masonic deeds of benefit cannot be reckoned, they are
never counted. The left hand heeds not what the right hand
doeth. They are unproclaimed, unseen, like the healing oil poured
into the wound, its flow is not visible ; that it has flowed is not
seen by the eye, until it has filled to the full the wound of the
afflicted. This, my brethren, this my hearers, is the real majesty
of that "Mystic Tie," so charming to the initiated, as it throws its
perpetual halo of religious light, and radiant beauty around those
immutable emblems, fixed by the founders of the faith, in beaming
lustre in our Temples, to animate the young, to cheer the aged
brothers ; to quicken the sluggish ; to temper the enthusiastic ;

but above all, to keep forever bright in untiring remembrance, those Divine precepts, which are at once the life, the light, the jewels and glory of Freemasonry.

During comparatively the modern advance of the Order, in its absolutely exclusive moral attitude, it has met, as in circumstances before in all ages, with stern opposition. When has reform, or proffered benefit not met opposition, nay persecution? Hostility by indifference or open warfare, attends always steps of advance. They increase, too, with the spread of all efforts of amelioration in human condition, often intensifying in degree, as the promised boon is silent, unobtrusive, intangible to the public eye in its work-ing. The priceless gem sees the light only by having the crusts embosoming it partially removed. Masonry also has met, perhaps it may again meet bigoted intolerance, despotism, the promptings of envy, a mingling of hateful motives, each and all but thickened crusts, impeding a march in a progress, that will not, cannot be stayed.

The Institution however, had taken deep root. The vital prin-ciple of Speculative Masonry was too strong, its influence was too potent, its purposes were too momentous, and resting confidingly upon its Book of Constitutions, adhering steadfastly to the "ancient landmarks," to obedience to rulers, with fresh adminis-tration, pointing to renowned annals, the "Order" has uniformly prevailed, just as it did at a more recent day, when unworthy men, — "Cowans and Eaves droppers," — essayed, with astounding impudence, to hurl into the vortex of political strife, — impelled by calculating, selfish baseness, — an Institution within whose potent charm they failed to enter, and which they could not appreciate.

Passing from this rapid contemplation of "Operative and Specu-lative Masonry," and from its condition in the "Old World," where the rust of time, the mouldering waste of age, has obliterated the precise details of an Institution, which has outlived both causes of destruction ; let us now try the motives, consider the influences, and then summon forth some of the doings, that the introduction of Freemasonry into New England has brought to pass, between

" high twelve," of the past, and the noon of the present century ;
a period covered by the records of " St. Andrew's," and more than
spanned by those of its noble parent body, who is pleased to recognize in our Lodge a child faithful to her adoption.

In approaching this branch of my subject, I am moved with more
than ordinary distrust in my ability to present such an estimate of
so paramount an era in Masonry, as shall do justice to my own
convictions ; and, what is of greater consequence, one that shall respond to the sentiments, in this regard, of the distinguished brethren and gentlemen, whose presence on this occasion is a gracious
recognition of the importance of the era, as it certainly is a mark
of respect to the Order, and to the Lodge of St. Andrew.   Moreover, the special intelligence of the fraternity in this part of Masonic
history, holds the speaker to what may be expressed as an embarrassing fidelity in statement of details.

Touching, then, the motives for establishing Lodges in this
country, the conclusion is irresistible that an earnest conviction of
the exalted character of Masonry, of its philanthropic design, of its
social, hospitable, and charitable character, was foremost in the
minds of the Masons, who in 1733 laid the first stone of their
cherished edifice here in Boston.   By this act, the founders of " St.
John's Grand Lodge" added another proof of the universality of
Freemasonry.   They saw in a territory so vast, so promising, and
so sparsely settled by different races, the need of an influence more
subtle and efficacious for good than either governmental or ordinary
social institutions can ever afford.   They witnessed eager, stirring,
absorbed, busy communities, who demanded rest to over-taxed facul-
ties, some healthy diversion, some other aspect in the scene of daily
life more joyously colored than the grim picture, which from the
earliest colonial time, had been set before the people, drawn and
deep shaded still in that day in the austere lineaments of " Puri-
tanism."   A holiday sketching-in must beautify, by pleasing contrast, the never so essential drudging details.   The outlook upon
the landscape must have the blending of softer tints and glowing
emblems as much as the grandeur of dignified outline.   These wise

founders foresaw, amid the usual discordant elements of individual interest, of such a necessarily rough state of society, a wide domain opening for the wholesome display of sentiments which could mitigate severities in civil and social relations, and infuse the charm of amenity and good fellowship through the land, for its happiness and prosperity. In one word, that divinely inspired idea so early taught in our steps towards the Light, which enjoins upon us to regard all mankind as Brothers, underlay, and was the superior motive towards gathering into fold the early Masons on this continent, organized Lodges, and made a beginning for good work.

If comparisons were pertinent, between old and new world Masonry, the thought might be ventured :— that abroad and heretofore, it had shone beautiful in theory, whilst here it promised to be the embodiment of a prime active daily duty. In the one land it was apt to be felt as an adornment of especial personal merit ; in the other, it was meant to raise the standard of general, popular regard.

In estimating next the influence and success which the introduction of Freemasonry secured, let us see into whose hands was its guidance first put ; for from this, in addition to the perfection of the tools confided to the workmen, are we to trace results, which have done honor to the Institution in this country.

Among the men who embraced our Order and became zealous in its observances, are names which are notably identified with the memorable eras of the colonies. Patriots, who nurtured the ideas, which spoke the nation into birth ; who stood by doing yeoman service in the fearful struggle which raised it to maturtiy, and who lived to see their fame grow with its strength, and be stamped with the prestige of world-wide renown. In the religious, military, and civil history of the Nation the Brethren were noted ; in science, in the arts, in professional careers, came good and wise men of all stations, who, drawing from the same fountain of inspiration, joined with steadfast attachment to Masonry. To a very surprising extent numerically, as also in point of high character, will this statement be in accord. It is not claimed that love of liberty, natural rights, moral and artistic culture, a well regulated society, had their sole main-spring from an order that make such aspirations cardinal points ; but rather that the constructive harmony inherent in Masonry, was adequate and marvellously consistent with them all. It is this adaptation to the infinite relations, social and official, in civilized communities ; in one word, it is this "Spirit of Masonry," more than the charm of apposite emblems, singular mysteries, or inscrutable secrets which has really given Freemasonry its clear record and universality from the year of Light.

Again, the political freedom, secured by the Independence of the United States, carried with it the privilege and opportunity of questioning the propriety of the existence of all Societies. This was a just claim of the people; but in theory and practice it was in marked contrast with that other set of political ideas, which in Europe gave to the jealous aristocratic few the sole right of opinion, a monopoly of influence, with the power of enforcement. Before both of these tribunals has Freemasonry been on trial. It is before that one, which is the most searching, and from which the most satisfactory verdict is taken, namely ; with the public opinion of a free people, that the order had now, for the first time in the world, come to be confronted. What has been the verdict ? Is the Lodge record of innumerable charities ? ay, the very absence of the record of benefactions ! in answer : No, no ; such things are not spoken of elsewhere, they shall not be here. Masonry does not need them in evidence ! Summon, instead, the good repute of the "Roll of Workmen ;" witness the uniformly conspicuous, and always courteous part borne by the Brotherhood on public occasions. Behold ! from the imposing ceremonial of a country's mourning to the scene of tenderest commemoration, where a few Brethren are assembled bearing "the sprig of Acacia," mingling a sentiment of fraternal sympathy with the wail of sorrow in the bereaved circle ! In both will the eye linger long, on the solemn but cheering emblems of the Mason's faith. Or, when moved by grand purpose, civic or associated enterprise rears the enduring monument to patriotism, high prized worth, to philanthropy, learning, valor, use

or art, there, too, Freemasonry pours forth its symbolic benison
in "Corn, Wine and Oil." Behold, too, amid the popular joy, with
pomp and pageantry on Gala days, the "Order" responds to the
general call and decks the scene with regalia adorned in jewelled
emblazonry, pregnant in meaning to the initiated. Even the
formation in this country of respectable, and doubtless excellent
so called "secret societies," imitations in "parts or points," of some
of the belongings of the ancient Masonic body, perhaps with other,
but worthy objects, are in some proper degree, a testimony to
our good name; or it may be solely to successful administration.

But these evidences, with the solicitation for admission to our
Lodges, are after all only the extrinsic evidence of popularity. One
true secret of the influence of Masonry in the United States, and
of the stand which it now securely occupies in all parts of society,
is, the opportunity presented by the genius of our whole social, as
well as governmental structure, for the development of that ancient
"landmark" of our Order, which rebukes artificial distinctions,
fostered by the caprice, the pride, the avarice of man, by reason of
birth, or any accidental advantages whatsoever; such distinctions
or ranks, as have been set up in other countries, to dash the manhood of men. — And here let me remark that Freemasonry, my
brothers, must be vigilant to keep bright its own inestimable teachings; in view of the baleful pride, and its consequences, which the
rapid prosperity of the American people often exhibit so conspicuously. In our times, we have need to value that noble sentiment
of "The Craft," which declares, "that it is the internal and not the
external qualifications which should recommend a man to be made
a Mason." A rigid, untemporizing steadfastness to this "land
mark," has not only promoted the moral grandeur of Masonry,
besides perpetuating its power, but it is instrumental for the common weal in a land where every honorable aspiration, and each
faculty of humanity has full scope.

Masons must recognize another, and it is the deepest cause of the
flourishing growth of that scion of the old Masonic tree planted in
this New England soil. It is the lessons imparted to the "Initiate,"

as step by step, from darkness to light, from the corner stone to the key of the arch, he is led into the mysteries of the craft. We must not, in every presence, lift that veil — more than it has been done already in operative Masonry — wrought by the cunning handiwork of illustrious craftsmen, our predecessors, which has proved immemorially so impenetrable a panoply for the protection of the Mason's faith, no less than for a positive public good ; but Masonry declares that "She would call all men Brethren," lifting her secret veil to — those who are duly and fully prepared ; asserting, likewise, that it is a preparation of the heart. Therefore, let us conjure you, friends, to believe that no step is made towards the "Mystic Tie" which does not inculcate trust in God, obedience to rulers, charity, hospitality, the sacred fulfilment of all obligations, and which by the most engaging method does not impress upon the mind the dignity of knowledge. No religious duty, no social tie, or public call can be neglected, consistently with Masonic pledges ; whilst from the first lesson taught to the "youngest entered apprentice," to the last moment, when the flickering light has dimmed his earthly tabernacle, these great truths are vividly impressed upon his attention by typical representations of perpetual remembrance, as unchangeable as is that all seeing eye, who deigns to recognize in their similitudes, symbols of the Creator's love for His creatures.

Before passing from this part of my subject, let me venture one other reflection on the inherent strength of the Masonic principle in this country, to wit : — In Europe, the "Lodges" have embraced members of exalted social and political position, who, separated by well recognized distinctions unknown here, have exercised an influence according to the degree of their elevation before the community. These Masons, by reason of an enlightened faith in Masonry, together with an ability to point everywhere in Europe at monuments proclaiming the services and skill of the "Operative Craft," secured to it on the one hand patronage, and on the other, respect and acquiescence at large. There has been another element of support abroad, to the Institution, equally unknown here.

12

It is the desire of oppressed subjects, for some secret point of concentration, for the safe interchange of convictions in civil emergencies. In this Republic how different is all this! Here, the unyielding note of clamor for individual rights, the stern cry for popular redress, those first, last, and always perpetual claims of freemen, are heralded with clarion tones in an asylum vaster than the arena of Lodges; while the cry will reach an auditory of the nation's great brotherhood. It must be so. Elsewhere there are aspirations in the breasts of a people which can only whisper in utterance. Let me not be understood as intimating that opposition to tyranny even, could be organized in Lodges anywhere, or that such hopes are a proper element of the hold of the Institution, — or that it has ever been so used; for reasons obvious to Masons such measures are impossible. The recent failure of Kossuth to move politically in our Lodges is an illustration of my point, both in its conception and utter failure. But it is suggested simply as a reason, why Masonry in nations less free than America, might possess a charm to the masses, which, however fallacious, did draw their aid to its support. This reflection, if it does not enhance, certainly does not take from, the still plain fact that Freemasonry in the United States has taken care of itself, without help from the patronage of any class, or the presence of the trophies of the Operative Brothers, or from any adventitious cause whatsoever; but by its own Wisdom, Strength, and Beauty.

My Brothers, these considerations are not only a striking tribute to the lofty claim of our Institution for universal regard, but they are significant of the paramount consequence of its introduction into this country. Such reflections seemed to me to be in sentiment, pertinent to this auspicious Centennial occasion; and, co-eval, as the record run over was, with the great Masonic revival of A. D. 1717, it seemed also, that they were both worthy of presentation to you, as signal events of the Eighteenth Century.

Brethren of "St. Andrew's:" after this long survey of the Masonic Institution, we come now to the history of our own beloved and venerable Lodge, — a history without a parallel, in the line of conspicuous Masonic events through which its members have been prominent actors.

The Lodge of St. Andrew, in its official relations, has occupied six positions successively. First, as subordinate to the Grand Lodge of Scotland; second, in recognition by a Provincial Grand Body, substantially of "St. Andrew's" own creation; third, in a qualified recognition of a Grand Lodge, caused by the exigencies of the American Revolution; fourth, by recognition in part, of the Massachusetts Grand Lodge; fifth, to comparatively, the anomalous position of an isolated Lodge; and finally, to the relation now occupied under the jurisdiction of the Grand Lodge of Massachusetts. During the whole of this period, and amid all these respective official relations of the Lodge, this body has uniformly worked under the original Scotch charter granted to it, one hundred years ago this night, bearing an endorsement, made forty-seven years since, of the Grand Lodge of Massachusetts, and one honored member, the venerable Zephaniah Sampson, recorded in 1805, who participated in the change last alluded to, is spared to us, and is present this evening. May the Almighty Architect guard and guide our Brother, and finally receive him into His perfect Lodge above!

But the proper history of "St. Andrew's" stretches its record even beyond the century, whose close we are met to commemorate. This history covers yet another relation; associated in its leading feature with the ancient usage, in the past ages of Freemasonry. It is briefly as follows:—In 1752 a number of Masons in Boston, who did not recognize the authority of the Grand Lodge of England, and in consequence the integrity of St. John's Grand Lodge in this colony, assembled to form a Lodge, in accordance with immemorial usage prior to A. D. 1721. This action was very properly called in question by "St. John's," whereupon those Brethren who were accomplished Masons, referred their action to the Grand Lodge of Scotland. This was in 1754. The Scotch Grand Body, as will be seen further on in its proper place, under the more formal proceedings of "St. Andrew's" for regular organization, did regularize these Masons, at the same time graciously recognizing the aforesaid immemorial usage; in other words, the good intention and acts of these Masons, insomuch as to set forth in their minutes, that the charter granted to regularize them was one of "New Erection," which technical phrase signified that the Body now constituted, had a beginning "in form" at some time, antedating the charter then and there granted.

The prime consideration, then, which presents itself in the history of "St. Andrew's," is this; why did its founders seek a charter in Scotland, when St. John's Grand Lodge of Free and Accepted Masons was already at work in ample form within the colony, on the same spot, and had been so for twenty years? The answer — and it is the most singular and prominent episode in modern Masonry — is, that the vigorous era brought on by the revival in the old "Order," A. D. 1717, was fertile in projects of reform, which culminated in 1738 in a so-called secession from the Grand Lodge of England, on questions purely local in Great Britain. A rival Grand Body appeared. An unbecoming strife was engendered. Whereupon the English Grand Lodge, in order to detect who of the Brethren were in sympathy with itself, and who were of the "secession" household, adopted a strange, frivolous, and uncalled for tampering with one feature of the Ritual. This unwise, gratuitous step of the Grand Lodge of England was cunningly seized upon by the other party, and made the most of by claiming for themselves the title of "Ancient Masons," because, in the matter of Ritual, the seceders had made no change whatever, but adhered strictly to the ancient landmarks, while they denounced the Grand Lodge of England, styling that Body "a Grand Lodge of Modern Masons." Thus the terms, "Ancient and Modern," wholly arbitrary in this application, came to be, in a portion of the Anglo-Saxon Masonic family, opprobrious names, designative only of two parties to a quarrel, both of whom were equally Free and Accepted Masons. No Masonic bodies but those strictly of English descent — and not all of them — took part in this quarrel. The Grand Lodge of Scotland, in particular, by prudent and forbearing conduct, uniformly exerted its influence to avert any pernicious effects of the controversy from the "Order" in general, and both sorts of so-styled brethren were invariably welcomed to its Lodges. This painful "Ancient and Modern" difference, lasted for seventy-five years in the mother country, and during the greater part of this period it embittered Masonic relations in the colonies. It really became a species of original sin in its working, seriously embarrassing innocent, upright made Masons in both "Ancient and Modern" folds. It is, however, an honorable fact to record, that in Boston, the light of reason and good sense soonest dawned. By the beginning of this century, an example of reconciliation was set, and in the year 1813 the notorious "Ancient and Modern" differences ceased to disfigure any portion of the clean escutcheon of Freemasonry.

Some aspects of the actions of men, when arrayed in heated partisanship, do partake of the grotesque; but outside the realm of mythical story, we search in vain for an absurdity parallel to this one.

In a fable of Voltaire, let me invoke a likeness of one feature of this "Ancient and Modern" contest, — so styled. In Babylon, at the time of King Moabdar, there lived a man of consequence, named Zadig. He was skilful, wise, and very popular. Now, in the city for five hundred years, the great political parties were the "Left Footers" and "Right Footers." It was an essential plank in the faith of one, that the Temple of Mithra should be entered with the left foot foremost ; and of the other, with the right foot foremost. It came to pass on a great occasion, that Zadig, for the first time must visit the Temple of Mithra, and very intense was the excitement between the "Left and Right Footers," to be assured on whose side the great man was. The day came. The avenues of the Temple were thronged ; the people of Babylon were breathless with emotion. Zadig advanced to the entrance, paused an instant, then jumped over the threshold with both of his feet together. This jump disposed of the question.

Saint John's Grand Lodge, — the only organized body of Masons in the colonies, — in the strictness of their fealty to the parent body, refused to affiliate with "Ancient Masons." Now among the brethren in Boston, about the middle of the eighteenth century, were a number of skilful brethren who were "Ancient Masons," who, unwilling to submit to exclusion from the practice of Masonry in Boston, unwilling also to ask any Erection, — if indeed it would have been granted, — from St. John's Lodge of "Moderns," availed themselves of an acquaintance with a number of "Ancients" at Halifax, and with one brother, of still greater intimacy, James Logan, who was in the colony at the time. Almost immediately thereupon, in the language of a contemporary writer, these brethren further associated themselves "with a number of Masons, many of whom, having been initiated in foreign countries, became emulous to cultivate the Royal Art under the Scotch Grand Lodge," and forwarded, in 1754, a petition to the Grand Lodge of Scotland for a Charter.

It must be observed here, that independently of this "Ancient and Modern" issue, the inference is plain, that a preference for Scottish Masonic authority, — whose purity was never questioned, — was present in the motive to go thither for a Charter, instead of seeking any rights and privileges from a strictly English source, the authority of which, howsoever perversely, was nevertheless disputed by a powerful opposition.

This petition, — with the recommendation of the Falkirk Lodge, in Scotland, — was presented to the Grand Committee of the Scotch Grand Lodge, at a sitting, held in Mary's Chapel, on the 22d of November, 1756, and approved. Thereupon a delay ensued of nearly four years; during which, St. Andrew's Lodge made certainly six Masons. These earliest records have become so mouldered or wasted, that no more candidates can be made out as having been carried through. Brother George Bray, who is named in the Charter, was the first one.

— The cause of this long delay is not surprising. A French war with Great Britain and her colonies, was one interruption. The correspondence of Bro. Logan with "St. Andrew's," during

these four years, shows many others, all, however, of detail, for the
business was new, probably without exact or sufficient precedent.
For instance: certain requisite names were omitted by the petitioners ; the name of the Lodge to be chartered was not set forth.
The customary adjustment for the Grand charity fund of the Masonic Infirmary of Scotland, — the guinea tribute, and half crown
initiate fee to Grand Parent Lodge, were to be determined, and
curiously enough, the ignorance, — strangely common abroad, even
in our day, of the geography of America, caused delay. Thus, the
Scotch officials on more than one occasion, addressed letters to
"The Brethren of Boston in Virginia." Lastly, in payment of
preliminary charges, "St. Andrew's" sent out a consignment of
"buck skins and other goods," valued at fifty pounds sterling
which, by some oversight, became "forfeit" to the customs and
when about to be sold in the British Court of Exchequer, fortu-
nately were saved to the Lodge. It is to be remarked, however
that, at no time, was there a shadow of objection started, as to
the standing of the brethren. —

At length, in the autumn of 1760, the Charter was received by
the hands of brother Wm. MacAlpine, a Scotchman, afterwards a
member of the Lodge, and the following are the minutes and extracts, from the books of the Grand Lodge of Scotland, concerning
its grant.

" Grand Secretary's Office, }
  Grand Lodge of Scotland." }

At a meeting of Grand Committee, held in Mary's Chapel, 22d November,
1756, *inter alia:* —

There was also presented to the committee a petition of sundry Brothers and
Free and Accepted Masons, residing in Boston, New England, praying to be
erected into a regular Lodge, under the sanction of the Grand Lodge of Scotland, and along with said petition, there was presented to said committee a
recommendatory letter by the Master and Wardens of the Lodge of Falkirk, in
relation to the said petition. The committee having considered the petition and

letter of recommendation. they remit the same to the consideration of the Grand
Lodge with this opinion. — that the documents produced along with the said
petition, are sufficient to entitle the petitioners to a Charter of Constitution.

QUARTERLY COMMUNICATION,
Mary's Chapel. 21st May. 1759.
inter alia.

Ordered. That the Charter of Constitution mentioned in the minutes of the
30th November, 1756, in favor of Isaac DeCoster and others, Brothers in
Boston, in New England, be expede under the title of St. Andrew's Lodge,
Boston.

Endorsed.   { From Grand Lodge Records,
A CHARTER OF NEW ERECTION.   {   Wm. A. Laurie, Gd. Sec.,
                                                    {   August, 1855.

The name of Saint Andrew was bestowed upon the Lodge from
the interesting fact that its petition for a charter was presented on
that Saint's day.

On the fourth of September, A. D. 1760, the charter was laid
before the Lodge, and in the same evening work was commenced
under it, by receiving Paul Revere, a goldsmith and engraver, as an
Entered Apprentice. This charter is numbered 81, of the Registry of Scotland, and not 82, as is usually given in current Masonic
documents. Lodge 82 in Scotch Registry is that of Blandford,
Virginia. This original parchment has always been in possession
of the Lodge of St. Andrew, and with the endorsement, as before
stated, of the Grand Lodge of Massachusetts, is the Masonic
authorization under which the Lodge has uninterruptedly, for a
century past, Received, Passed, and Raised Masons.

Isaac DeCoster, who was in Scotland, pending the proceedings
for this charter, had been designated by Bro. Logan for the office
of Master, and he held that office from April 10, 1756, to July 10,
1760, notwithstanding his absence. Bro. DeCoster had previously

been a member of a Lodge in Halifax, Nova Scotia, and on his coming to Boston, was refused, admission as a visitor to the old First Lodge of the town by two votes, because he was an " Ancient Mason." His instructions to St. Andrew's, during his Mastership, and while absent, are curiously imbued with the controversial Masonic spirit of that day.

The earliest Lodge meetings were held at Bro. Whateley's Inn, and occasionally at private houses ; but the organization of the Lodge on its official New Erection, took place in the Long-room of the Green Dragon Tavern. On the receipt of the charter, in September, 1760, the meetings were held at the Royal Exchange Tavern, King street, — now State street, Boston, and continued there until the purchase, — for £466, 13s. 4d. — of the Green Dragon Tavern, March 31, 1764. After this celebrated Inn came into the possession of the Lodge of St. Andrew, it was known also as Freemason's Arms, and the apartments occupied by the Masons, as Mason's Hall. This estate has ever since been the property of this Lodge ; it began to meet regularly here April 13, 1764, and assembled here continuously up to 1818.

We may well imagine the exultant joy which the "Ancient" Masons of Boston felt at the realization of the fact of a charter in actual possession, from so exalted a source as the Grand Lodge of Scotland ; and on the other hand, the chagrin of the "Moderns" at the successful erection of a Lodge by their opponents, whom they had denounced, and had striven to keep out of the Lodges of the town. Besides this very natural feeling, here was a rival body in a common jurisdiction with at least a title from an undisputed parentage, who could make Masons, and exercise all the functions, rights and privileges of Ancient Free and Accepted Masonry. In other words, what before was a scattered number of unregularized brethren, whom the close organization of a sole recognized body could treat in Masonic relations, as they saw fit, had now become a legally constituted Lodge, under the latest laws and best established form of the institution. Moreover, this rival body was knit together in the strong bond of zealous, quickened sympathy, with resources in "basket and in store," and ample skill in knowledge of the craft.

It is pertinent however, to remark here, that the intelligence of Boston Masons on both sides of this unhappy division, did show them how meaningless — certainly everywhere outside of England — was the nature of this "Ancient and Modern" contest. Both sides knew that each were lawfully made Masons, and the conviction must be forced upon the careful reader of the annals from 1750 to 1800, how little of plain dealing, of proper tact, was really necessary to banish forever the whole of it to England, where the quarrel belonged. The analogy in this, to all human concerns, discovers the same old working ; namely : — that it is ever the little irritations which do most annoy, and are longest endured, whilst a cause of decided magnitude is more likely to be promptly and intelligently disposed of.

Notwithstanding this jubilant feeling, "St. Andrew's" courteously presented their new charter to M. W. Bro. Gridley, Grand Master of St. John's Grand Lodge, for his inspection, claiming also, fraternal recognition and fellowship. The Grand Master did recognize the authentic character of an act of the Grand Lodge of Scotland, but persisted in refusing all Masonic intercourse with the Lodge, asserting that the Scotch Grand Lodge had been deceived ; that the brethren of "St. Andrew's" were clandestine made Masons ; that the charter was an infringement of the jurisdiction of "St. John's" Grand Powers, and that the brethren could only be regularized by "St. John's," on payment of "the charge for entertainment." Such was the language of a vote of this Provincial Grand Lodge, and but for the hospitable customs of the Order, in that day, would be deemed discourteous, as well as reproachful. It is mainly significant now, as proving what has been before characterized as the substantially frivolous ground of difference between these "Ancients and Moderns."

In the above paragraph are grouped the positions and attitude of St. John's Grand Lodge in their relations with "St. Andrew's," from the beginning of the latter named Lodge up to 1767. On repeated occasions, proper efforts were made to bring to pass, courteous and friendly relations. These efforts went so far as to attempt to reconcile entirely the "Ancient and Modern" issue in this colony; and it is but reproducing the truth of history to assert, that "St. Andrew's" acted the most creditable part throughout. Our Lodge, however, continued to receive the visits of the so-called "Moderns," and admitted them to membership even, without reciprocity on the other side. At length, impelled by self-respect, "St. Andrew's" closed its doors against them; but not until a vote peremptorily "forbidding all members of Lodges in the jurisdiction of 'St. John's' visiting a Lodge of Scotch Masons, so called, in Boston," had been passed by their opponents. Frequent correspondence with the Grand Lodge of Scotland furnished the entire concurrence of that distinguished Body, in all the steps of our Lodge. Yet a spirit of vindictiveness and surly conduct animated the "Moderns" for these nearly ten years.

Meanwhile, the Lodge was actively at work, and did not omit giving suitable publicity to its valued charter. In the newspapers of the town as early as 1761 and afterwards, advertisements noting celebrations of the "St. John's Festival," appeared in the following style, — "St. Andrew's Lodge, holding by authority of the Rt. Hon. Lord Aberdour, Grand Master of Great Britain, will celebrate, etc., at the Royal Exchange Tavern."

Candidates came forward freely, many prominent men took membership; among them were Joseph Warren, "made in" 1761, John Lowell, Dr. Jeffries, the elder Andrew Sigourney, Bros. Deshon, Carter, Mayhew, Danforth, Paine, and other leading men in colony and town affairs. A set of by-laws were borrowed from Halifax, and frequent amendments showed a rigid scrutiny, in the welfare and decorum of the Lodge. We cannot be indifferent to anything about the ways and means of these manly Masons, to set up a good Lodge, surrounded as they were by unfriendly brethren who watched with jealous eyes every movement of "St. Andrew's." It must be borne in mind, that it was not for a day, or occasion, or single issue, our predecessors had to face opposition; but the

settled, radical hostility of a whole Order, outside their own ranks for
half a century. Alone and singular, these devoted men stood to
their tenets through good report and through evil report. Wise
and wary as in duty bound, they husbanded all resources and made
every means conspire to form a creditable Society, one which
should attract initiates, and win and keep the respect of all high
minded Masons. Nothing was left at loose ends, lax, or rusty: Indeed, their administration of affairs, no less than their "work,"
was in marked contrast to everything of the sort about them in
the province. The number of members was early limited as a pre-
cautionary step ; convivial practices, usual at that age, were forbidden by " St. Andrew's " in " working hours," — promptness, attention, civility, and decorous behavior, were secured by fines and
penalties, which were rigidly exacted. Six pence for tardiness, two
shillings for three times absence. If a member was at all disguised
by the " good cheer " of the times, he must hold his peace during
the session ; outside in his daily walk, every one must be circum-
spect, reticent of his speech on Lodge business ; must not keep
company with clandestine Masons. Once the secretary was obliged
to apologize for doubtful language in a public town meeting, touching the institution, — the degrees must be given on due examination, and with proper lapses of time, if otherwise, for good reason,
the candidate must pay " the reckoning." Smoking in Mason's
Hall was prohibited, and it must be cleared at the closing. But for
all this, the Lodge was made inviting and generous in welcome.
The call to "refreshment" fully met all the need ; the " closet
stewards " were important functionaries, who added to their " skill
in the craft," a measure of skill in the knowledge of this world's
good things ; but they too must be enjoined to duty ; the liquors
were to be good, and bountiful in supply. Thus kindly cheer prevailed, nature got a pleasant jog, and " the balance was always kept
right adjusted." Again, the treasure chest was frugally cared
for. If the fund reached £12, it was to be put in a Province note
on interest. Above all, sweet charity hallowed every scene ! Scarce
a meeting but the silent vote told the brother's devotion at the

precious shrine, and when the Lodge's purse fell below the mark, the hat went around. For half a century, — ay, till the far-seeing forethought of this able ancestry of ours had placed " St. Andrew's " full handed in her treasury, this time-honored custom, all cocked hat and leather breeched, anon in ruffle shirt and silver buckles, from " East to West and South," appeared gathering in its harvest of blessed tribute, to be scattered as widely to the household of the faithful first, and next beyond. Then the " Stranger's fund!" There was help for the stranger always.

In all relations " St. Andrew's " was prompt, efficient and prosperous. Regular correspondence with the Grand Lodge of Scotland was kept up ; this was continued in the files until 1809. Exact direction in Masonic matters was solicited, and responded to. In 1762, Bro. James Logan of the Falkirk Lodge who had been, from the commencement, an earnest co-worker in behalf of the Lodge, was made its representative in Grand Lodge. At a later period, the Grand Secretary performed this office. Brother Logan was presented for his valuable services, with two nice buckskins for gloves, and small clothes. The gloves he gave to Brother Alexander MacDougal of the Grand Lodge. " Ancient Masonry " became popular, and the brethren began to consider the calls for more Lodges. In October of this year application was made to Scotland for leave to confer the Royal Arch degrees ; also, for Grand Lodge powers in order to form more Ancient Lodges. The following year, 1763, the Lodge, — on learning that Colonel Young was in America, with a commission as Provincial Grand Master, — recalled their request.

The greatest harmony existed. In a letter to Scotland just after the purchase of the " Green Dragon," they say " We have the most magnificent Lodge in North America, and the most numerous in these parts." For the first period of twenty years, the books show the names of some five hundred candidates, a greater number than for the next similar period.

Again, in 1766, renewed attempts were put forth for some sort of fellowship, with St. John's Grand Lodge and its affiliated brethren. "St. Andrew's" courteously extended civilities by the hand of its members, several of whom were men of the highest standing in the Province. These acts only again encountered indifference, capricious conduct, or positive rudeness. But "St. Andrew's" persisted in invitations for formal visits, and by well directed purpose towards showing the Modern Grand Lodge, its own continued upright acts, and legal authorization. However creditable to our predecessors; the narrative detail of these doings would be gratuitous now, if not altogether a wearysome exhibition of an honest desire for "a happy coalition," encountering a querulous indifference; and we gladly hail the more promising era of 1767. By this time then, the position of "St. Andrew's" in every point of view had become so firmly established, that other motives besides those cardinal principles, which should alone have actuated the "Moderns," were apparent in response to the Lodge's desire for peace and reconciliation; an event also occurred in September of this year, which hastened more courteous relations. This was the offer of "St. Andrew's" to join the Grand Lodge in celebrating the obsequies of their late M. W. Grand Master, Gridley, which, being unanimously accepted, became the occasion of an interchange of Masonic courtesies on the day thereof. Not long after, Richard Gridley of "St. John's" was made chairman of a committee, whose business it became to reconsider the denunciating action of that Grand body, which had been exhibited in January of this year. In May, 1768, this committee submitted their report. It is a lengthy review of the controversy, winding up in conclusion with this language : —

"That inasmuch as the brethren of St. Andrew's Lodge have resolved to embrace every method consistent with the good of Masonry, and their own honor, to promote a social intercourse with persons whom they so highly esteem as brethren and friends, we, the Grand Lodge, doubt not the Lodges under this jurisdiction will ever show as great a zeal to promote love and friendship as any Lodge whatever."

The subtle vein of mockery in the above was not suffered to

hinder any longer, proper relations between the bodies ; and their intercouse thereafter assumed a different, and more agreeable footing. Formal visits were interchanged ; and controversy in an obnoxious sense ceased. But there came to pass no " happy coalition," and presently " St. Andrew's," with the highest consideration for its own welfare and the general good of its Order, took measures for one of the most important steps in its own history, and of Massachusetts Masonry, namely : — the erection of Grand Lodge powers in the interest of "Ancient" Free and Accepted Masonry.

The successful erection of a second Grand Lodge at the instance of a single Lodge, and that an isolated branch of the colonial Masonic Order, was not only in itself a conspicuously interesting event, but as the sequel proved, it became the means of giving force and unbroken continuity to Massachusetts Masonic jurisdiction. All this the new Grand Lodge did, by persevering " in work " through the distractions caused by the American Revolution, and the political settlement of the State afterwards, — a period of sixteen years ; during which time St. John's Grand Lodge virtually held their own powers in abeyance. In this place a sketch only can be made of those transactions, as follows : —

The Lodge of St. Andrew, in 1768, finding that a coalition of the Masons of the colony could not be accomplished, and that the interests of " Ancient " Masonry must suffer for the want of a superior body, joined with three army Lodges in a petition to the Grand Lodge of Scotland for the appointment of a Provincial Grand Master, designating for that office their own Master, Joseph Warren. The petition was granted. The commission was received the 19th of September, 1769 ; it was brought over by Capt. L. Frazier, who was thanked by vote of the Lodge for his great care thereof. Bro. Paul Revere was directed to make suitable jewels for the Grand officers, at the expense of " St. Andrew's," and on the ensuing 27th of December Joseph Warren was inaugurated and saluted, as Grand Master in Mason's Hall, Green Dragon Tavern, in the presence of the Lodge of St. Andrew and the British Regimental Lodges Nos. 14 and 29. The powers of this Grand Lodge, styled Provincial, but not strictly Provincial in the sense of that term as used in Great Britain, — gave the right to establish Lodges ; possessing from the nature of the case, really inherent and independent Grand Lodge powers, with the single exception that it was required to make returns of charters issued, but paid no fees.

In March, 1772, another commission made Joseph Warren, Grand Master of Masons for the whole continent. By virtue of this authority, in 1773, he appointed Joseph Webb, Deputy Grand Master. On the 17th of June, of memorable memory, Grand Master Warren fell on Bunker Hill! In April, 1776, his remains received an imposingly solemn burial by Massachusetts Grand Lodge. The Hon. Perez Morton, a distinguished member of St. Andrew's, delivered an oration on the occasion of the obsequies, which has ever been marked for its eloquent language, and dignity of sentiment

It is not surprising, that in the infancy of Masonic jurisprudence, the death of Warren was erroneously deemed to have terminated the existence of this Provincial Grand Lodge. The Lodge of St. Andrew proposed to forward an application for a new appointment on the theory that Warren's commission died with him ; the application was sent out. Meanwhile, the importance of preserving Grand Masonic relations ; as they declared, " to soften the rigors of the war so seriously interrupted by the siege of Boston," caused the brethren to proceed to the election of a Grand Master. Consequently on the 8th of March, 1777, the Deputy Grand Master Joseph Webb was unanimously elected Grand Master. With the exception of the Master of St. Peter's Lodge, Newburyport, and a Past Master of Tyrian Lodge, Gloucester, also a member of " St. Andrew's," all the brethren who made this election, were members of the Lodge of St. Andrew. This step, at the time, was clearly Provisional, and without any declaration whatsoever ; but before the close of the century, — owing to the progress of events, — this act came to be regarded, by this Grand Lodge, — or by a few distinguished Masons who expressed themselves on the subject, — as a Masonic declaration of independence, and from its date, as being the earliest similar declaration by any Grand Lodge of America. It will be necessary however, to remark in this regard, again, that the body who elected Grand Master Joseph Webb in March, 1777, did not make any declaration of independence; neither could it be reasonably supposed that it contemplated so decisive an act at that moment, for this reason, to wit: the brethren who made that election — 8th of March, 1777, — were all members of the Lodge of St. Andrew, with the exception of the Master of "St. Peter's;" and "St. Andrew's," from first to last, or until the year 1807, positively and with remarkable persistency refused to do any act whatsoever, tending to cut clear of a certain Masonic dependence on the Grand Lodge of Scotland; farther on this will appear more unequivocally.

In this condition, the "Ancient" Grand Lodge continued in good service, uninterruptedly, until the 6th of December, 1782. At this time the Independence of the United States being considered secure, the "body" reviewed its position, and after serious deliberation, decided by the issue of a famous manifesto, to renounce allegiance to Scotland, and become a "Massachusetts Grand Lodge of Ancient Masons." This was done at the day and date above given, and M. W. Bro. John Warren, a brother of the first Grand Master, who was "made" in "St. Andrew's" April 18, 1777, was chosen Grand Master. Fifteen days after the making of the manifesto, in a reply to an invitation to celebrate the approaching St. John's Festival, "St. Andrew's Lodge" declined, by a vote of 30 to 19, to acknowledge that the Massachusetts Grand Lodge is independent of the Scotch Grand Lodge, as set forth in the aforesaid manifesto.

Up to this time, the exigency of the war and the absence of advices from Scotland, induced "St. Andrew's" silently to acquiesce in all suitable measures for keeping intact, the great step in behalf of "Ancient Masonry," which the Lodge alone had felicitously inaugurated and now sustained almost singly; but at the idea of utterly drifting away from the pure source of the ancient current in Scotland, it hesitated. Thus the saying of the day, "When Massa-

14

chusetts breaks from Scotland, 'St. Andrew' will break from her."
Still, there was a radical divergency of opinion on this question in
the Lodge, and it resulted, as will presently appear, in a vital one.

During the year following, 1783, the Lodge continued to send up
its Master and Wardens to Grand Lodge, but the representation
was made under a reservation. This year, the National Peace was
declared, on which event the Lodge decided to discontinue its representation, and give notice that "it held" only under the Grand
Lodge of Scotland. There was intense excitement on this question ; the determination was rampant to make changes in harmony,
if not in compliment to the new order of things in the young
nation. Again the subject was pressed in the following proposition : "Shall the Lodge pass under the jurisdiction of Massachusetts Grand Lodge, or remain by the Grand Lodge of Scotland?"
By vote, Jan. 22, 1784, of 29 to 23, it was again decided to hold
only by the Scotch charter. Absent members were required to
vote, and thereby this majority was increased. Bro. Paul Revere
headed the minority ; he demanded a hearing. A compromise of
opinion undoubtedly could have been effected, by changing the
name of the Lodge to that of "The Rising States Lodge," and this
was once actually voted, but subsequently reconsidered. Bro.
Revere persisted, and a painful controversy ensued, which was
ended by the retirement of twenty-three members, who immediately
started a "Rising States Lodge," September 4, 1784, chartered by
"Massachusetts Grand Lodge," with the right of dating from November 30, 1756. "St. Andrew's" was sued at law for a division
of its funds, and by the arbitration of referees, they were so divided.
But this defiance of Masonic law resulted unhappily : the new
Lodge quarrelled among themselves, making a sorry figure in the
Order, and in 1811 it dissolved. We may be permitted to utter
this reflection on these untoward transactions of "St. Andrew's"
men, that in the tumultuous emotions of these intensely patriotic
brethren, it is not altogether surprising that the gentle whisperings
of Masonic law should have gone unheeded.

In reviewing these important proceedings of the years 1782-5,

— which seriously influenced the course of our Lodge for a quarter of a century after, — historic justice requires of us to consider the respective positions and relations of the new Massachusetts Grand Lodge with " St. Andrew's." In general, then, the position of the Lodge of " St. Andrew" was this: the Lodge held, that independently of all questions of loyalty, expediency, or other considerations, that Masonic law and propriety demanded, after the death of Grand Master Warren, a reference to Scotland for a new appointment, or, in view of the independence of the colony, a reference to the Grand Lodge of Scotland for its approval of the act of declaring the Provincial Grand Lodge an independent one. On the other hand, the position of the new Massachusetts Grand Lodge was this; that body held that it had an inherent right in the circumstances under which it found itself in the Revolution, to make a declaration of its own independence. This body claimed that the preservation of Ancient Masonry on this continent required such a step; moreover, as a precedent, the Grand Lodge cited the successful erection of the different Grand Lodges in Great Britain and Ireland, affirming "that it was clear that some of them must have originated in assumption." In a full and very able report of a committee, on which Hon. Perez Morton was chairman, this position of Massachusetts Grand Lodge was argued, and five resolutions, — the second one being the famous manifesto before alluded to, — embodied reasons for declaring independence. This report was deliberately considered, "paragraph by paragraph," on Friday, Dec. 6, 1782, and adopted. Thus a controversy was commenced with the Lodge of St. Andrew, which was at times bitter, and always exciting. It lasted till the 23d of May, 1785, when by a formal letter, " St. Andrew's " notified the Grand Lodge that "it declined to entertain further the subject of joining the Massachusetts Grand Lodge, and would neither make nor receive any more communications upon that question.

And now, " St. Andrew's " was again alone. After fifteen years of Grand Lodge affiliation, she was forced by convictions of the same high sense duty, which had impelled her to seek across the

ocean for a purer spring of Masonry; she was forced, I say, to
cut clear from those fond associations, in which she had been the
prime moving master spirit, and again stand out an isolated Lodge.
Thus the Lodge proudly, but not defiantly, stood for a quarter of a
century longer.

This absolute severance of Massachusetts Grand Lodge with its
affiliated "Ancient Lodges," from "St. Andrew's;" the violent
separation of a favorite child from the mother who had borne it,
amid struggles and trials, from weakness to assured maturity and
strength; at the moment, too, of the estrangement of half her own
household, was a crisis indeed, demanding wisdom and the firmest
resolution to support. But these bereavements, with its attendant
legacy of loss of a moiety of its funds, and ill will, was far from all
of the perplexity which was imposed in 1784, upon this heroic
Lodge. The pressure upon "St. Andrew's" from without the
Order from the community at large, was potent. A prolonged
national contest, which had worked up to the highest pitch every
faculty of the people, had been brought to a glorious conclusion.
An intense American feeling, mingled with hatred of everything
British, became the public sentiment of the hour. A positive determination that would not endure debate, to affiliate with nothing
whatever, that was tinged with English associations, was upper-
most in the minds of the people. Such feelings pervaded the
smallest matters. The names of buildings, squares and streets
and societies, even of persons, were changed. A universal wish
to introduce names popularly designative and dear to the national
heart, was loudly demanded. Lodges new and old, took names
indicative of the altered state of things. Pennsylvania had even
proposed a United States General Grand Lodge, with Washington
at its head;—a project which "St. Andrew's" declined unanimously. It was not surprising therefore, that the Masonic Institution, in whose bosom was a large proportion of the leading
actors of the Revolution of 1776, should feel the force of freedom's
swelling tide. In the patriotic claims of a common sentiment, it
is not difficult to imagine that zealous brothers, some of whom had

been doomed as martyrs in the cause of a people's regeneration, did stand ready to blot out the style of a single Lodge, ay, its existence, rather than see in it, a perpetuation of the least memento of allegiance to the mother country. With the light we have in the glowing blaze of national success, it is plain what we should have done in the crisis. But we are to remember that our gallant predecessors stood in a lurid light, compared to that vouchsafed to us.

The majority of the Lodge, headed by Bro. Wm. Burbeck, — who had been Senior Warden of the first Lodge of "Moderns," in Boston, but quit it preferring to cast his lot with "Ancient St. Andrew's," and one of its original grantees, — stood firm, resisting all popular innovations upon Masonry, as they viewed them. These brethren sympathized in patriotic impulses, no less fervently than the great body who cut loose from "St. Andrew's;" but besides all questions of the assured independence of the country; their course of action is to be interpreted by two main considerations. First, — the "Ancient and Modern" controversy, was still virulent abroad, and in an uncertain state of abeyance at home; in their minds the absolute purity of Masonry might yet be involved in the issue; whilst, as for them and their household, they meant to stand by the sure "landmarks," and their direct lineage from the Grand Lodge in Scotland. This secured indisputable integrity, if it was kept uninterrupted. Second,— they knew that Freemasonry was, in the best sense, on a distinct plane from all usual societies of the times, and if such an Institution was suffered to yield to popular clamor on any crisis, however momentous, or commendatory in itself, the "Order" might again and again do so, when weak brethren were at its helm, and a stormy look out impended. Our trusting predecessors felt that external influences should be kept aloof, or at all events they had a conviction that the eldest human society had no safe current save its own, in the absence of emergency, and should always move with deliberation. Then too, the future and opportunity were before them; and the record shows that these brethren looked forward to changes under much more auspicious circumstances. It was felicitously providen-

tial, that some of these noble members, who bore without faltering
the heat and burden of the day of those crises in "St. Andrew's,"
did live to witness its thorough consummation, on its proper merits
in due form, in profound peace, when Masonic and civil discord
were hushed by the free will and accord of all concerned.

After ten years of vexatious isolation, another crisis came on the
Lodge, in a Masonic measure which, with the light that we now
have, must be pronounced as eminently for the good of "the
Order." The United States grew ; its cardinal theory of strength
by union contained something real, tangible ; its very idea was a
charm to all hearts ; its bare statement served as a powerful argument, and "St. John's" with Massachusetts Grand Lodge made a
union in March, 1792, forming the Most Worshipful Grand Lodge
of Massachusetts ; a venerable body, which has ever deserved and
received the profound and universal respect of the fraternity ; a
body also, which in its full official title, incorporates in graceful announcement, eternal oblivion to the old time "Ancient and Modern"
disagreement.

Again the Lodge of St. Andrew stood out. The time had
not come to cut clear from Scotland. Reinforced by able members
who were in full sympathy with its policy, the Lodge refused to
have anything to do with the Grand Body. Whatever may be
thought of the expediency of such refusal, there certainly was a remarkable consistency in this unwavering attachment to the Scotch
charter, with the prospect of being left alone and isolated from all
other subordinate Lodges. The union of the two Grand Lodges
being perfected, with the almost universal acquiescence of the whole
fraternity of the country, the new body, — after using invitation and
persuasion to bring to pass a thorough unity of sentiment in the
Order, — at once took stringent measures, which bore hard upon
"St. Andrew's" in its solitary position. Among these measures
passed by the influence of "Massachusetts" and in pursuance of.
the resolve in 1797 of her own Grand Lodge, was the resolution of
Grand Lodges in other States to the following effect : —

"All Masons under our jurisdiction are forbid to hold correspondence or communication with any Mason or Masons, citizens of the United States, who hold authority under, or acknowledge the supremacy of any foreign Grand Lodge, or who do not by their representatives communicate and pay their dues to the Grand Lodge of the State where they reside."

Thus stigmatized, the Lodge of St. Andrew pursued its career, husbanding its resources, punctilious, faithful and courteous in all its acts. As time passed on, a certain respect for the firmness to principle which the Lodge exhibited in the very tenacity of its loyalty to "Scotland," was the means of "St. Andrew's" being permitted to share with the Order at large in occasional Masonic civilities. The personal weight of character also of the members, prevented such utter ignoring of the Lodge, as the policy of the Grand Lodge contemplated.

Let us now, for a moment, relieve this narrative of a quarter of a century of isolation, by recounting some of the trophies which have given a special renown to "St. Andrew's." I refer to the course of the Lodge, and of the course of its members as patriots.

In the "American Revolution" the scenes in Mason's Hall, like those of Faneuil Hall, have become historical. With one or two exceptions the members were all zealous partisans in the patriotic cause. During the siege of Boston the Lodge was closed, and the building was used as a hospital, and for the benefit of the poor. But after the British were driven out, the Lodge meetings were large and enthusiastic. On one night in December, 1777, there were thirty-five visitors present, and twenty-nine names were presented for membership. In fact, it is pertinent to remark here, that the Lodge of St. Andrew performed a conspicuous and a very essential part in carrying the Masonic Institution through these eight years of war. The Grand Lodge itself was almost a duplication of "St. Andrew's." For several years prior to the Declaration of Independence, covering all the period when this most memorable event since the Christian era was conceived and matured, if Faneuil Hall was the "Cradle of Liberty," then the "Green Dragon" held the nursing arms of those who certainly fondled the lusty child of '76. "St. Andrew's," was a North End Lodge, and its Masonic "work" constantly alternated with the secret meetings of those ardent patriots who controlled all the early revolutionary movements. The men were the same in both. The walls of the old "Green Dragon" offered for the service of the country, embraced the asylum of those noble hearts which sternest beat in response to the demand of the hour. It is impossible to separate the Lodge from the fullest accord in the entire struggle. Enough for the institution, that in making such men good Masons, it made them also trusty patriots, giving them one and all a common tie, which in the hour of peril, inspired them with the firmest mutual confidence, for their own protection, to the end at last of the nation's independence. The roll of members and of visitors increased in an unexampled manner ; an act of incorporation was voted for ; officers of the army who were Masons, — as nearly all were, — had invitations to visit constantly. Major-Gen. Lincoln was complimented with the degrees without fees ; his "St. Andrew's" diploma is still kept by his family as a memento of the period. Committees were raised to look after prisoners of war and distressed foreign brothers. On one occasion four Dutch masons who had been stripped by a captain at sea, were brought to the Hall, and the Lodge gave vent to its patriotic impulses by voting relief to brethren who had been "robbed by one of Tyrant George's frigates." The secretary responds to the scenes he witnesses by writing at the foot of his records, "God save the country," again, "God save the Lodge." In the winter of 1777 the distress in Boston was great, and at one time the members voted £250, for general relief. The Overseers of the Poor officially returned thanks to "St. Andrew's" for this timely charity. The Grand Lodge of Scotland in the same way thanked the Lodge for "attention and kind offices to British brothers, prisoners of war." Your files are replete with evidences of the unremitting care for individual distress during the Revolution. But after all, the "Green Dragon" is a national landmark of the great struggle ; what was done there, and the men who did it, is a part of history, we must not wholly appropriate the fame.

I cannot forbear however, to quote from the records of the Lodge, an incident illustrating the part which "St. Andrew's" men took in the boldest private deed of revolutionary annals, one too, which has rung round the world.

Col. Henry Purkett, a revolutionary officer and an honored member of "St. Andrew's," — whom some of us can remember in his seat in this Lodge, — was one of the "Indians" who threw the British East India Company's Tea overboard on the memorable night of Dec. 16, 1773. Our brother the Colonel, by what he used to say to us, as well as by what he did not say, declared that the "Boston Tea Party" was got up at the "Green Dragon Tavern," and in St. Andrew's Lodge. Paul Revere was a leader in the party, and at this time he was influential in the order. The records of course are Masonically silent ; but their very silence speak with no uncertain sound, as follows : —

The 30th of November, Saint Andrew's night, was the occasion of the annual election of Lodge officers, uniformly with full attendance ; on this election night previous to the 16th of Dec. 1773, there were but seven members present! The ceremonies were passed, but the secretary closes his record thus : " N. B.— Consignees of Tea took up the brethren's time." On the 2d of Dec. the Lodge met and chose its officers, John Lowell, Master ; on the 9th another meeting ; nothing unusual then. But on the 16th, the memorable night, the Lodge met again, with only five present ! and the secretary finishes up : no record at all, in fact ; by a significant flourish, such as never before or since, set off the decorous record of "St. Andrew's." Now, with Bro. Purkett's testimony and our own records, we will leave the whereabouts of our members to a jury composed of all their countrymen.

To resume ; notwithstanding the peculiar attitude of the Lodge of St. Andrew between the years 1782 and 1809, a certain prestige hung over the stout-hearted Lodge, that went far towards softening the resentment which Masons were obliged officially to entertain for a single body who held out against the Grand Lodge of Massachusetts, and who would not embrace the popular sentiment for union and Masonic nationality. Expressions of regret began to take the place of sweeping condemnation, and "St. Andrew's" was looked upon as a prostrate column, or as a child without a parent, or with a parent too distant for any good, while here was one at home ready and anxious to adopt. Near one hundred Lodges belonged in the Commonwealth, and with "St. Andrew's" the Masonic edifice would be perfected. Here and there a friendly greeting from distant Lodges, who had some old association with the earliest "Ancient Lodge," would be received, always urging union. The town of Boston was now united to Charlestown by a bridge. The brethren on the other side of the river were no more to be styled "sea-faring," as of yore, and "King Solomon's Lodge" ventured to make "St. Andrew's" a friendly call in full regalia. The Grand Lodge itself held out the "olive branch" by bringing forward an article in its Constitution, whereby a Lodge holding under a foreign jurisdiction could "come in," preserving its charter, and its rank by date.

The death of Washington too, at the close of the century, filling all hearts with sorrow, united the entire brotherhood in one common bond of sympathy. On this event "St. Andrew's," with other Lodges, was draped in mourning, and its members responded with their brethren at large, in every testimonial of Masonic respect, which was prompted by the sad occasion. In short, opportunities were made propitious, and all things gradually conspired to the union of this last Lodge with the Grand Lodge of Massachusetts.

In June, 1798, the Lodge was specially convened to consider Masonic relations, and it was decided 19 to 8, to address the Grand Lodge of Scotland on the question of "St. Andrew's" passing under the jurisdiction of Massachusetts. A committee was appointed to write that Grand Lodge. In December, 1799, the answer from Scotland was received. In this, the Scotch Grand Lodge kindly acknowledge their relation, but substantially leave untouched any decision in regard to what "St. Andrew's" ought to do. The Grand Secretary however, remarks, " that inasmuch as the Massachusetts Grand Lodge has not been recognized by either of the

Grand Lodges in Great Britain, " St. Andrew's" is not bound to consider them as entitled to the character of a Grand Body." On the 9th of Dec. the Grand Lodge of Massachusetts itself, sent a committee to confer with the Lodge on the subject of union. On the 19th this conference was committed to select committee, and at a special Lodge on the 10th of Feb. 1800, they report that they are equally divided in opinion as to what course to advise the Lodge. Whereupon an attempt was made to send a new committee to confer with the conference committee of Grand Lodge. This was negatived by a vote of 21 to 6. It was then decided that the secretary should send a letter to Grand Lodge explaining to that body the feelings of " St. Andrew's " in regard to the proposed conference for union. The secretary at once submitted the following : " St. Andrew's Lodge, after having been recently acknowledged by their parent, cannot with justice to themselves renounce their allegiance, nor do they feel that any Grand Lodge could receive them under its jurisdiction, without dishonoring themselves by such a reception." But this letter goes on to say, that " should any occurrence take place that we can with honor embrace, and that will justify us as a Lodge in acknowledging your jurisdiction, we shall not hesitate a moment, being fully convinced from experience, that we should thereby be relieved from much anxiety and trouble."

The subject so far as any official act of " St. Andrew's" was taken, — save by incidental discussion in 1803, – 4, – 5, — was heard of no more until the fall of 1807 ; meanwhile, there was an excellent feeling of cordiality constantly growing up between the parties. The " Ancient and Modern " phantom had vanished ; the lingering sentiment of Masonic fealty to Scotland alone, was in the way. In April, 1804, a delegation from " Mt. Lebanon Lodge," and in the name of that respected body, formally visited " St. Andrew's," and in a very delicately courteous manner expressed a desire for mutual intercourse between the brethren. The members of " St. Andrew's " heartily embraced the delegation, and instantly appointed five of their prominent associates to return the visit. " St. John's " also visited officially. At length, in October, 1807. the

great measure was again brought forward. A very able committee
was formed, with Andrew Sigourney chairman, to whom was entrusted the subject of a thorough examination of the financial and
Masonic relations of the Lodge with the Scotch Grand Lodge, and
it was also their duty to review the action which had taken place
between "St. Andrew's" and Grand Lodge of Massachusetts, in
committee and otherwise, on the whole matter of the proposed
union, then to report in full, with such recommendations as they
should see fit. Prior to the annual meeting in November, this
committee presented their report in writing to the Master. It is a
long, admirable, and explicit statement of the whole subject matter,
containing also an account current of the work of the Lodge, with
reference to an adjustment in full of the "dues" to the Grand
Lodge of Scotland. There is no mention, however, of the reasons
which stood in the way of an earlier conclusion on the question of
the union. The report closes as follows : —

"Your committee are therefore of opinion that the full sum due the Grand
Lodge of Scotland be remitted ; and that if St. Andrew's Lodge can be received under the Grand Lodge of Massachusetts, with honor to themselves and
the said Grand Lodge ; then that the Grand Lodge of Scotland be requested to
give St. Andrew's Lodge an honorable dismission, and discharge them from
being any longer their subjects. Your committee, conceiving that it would tend
much to the honor, increase, and prosperity of St. Andrew's Lodge could they
have a head with whom they could often and freely communicate, and to obtain
this object, your committee are of opinion that a committee should be appointed
to confer with the Grand Lodge of Massachusetts, to know in what manner,
and on what terms, St. Andrew's Lodge would be received by them, and to consult on the best method to be pursued to obtain an honorable discharge from
one, and reception by the other."

At the annual meeting, Nov. 30th, the Lodge accepted this report, and voted to remit its dues to the Grand Lodge of Scotland,
also to request a discharge, and to communicate with the Grand
Lodge of Massachusetts to this effect. On the 5th of December
the committee of the two bodies met in conference ; at which a full

understanding having been arrived at, Brother Elisha Sigourney, in behalf of "St. Andrew's," officially accepted the proposal for a union, after the necessary advices should have been received from Scotland. This action was done the 15th of December, 1807.

In the meantime, St. Andrew's Lodge, at a special meeting Sept. 7, 1809, having obtained an honorable discharge from its Honored Scotch Parent by remittance in full of £90, for all its dues, appointed a committee to attend a Communication of the Grand Lodge of Massachusetts, to be held on the 11th instant, and inform them "that, at the annual meeting of Grand Lodge, 'St. Andrew's' will become one of its members, agreeably to the Communication made in December, 1807." Accordingly, on the 11th of September, the committee was most cordially received by the Grand Lodge and assured that "the Grand Lodge of Massachuetts, with the most heartfelt satisfaction, anticipated the happy and pleasurable consequences of this union, and promise a paternal regard to the integrity of 'St. Andrew's.'" The committee were then invited to seats, and "to participate in the festivities of the occasion." Nothing now remained but to perfect the official acts which must accompany the change of jurisdiction, and both parties awaited with becoming impatience, for the felicitous consummation. The 11th of December, 1809, came, and the Master and Wardens had taken seats in Grand Lodge, when the Grand Marshal informed the M. W. Grand Master that "St. Andrew's Lodge had taken seats for the first time as a member of Grand Lodge, and it was probable that the Worshipful Master had some communication to make." Whereupon the Master of "St. Andrew's" arose and addressed the Grand Lodge in an eloquent speech, to which the Grand Master, grasping the hand of the Master, responded with a hearty fraternal welcome; thereupon directing the Charter of the Lodge to be countersigned and recorded. The annual election then proceeded, when it appeared that a member of "St. Andrew's," — Andrew Sigourney, — had been unanimously elected Grand Treasurer, a mark of high respect to this Lodge.

The beautiful ceremonies, attending the cement of the last link in the bright Masonic chain of Massachusetts was not yet finished ; nor the season of official rejoicing over. On the ensuing 12th of April, the M. W. Grand Master, with all the other Grand officers, visited " St. Andrew's " at " The Green Dragon," and here in the ancient historic hall, the supreme dignity of Grand Lodge, and high Masonic etiquette, gracefully yielded to the emotions which filled all present, for a hallowed moment of most hearty fraternal love, brother to brother. The addresses on this grand occasion were admirable and replete with sentiments of reciprocal regard and satisfaction. True Masonic hospitality chastening a scene that testified to complete Masonic harmony in Massachusetts, after nearly three quarters of a century of discord.

We must not linger on this pleasant memory. The glistening eye of our honored brother yonder, tells us better than any words of mine can do, how at this bare recital, there wells up in his bosom, grand emotions at the remembrance of that scene in which he, forty-seven years ago, then Junior Warden of " St. Andrew's," bore his full share.

Brethren of " St. Andrew's :" we need not review this long narrative of progress to the point, when our Lodge first hailed, as its adopted parent, the Grand Lodge of Massachusetts ; that period of more than half a century of a Lodge Militant, those oft recurring crises, those manly spirits who so bravely pressed onward under the sole support of honest convictions. You cannot forget them. No! It is past, without one stain of reproach on " St. Andrew's," and we are the gainers, just as our successors shall be gainers, if we, in the face of prosperity, are as faithful as those predecessors were in adversity.

And now, to look beyond the historical sequence of events, which at last culminated so felicitously; let us see what was the prime cause of the persistent action of our early members ; what great motive underlied the steady reluctance to enrol " St. Andrew's " at once, as other Lodges did themselves after the Revolution, under a jurisdiction here at home. At an early period, as

we have seen, the "Ancient and Modern" Masonic issue was a
sufficient motive ; but as time wore on, this gave way before the
good sense of the "Order" in America, and died out making "no
sign." We are therefore, left to declare that it was the Charter,
possessed by the Lodge which really made this distinguishing feature of its policy, becoming at last the sole cause of its long isolation. Let us then devote a little space to the jealous regard and
watchfulness of this Scotch Charter.

A. D. 1760, the Charter of the Lodge of St. Andrew first comes
to view, in presentation to the Grand Master of "St. John's." He
admits its legality, but declines to recognize the grantees as regular Masons. These grantees, finding that no "happy coalition"
was likely to take place with the fraternity of the colony, at once
fell back upon this piece of parchment which empowered them to
work. In 1768, one of these grantees on retiring from the chair
of the Lodge, retained the Charter in his own hands. In 1771, the
Lodge made a demand for it ; Bro. Burbeck refused this demand.
The majority of the Lodge must have silently acquiesced in its
secretion, for at the next election, he was invited to serve again as
Master, but would not accept. In 1773, a formal vote was passed,
requiring the Wardens to ask for the Charter. To this brother
Burbeck gave no answer. Thereupon, a dispensation was asked
of the Provincial Grand Lodge until a copy could be got from
Scotland. The dispensation was granted. The Lodge then voted
to send out for a copy of the Charter, but this does not appear to
have been done ; at any rate, the Grand Lodge of Scotland took
no action. In 1776, another demand was made with the same
refusal. Repeated attempts followed, to suspend brother Burbeck.
In 1785, this brother died. On his death bed, with a solemn injunction he confided the Charter to brothers Jas. Carter, Master,
and Elisha Sigourney, a Warden of "St. Andrew's." These
brethren made this known to the Lodge, and by its vote, they
were requested to retain it till further orders. In 1789, brother
Sigourney was "requested to lay the Charter on the table each
Lodge night ;" the Secretary was directed to read it at the annual

meeting, to have it transcribed in the Records, and a notarial copy
made in due form. In 1790, the "Royal Arch Lodge," was "indulged with the use of ' St. Andrew's' Charter, so long as a majority of its members were also members of this Lodge." The next
year after the formation of the Grand Lodge of Massachusetts, the
validity of the Charter was fully discussed in the Lodge, and it
was voted to be good, and letters were sent to Scotland asking
the approbation of the Scotch Grand Body, in all proceedings.
Six years passed without a reply, — a season of unusual perplexity
to our members, — finally in 1799 an answer came fully confirming the Charter, and the course of "St. Andrew's," with many
expressions of regard. The preservation of the parchment continued to cause anxious solicitude. In 1804 on one occasion, it was
not forthcoming, and a committee was sent out to bring it in.
Again, it was absent; but on discussion, the Lodge concluded
to wait for brother Sigourney, and subsequently by vote, this excellent brother was made responsible for the safety of the Charter.
At last, December 14 1809, three days after St. Andrew's Lodge
had taken its seat as a member of the Grand Lodge of Massachusetts, brother Elisha Sigourney arose, and thus addressed the
Worshipful Master of St. Andrew's Lodge : —

" Having received this Charter from the Right Worshipful brother William
Burbeck on his death-bed, under a solemn injunction never to give it up until
the difficulty, which then existed between the Grand Lodge and "St. Andrew's,"
should be settled, which change has been approved by this Lodge, and that
happy time now having arived, I with pleasure divest myself of the trust reposed
in me, and in the presence of the Lodge commit this Charter to the R. W. Master, whose rightful privilege it is to take charge thereof."

The Charter was again recorded, and it has ever since occupied
its appropriate place in the archives of "St. Andrews."

The written records of these proceedings, running through a
period of over forty years, are interesting, but I am of the opinion
that the unwritten record concerning this Charter, which was securely kept, would possess a deeper interest to us. The whole

story can never be told; but with the help of tradition, through old members, the following conclusion, I think, is to be gathered :

Brother Burbeck was made in, and became Senior Warden of the First Lodge in Boston ; but withdrew, preferring to pursue his Masonic career with " Ancient St. Andrew's." He was an earnest man of positive opinions. Now at the time of his seizing this Charter, he was the only active member, if not the only one alive, who was named in its grant. With Burbeck's Masonic intelligence, identification with " St. Andrew's," and great services, this Charter grew to be of marked value in his eyes. He saw too, from the time of the erection of the Provincial Grand Lodge a constant uneasiness on the part of Paul Revere and a number of his friends in the Lodge, violently to cut clear of Scotland and every British association. Burbeck was not without the secret acquiesence of the majority, in the step he took. As the feeling waxed hotter, he placed the charter under the guns of the fort in Boston Harbor, where he was stationed as an officer. Time passed. It was not policy for the majority of the Lodge to refuse utterly the call for the Charter by the minority ; but they trusted in Burbeck's determination. The revolution was a severe ordeal for the Lodge ; Revere became rampant to blot out the Scotch parchment, and the Lodge jewels and papers had to be guarded, — even secreted. Burbeck was loyal to his country, but he held on to the Charter. The Lodge tried suspension, then voted him back conditionally ; he got back without conditions. The grand projects of the times found him resolute. The minority of the Lodge withdrew membership ; the " Rising States " began its prurient career, " St. Andrew's " withstood the internal, as it had the external storm. The new Lodge became vindictive, unscrupulously hostile to " St. Andrew's " always, — even to the moment of the full accomplishment of union in 1809, when the " Rising States " dissolved, under stern rebuke of all Masons, and under the breath of " St. Andrew's " in Grand Lodge. But to return to Bro. Burbeck :— in 1783 he saw that between the claims for absolute independence in all possible things, the probable union of the two Grand Lodges, and the lurking re-

16

mains of the " Ancient and Modern " controversy besides ; Burbeck
saw that harm might yet befall his beloved Lodge if its Charter was
not preserved, and he with his friends were still steadfast.   In
1785 Bro. Burbeck, admonished by his infirmities that he must
shortly render up earthly trusts, called to his death-bed his firm
friend and coadjutor, Bro. Elisha Sigourney, and handing to him a
munificent donation "for the relief of indigent brethren and their
widows," all of which he did in the name of an unknown friend ; he
placed the Charter in Sigourney's hands, under the same pledge, as
he declared to keep it sacredly as he had done.   The sequel in
1809, by Bro. Sigourney, has already been given.

    This Charter is believed to be the only one now in existence from
a similar source, in the United States.   In Canada there are Lodges
with Charters from the Grand Lodge of Scotland.   It is the oldest
Charter in the jurisdiction of Massachusetts.   But it is not from
these facts, nor from the special incidents touching its preservation,
that we should alone esteem it.   If I have not utterly failed in my
endeavor, you will have gathered enough of the course of our Institution to discover that while Freemasonry does not change, yet its
position in its relations to men, at one or another period of time, is
not always permitted to remain the same.   The infirmity of mankind, we all know ; the infirmity of men as Masons, I have not
been able to conceal.   In the past one hundred years, notwithstanding the greater degree of intelligence, our Order has encountered
its " Left Footers and Right Footers," and those who could take no
" step " at all, perversity or an intense national sentiment has
closed our " Temple " to the regularly initiated.   In the mutability
of all things human, the immutability of the great principle, — the
ancient landmarks, — the sacred title deed of the lawful right of
our successors, may be made to tremble in the balance, between
some " Ancient and Modern " controversy yet to be developed from
the womb of the future.   The vast Masonic family now pursue
their perfect work in harmony ; not a ripple breaks in wanton defiance near the " Three Great Pillars," not a shadow dims the efful-
gence of the " Three Great Lights,"— the Square, Level and Plumb

everywhere enjoin obedience from willing hearts! Let us fervently hope, that neither discord nor division shall ever invade the Institution! But if it shall be otherwise ordered! If "St. Andrew's" is again put upon her defence, the Lodge can rally upon a Charter from a fountain source so high that its purity never was questioned. In the factions of the past, or previous centuries, the Grand Lodge of Scotland has been arrayed neither upon the one side, nor the other; but her arbitrament has become rather a palladium of Masonic rights. The grant of "St. Andrew's" Charter is a notable case in point, — the historian of this ancient Scotch Body will not fail to recount others, — from the hour of our Charter's date until the present, "St. Andrew's" has been courteously loyal to Ancient Craft Masonry, — the Grand Lodge of Scotland has uniformly held unwavering confidence in the wisdom of this grant.—On this, our Centennial Day, in the presence of her honored representatives the Grand Lodge of Scotland bids us take note of its confirmed approval. Our Charter bears too, the endorsement of the Most Worshipful Grand Lodge of Massachusetts, an act done under circumstances which, as the Order stretches down the ages, will ever reflect increased honor upon all concerned. Such considerations give a value to our Charter, which the recurrence of an hundredth or a ten hundredth birthday, can only alike commemorate.

For more than two generations, covering the period to this moment, during which "St. Andrew's" has pursued the even tenor of its way in the present beneficent jurisdiction, a leading feature of its history, discovers abundant testimony to the sagacity of the Lodge's early members, and to the wise prudence of those who come after them in the control of affairs. The brethren before me, who, in the vigor of early manhood chose their Masonic career in this Lodge, can now in the maturity of riper years, look back with pride and satisfaction upon their own faithful response to the important trusts committed to them, and to the substantial good fruits in charity and hospitality borne of their fostering care; but in the face of the cherished memories of those who have passed on, it will be the choice of the living to wait for their encomiums. But yet, while we do not stop to place garlands on all the living, there are nevertheless epochs in the progress of human societies, which in the narrative cannot be separated from the heroic men who controlled them. We may therefore for once anticipate the faithful chronicler of Masonic history for the past quarter-century, a period, during which, save at its commencement, the Masonic firmament of this State has shown a clear sky, no star dimmed or absent; we may, I say, anticipate the faithful chronicler in his estimate of a brother, when he meets the story of one dark portent which threatened to obscure the bright azure, like as some foul pestilential miasma that the sunlight dissipates. We shall see him then, pause over the record of A. D. 1833, to eulogize the author of the "Memorial" to the Legislature of Massachusetts, which wielded — a shining weapon,— from the lofty citadel, and by the resolute hand of the Most Worshipful Grand Lodge of Massachusetts, fell, a besom of destruction upon long matured Anti-Masonic plot and counter-plot. It will be written too, that this dismaying, annihilating blow at the whole fabric of a political party's devilish handiwork, as instant, as bold, as perfect as an electric shock, was, all in all, the fine intellectual accomplishment of a Master of our own "St. Andrew's." We must not forget to honor the paramount service of a Brother who honors us by his Lodge association, and who does honor to a whole fraternity at large, whom he has so long, so prominently, so usefully served, with conspicuous ability.

This tribute to one of the oldest members of the Lodge of St. Andrew, is certainly due to a brother, who far beyond any other member of the Order in New England, bore the sharp point of persecution in behalf of his Lodge, and in behalf of the integrity of Masonry, during the seven years crusade against the Fraternity, which swept over social, no less than political relations at the North a quarter of a century ago, with an intensity of bitterness, that can scarcely be understood by those who were not eye witnesses to the envenomed scourge of Anti-Masonry. I would have gladly got on to my close without mention of this hateful epithet, — thrusting it from me as a reeking abomination,— fit only for that pit of condemnation, to which it has been long since consigned by common consent. But you have a right in this place, to hold your speaker answerable for fidelity to his topic, and your successors have a right to demand equal fidelity to all the record which has concerned "St. Andrew's." Suffer me then, as a matter of current history in the past, — in which too, our Lodge was identified, — to reproduce in the briefest manner, a strange episode in the progress of Masonry.

In the autumn of the year 1826, a ruthless attack upon the Masonic Institution broke out in western New York. Encouraged by unprincipled politicians with a strong leaven of religious fanaticism, this Anti-Masonic blast swept over the Northern States of this Union like a sirocco of the desert, burying beneath its blistering sands, the cherished elements of social, civil and political life. In the not overdrawn language of the day — "The ties of friendship and kindred were sundered, the springs of sympathy were dried up, confidence between man and man was destroyed ; the demon of madness and persecution ran riot through the community, the prominent and active members of the Masonic Institution were thwarted in their business, denied the lawful exercise of their civil franchises, driven from public offices, from the jury box, from the churches ; subjected to insolence and contumely, hunted down as felons, and only saved from assassination through the cowardice of their persecutors."

In 1827, these malignant features of Anti-Masonry appeared in Massachusetts. In the year following, it was rampant in the politics, and in the churches of the country towns, assuming a distinct party organization. By the fall of 1830, this party, gathering around it the worst elements of political corruption and fanaticism, had so increased in numbers, as to control the elections in small towns, and presently this Anti-Masonic party became an acquisition to be courted and bid for, by the great national parties. This gave it an extraneous importance far beyond its real consequence, and at last the Anti-Masons measured so much in the scales of political iniquity as to give them what is called "the balance of power," and they at once displayed the most unscrupulous audacity in hostile acts against Masons and everything belonging to the Order.

The community outside the infamous plotting against individual rights and private judgment, and especially right-minded people from the most intelligent classes who were not of the " Order," at length feeling the injustice of these high-handed proceedings, urged upon the Grand Lodge of Massachusetts the propriety of officially protesting against the vile denunciation, and to make an authentic statement of the principles inculcated by Freemasonry, of the obligations of the " Society" to God and as citizens. On the 31st of December, 1831, the well-known paper entitled " A Declaration of the Freemasons of Boston and vicinity," was published. In all, some six thousand names were attached to the declaration. The effect was good. The common bond was strengthened in the fraternity, the position of the Grand Lodge was more assured, and the confidence of the ingenuous portion of the community was confirmed. The mischievous tendency of political Anti-Masonry, however was not allayed. The excitement increased in degree as the leading parties of the State became more evenly balanced in the strife for ascendency, and the Anti-Masons demanded and obtained a share in political offices and in the Legislature.

And now for the clear understanding of the severe crisis that we are approaching it is necessary to go back in point of time, for a moment, and to state an embarrassing contingency in which the Grand Lodge of the State found themselves during the very height of the power of this despicable Anti-Masonic faction, and which further aggravated the whole matter. The story is as follows : —

In 1830, the Grand Lodge being obliged to vacate the old State House, — then about to be required for city uses, — purchased the land on which this Masonic Temple stands where we are now assembled, and on the 30th of October, laid the corner stone of the present structure. It was then a corporate body holding a charter granted by the Legislature in 1817, with authority by law to hold

property not exceeding eighty thousand dollars, — further restricted
to twenty thousand of real, and sixty thousand of personal estate, —
denominated the GRAND CHARITY FUND. As the building of the
Temple progressed, the Grand Lodge found itself under the necessity of asking the Legislature for a modification of its charter, to
enable it to hold a larger amount of real estate, and a proportion-
ably less of personal. Accordingly, in January, 1831, a petition to
this effect was presented, and here I resume the thread of the narrative, dropped above : —

The Anti-Masons in the House are supposed to have numbered
about thirty, who, on presentation of the Grand Lodge petition for
this proper and reasonable modification of its charter, broke
forth in bitter denunciation of Masonry. The petition went to
committee. At once the " Heathen raged ; " remonstrances swept
over the Commonwealth ; no crime in the decalogue was left un-
committed by the Masons ; the Order must be investigated ;
persons and papers must be sent for ; the charter must be taken
away ; these were the demands up and down the land, and sixteen
thousand Anti-Masonic petitioners said amen. Towards the close
of the session Hon. Wm. Sullivan, chairman of the committee,
reported in favor of the Grand Lodge ; but the question was in-
definitely postponed.

The Masons, undaunted, completed their Temple, and dedicated
it in June, 1832. But the embarrassments of the Grand Lodge
were fearful ; a second petition would have met a similar fate with
the first. The whole structure and estate stood involved in for-
feiture to the State, unless relieved by some modification of charter,
and no relief was to be expected from the Legislature under the untoward circumstances. For no sooner had the Grand Lodge been
driven out defeated from the State House, than the Anti-Masons
went on with their petitions ; new names were rapidly added ; in
short, the demand was for investigation and annihilation of Freemasonry. The fiery ordeal had got to its hottest. The Grand
Lodge, sorely exercised, considered every expedient ; able committees sat in vain, but no agreement ; nothing was determined ; the

worst impended. The emergency was met, — as I have before stated, — by the then young Master of "St. Andrew's," in the following vote: —

Voted. That a committee be appointed to consider the expediency of surrendering the Act of Incorporation of the Grand Lodge, and report at the next meeting.

This vote was adopted, and a committee appointed consisting of R. W. Francis J. Oliver, Augustus Peabody, Joseph Baker, John Soley, and Charles W. Moore. This was on the 20th of December, 1833. On the following 27th, the committee submitted a "MEMORIAL,"—a surrender of the Charter, — which was unanimously adopted without amendment, and ordered to be presented to the Legislature with the Act of Incorporation.

This memorial, signed by the Grand Master and Wardens, was presented on the first day of the session, January, 1834, by the Hon. Stephen White, a member from Boston. It caused the wildest excitement, but after a stormy opposition it was adopted and the Grand Lodge was relieved of its embarrassment; its property was saved.

The "DECLARATION" of 1831, the "MEMORIAL" of 1833, — both written by the same hand, — and the triumphal acquittal on a charge for libel, in the same year, of the author of these celebrated documents, were the three blows which killed Anti-Masonry in Massachusetts, and redeemed the Masonic Institution from seven years of obloquy and unparalleled opposition. During this terrible crusade the Lodge of St. Andrew never shrunk from any responsibility, nor for one moment hesitated in its whole duty, with its money, its influence, and its vote. And, amid here and there instances of faint-heartedness, silent withdrawals, and wreck of long-standing cherished Masonic affiliations, "St. Andrew's," through its members, stood first and foremost, close in its hearty allegiance and its counsel to the Grand Lodge.

Brethren of "St. Andrew's:" We are drawing nigh the close

of our first Centennial Epoch, and one duty remains to be fulfilled : but we in vain attempt to do it justice ; the task is a willing, a grateful one, but we have not the means for response ! This we know ; St. Andrew's Lodge has been spared ! Her name fills a proud niche in the Temple of Masonry. But to whom among their associates belongs the honor of guiding, and guarding the Lodge through the past ! Where all are held in venerated memory, upon whom shall we bestow the mention of degrees of fame ! In the recollection of a few names, which have been, or may be selected from some peculiar prominence, or from circumstance of official position, we are not to be unmindful of that glorious roll of members who have left behind an honorable record in silent votes of loyalty to their Order, and to their Lodge. And yet again at a critical moment, radical differences of judgment have almost destroyed the Lodge, and once "St. Andrew's" was rent in twain ! But brethren, those Masons gave the same pledge that we did, they hearkened to the same injunctions ; they worshipped at the same altar ; they were zealous patriots and good men ; in a part of their action, they certainly did this Lodge a great wrong ! But we will forget, we will conjure a loved association of this day, and with old Scotia's truest bard, a brother Mason too, declare : —

> " Who made the heart ; 't is He alone
>   Decidedly can try us,
> He knows each chord — its various tone,
>   Each spring its various bias ;
> Then at the balance let 's be mute,
>   We never can adjust it ;
> What 's done we partly may compute,
>   But know not what 's resisted."

My brothers, if you had gone, as I have gone in the fulfilment of your summons, over the records of "St. Andrew's," you would have been eager to place a tribute here to Burbeck, Barrett, Warren, Webb, Palfrey, Danforth, Deshon, Carter, Morton, Webber, Green, the Sigourneys ! ay, the succession stops not here : In fraternal as-

17

sociation with these names, though not permitted to share the same service, there will leap to our lips with fresher grief, the honored names of Purkett, Fowle, Smith, Hutchinson, Hunt, Suter, Washburne, Rayner, Chickering, Loring! Alas! no human thanks can avail, — these brothers have their reward, — we will cherish their memories!

If my voice shall reach the ear of those venerable brethren — Hammatt, Lash, — who hallow our Festival by their presence to night, giving us living associations of that interesting day and occasion, when this last Lodge took its place under the Grand Lodge of the Commonwealth, — these words do thank them for the many fraternal acts which our records testify to, of their kindly participation in smoothing the way towards that happy united sentiment now jubilant in the Masonic family of Massachusetts.

I feel that in your hearts, you bid me linger longer on the memory of three of our members, to whom it surely was given to be of invaluable service to their Lodge, and who no less, were an honor to the several civic and Masonic trusts which they long filled.

Elisha, the elder of the Sigourneys, became a member of " St. Andrew's " in 1778 ; he stood with Burbeck in the memorable care for the Charter ; he was a wise, competent and liberal Mason, and to a remarkable degree in critical junctures, he held the confidence of the Order. Elisha Sigourney lived to see his labors nobly crowned by the union of his Lodge with the Grand Lodge : and died in 1811. The Sigourneys were Huguenots, a capital stock ; this Lodge has never been without men of that fine race.

Andrew, the younger, and the third of the name in the Lodge, was made a Mason here in 1791, and died within a few weeks of James Farrar, in 1820. To the admirable combination of qualities in heart and hand, which must claim from the Order in this State, love and reverence, Andrew Sigourney added a conscientious, generous devotion to the important concerns of his Lodge, which demands our gratitude ; honored in every walk of life ; in all Masonic measures of importance, he ably co-operated for the best and truest ; but to this brother alone is the credit due, of carrying out those thorough investigations into the condition of the Lodge, whence came, not only the reduction to systematic method of all matters of record and account ; but a complete comprehension of all its concerns. Through life his integrity was spotless ; on " St. Andrew's," in her delicate relations with the Grand Lodge of Scotland, financial and fiduciary,— and on all Masonic organizations,—he shed the bright lustre of his own honor. For almost thirty years of uninterrupted services, civic and Masonic, did this noble man respond with unsurpassed capacity and zeal, — at last he dropped his mantle, and " St. Andrew's," — blest ever in its hour of need, — caught it up and placed it upon his worthy successor, John James Loring ! The history of " St. Andrew's " would be incomplete without mention of Loring and the Sigourneys ! Ay ! the Temple of Masonry is illumined by the graces of their characters ! They are gone ! — but united in the Supreme, the perfect Lodge above, their memories are treasured below.

Brethren of " St. Andrew's," Let us be true to our own responsibilities, as present workmen in the great Temple of Freemasonry ; remembering that by good work only can it be handed down the ages to come. We are, each generation of Masons are equally important links in the time-hallowed ancestral chain, — may it with us be kept ever bright ; may we remember also, that we are the successors of men, whose love for the rights of man, — whose sturdy patriotism led them to do yeoman's service for a Nation's Independence. We too, are the successors of Masons whose love for Ancient Free and Accepted Masonry drove them to seek in a distant land a clear title empowering them to work. We also are the successors of brethren whose convictions of right, — whose skill " in the craft," — whose patient endurance to the end helped to give the Masonic fraternity of the Commonwealth an honorable affiliation. The life long pathway of these brethren was beset with difficulties ; ours, under a felicitous union and ample possessions, is made easy before us. Let not our course be wayward. In the absence of such pressures as our predecessors bore, it becomes us to avoid all thought of minor differences, if any arise, and aspiring to the just dignity of our glorious inheritance, work onward, upward as they did, in the spirit of Masonry !

The hundred years are complete! The eventful series is accomplished ! We stand on the threshold of another century! The genius of the age bids us look forward, heeding the lessons of the past ; but abiding upon ourselves. Thus are we to make history. Thus, have we our own responsibilities, and thus alone, must our memories encounter the test hereafter. Let us, let each generation of Masons be true to themselves ; then shall centuries go by filled with blessings, and Centennial Days shall herald grateful memories.

NOTE. The "DECLARATION," — with the names of " St. Andrew's " members who signed it, — and the " MEMORIAL," — a perpetual defence of Masonic principles, — to which allusion has been made in the Oration, will be found in the closing part of this book : Both of these papers were written by R. W. Charles Whitlock Moore ; who was born in Boston, March 31, 1801 ; made a Mason in Kennebec Lodge, Hallowell, March, 1822 ; and a member of the Lodge of St. Andrew, in October, of the same year. During the height of the Anti-Masonic persecution of " The Order," — for important considerations, besides his eminent fitness as an accomplished Mason, — Bro. Moore was chosen Master of the Lodge, and he is now (1870) its Senior Past Master and oldest member.

ORIGINAL ODE.

By Bro. Henry Grafton Clark, M. D. Music by S. P. Tuckerman, Esq., and sung by the Choir.

St. Andrew's Eve ! From yonder tower
As tolls the bell the passing hour ;
As silent glide time's ebbing sands,
A century completed stands !

St. Andrew's Eve ! Well met to-night !
To celebrate the century's flight,
And gather, ere it disappears,
The harvest of a hundred years !

A memory, and a tear, for those
Who lie in dreamless death's repose !
Let green acacia deck each grave,
And solemn cypress o'er it wave !

Grey moss creeps o'er the castle walls,
Of Aberdour's ancestral halls ;
But still our charter stands as fair,
As when the Douglas sealed it there.

So fade the past ! The present yields
Its fruits and flowers from fairer fields ;
For Beauty's radiance lights the East,
And loving friends will grace our feast !

The crescent moon her silver shield
Has lifted o'er the golden field ;
Come, let us bind our ripened sheaves,
And garland them with Autumn leaves !

After the conclusion of the services in the Grand Hall, the Worshipful Master directed the Marshal to form a Procession and to escort the audience to the Banquet.

The Feast was provided by Bro. J. B. Smith. Here abundance, superb elegance, and exquisite taste were so nicely blended as to command admiration and praise from the entire company. The tables were beautifully set forth with a profusion of choice flowers. The Thistle bloomed on every table, and an elegant bouquet was presented on every plate. The whole scene, in a word, — under the rich canopies, and emblazoned adornments of the noble hall, together with the jewelled guests standing in the brilliantly contrived light, — was enchanting to the gaze.

THE BANQUET.

NON NOBIS DOMINE, BY THE CHOIR,
ACCOMPANIED BY J. H. WILCOX, Esq., ON THE PIANO.

INVOCATION,
BY WORSHIPFUL BROTHER REV. WM. ROUNSEVILLE ALGER.

ADDRESS OF WELCOME,
BY
W. BRO. SAMUEL P. OLIVER,
MASTER OF THE LODGE.

Ladies and Gentlemen : —

It is an ancient and beautiful custom of our Order that at stated periods the workmen shall be called from labor to refreshment. With our ancient Brethren it was a matter of necessity that at high twelve of each day the sound of the axe and the hammer should cease, the plumb, square and level be laid aside, and the trowel be still for a season, that they might refresh and strengthen exhausted nature, and enjoy the rich privilege of social intercourse. In more modern days this time-honored and hallowed custom has been figuratively though strictly observed, and few are the occasions when refreshments are provided.

But in remembrance of this joyous custom, the Lodge of St. Andrew, at the close of one hundred years of labor, at this her high twelve of existence, now calls her craftsmen to refreshment. How readily do they respond to the unfamiliar but well remembered call!

As her representative upon this occasion, it becomes my official and grateful duty to bid you welcome to her family gathering. As we gather around this festive board, our bounding pulses are stilled, our exultation subdued, as we miss from their accustomed places, the loved and honored forms of some up to whom we have always looked for counsel and approval. They have gone forth on the level of time to the boundless realms of eternity, and are there engaged in admiring the fair proportions of that Temple, not made with hands, eternal in the heavens. Yet, what to us is loss untold, to them is gain unspeakable ; and with sinking, though reverent and grateful hearts, we desire to say, " So mote it be." The sweet remembrance of their virtues shall last till time shall be no more.

Our sorrow, however, is turned into joy as we see before us others equally loved and venerated, who for fifty years have been true and faithful Craftsmen, who have devoted to our Order, the vigor of youth and the energy of manhood, and now adorn it with the love of their declining years. Their virtues are placed on perpetual record.

The Grand Lodge of Massachusetts, that good old mother of us all, sends us her parental blessing, and is with us in the persons of her Grand Master and Wardens, whose countenances, everywhere welcome, now beam with the brightness of friendship and brotherly love. That other parent institution, from whose great heart we first drew the stream of life, the Grand Lodge of Scotland, greets us from across the waters, and through her representatives, bids us God-speed. Our sister Lodges, also, have sent hither their most skilful workmen to join in our counsels and in our festivities.

The good old Commonwealth of Massachusetts, though in our day of darkness and trial she stood aloof and heard not our cry of supplication, now sends to us her Chief Magistrate, not in his official robes of state, but in the simple garb of a Mason, to honor the occasion and heighten the festivity.

Though not clothed in a garment such as we would have him wear, yet in his heart prepared to be made a Mason, the ever welcome Head of our beloved city, laying aside his official gavel, sits down with us to-night, a willing and honored guest.

And last, but far from least, woman, the mother of Masons, forgetting those hours of loneliness and watching, forgiving us that we hold secrets she may not share. the embodiment of the Faith, Hope and Charity of our profession, is here to-night to soften, refine. and grace our jubilee.

And now, having with us Age, Manhood. and Woman, wisdom to contrive. strength to support, and beauty to adorn our undertaking — why need I longer delay to proclaim from the East to the West and the South, welcome. thrice welcome to the festivities of the Lodge of St. Andrew !

On removal of the cloth, the following

ORIGINAL SONG,

WRITTEN FOR THE FESTIVAL,

BY

BRO. E. T. WILSON, M. D.,

WAS SUNG.

AIR — " *The Star Spangled Banner.*"

Through the years that glide by, through the centuries' flight,
  Through the lapse of old time and decay of the ages,
Fair Masonry stands in perennial light,
  And writes her long record on adamant pages.
In the sunshine of truth, in perpetual youth,
Still she strikes for religion, for right and for truth.
  All hail to our Order, and long may the flame
  Of science and charity blaze at its name !

When the Temple first sprang towards Jerusalem's sky,
  And pillar and dome were fixed in their places,
Our Brethren worked 'neath the ALL-SEEING EYE ;
  As He taught, so they piled up its manifold graces.
We labor no more, like our Brothers of yore,
But the structure of virtue we build o'er and o'er.
  All hail to our Order, and long may the flame
  Of science and charity blaze at its name !

In Columbia's childhood, and long ere the time
  When she cast off the chains which her powers were repressing,
Our fathers brought o'er from a far distant clime
  The mark and the watchword, the faith and the blessing.
Keep the names blazoned fair, spite of rust and of wear,
Of the Masons who placed here the corner-stone square.
    All hail to our Order, and long may the flame
    Of science and charity blaze at its name !

In the work of our vows never weary or faint,
  Doing good in the path by our fortune allotted :
Let us be like our patron, old Scotia's saint,
  The gentleman, soldier, and Christian unspotted ;
His example so true, so genial, still view
In doing the labor our hands find to do !
    All hail to St. Andrew, and long may the name
    In our bosoms enkindle an emulous flame !

— ·-··ᴏᴏᵢ·ᵥᵢᴄᴏ——

BROTHER CHARLES ALLEN BROWNE, officiated as Toast Master.

Among those who responded to sentiments, were the

Most Worshipful WINSLOW LEWIS, M. D., Grand Master of the Grand Lodge
of Massachusetts.

Right Worshipful JOHN T. HEARD, Senior Grand Warden.

R. W. CHAS. R. TRAIN, Junior Grand Warden.

BRO. SAMUEL G. CLARK, Representative of the Grand Lodge of Scotland.

His Excellency BRO. HENRY J. GARDNER, Governor of the State.

His Honor ALEXANDER H. RICE, Mayor of Boston.

REV. BRO. WM. ROUNSEVILLE ALGER.

R. W. CHAS. W. MOORE, Grand Secretary of M. W. Grand Lodge.

I⁸

SPEECH OF THE M. W. GRAND MASTER.

The Most Worshipful Grand Master, WINSLOW LEWIS, in behalf of the Grand Lodge, said : —

Worshipful Master —

As the official exponent of the Grand Lodge of Massachusetts, as the Grand Master of the most venerable Masonic organization on this continent, I deem it and feel it to be the great feature of my official life, that the Centennial observance of St. Andrew's Lodge has occurred during my occupancy of the East, and that it is my high privilege to congratulate the Brethren on this, their festal day (which may well be termed the climacteric year of their existence), and to share with them the felicitations which exhilarate and cheer them on the completion of the hundredth year of their prosperous and honorable career.

Of that career, your faithful orator, and historian for the occasion, has portrayed its incipiency and progress, its onward and upward advance, its relations to the Order, its services, through its members, to the great cause of Free Masonry, as well as indirectly also to that of liberty and independence, in their capacity as citizens ; and before taking my seat I cannot resist the inclination I feel, to pay the tribute of acknowledgment and thanks so eminently due to that distinguished Brother, who has contributed so largely to the interest and success of the occasion, by the eloquent and appropriate words he has spoken to us. I believe that I only give voice to the sentiment of all who have enjoyed the felicity of listening to him, when, I tender to him the sincere thanks of all, and award to him the grateful praise of having acquitted himself of the laborious and responsible duty imposed upon him by his Brethren, in a manner worthy of his subject and of his own reputation as an accomplished Mason. For the handsome terms in which he has spoken of the body over which I have the honor to preside, he has my personal thanks. In a word, your orator has presented to his auditors, the honorable path in which St. Andrew's has ever marched, and which has conducted it to its present culmination of success. Well may your hearts respond with pride on this the " white day " of your organization.

And well may you say in the words of the great poet : —

> " After my death, I wish no other herald,
> No other speaker of my living actions,
> To keep mine honor from corruption ;
> But such an honest chronicler as Griffiths."

Thus far as Grand Master — but I leave the Chair and take my place among you, as one of your Lodge, as a "quasi member," for you have constituted me as such by your courtesies, your hospitable kindness, extended for so many years. Among you are the most loved friends of my Masonic life, my greatest social support, the hearts on which I lean, and which have never failed in their sustaining power. Words are but poor tributes to pay my dues to this Lodge. If there was a better coinage you should have it, golden cannot express it, and for my happiness in the future, let me hint that it is my ardent wish, that the indebtedness may never be diminished.

If this connection may be continued, and my life be spared for another decade ; if these friendships may endure till old age — the " three score years and ten " — come, then I shall feel that in true friendship's foliage, there is no " sere or yellow leaf." — In the silent register of my heart, " St. Andrew's " will live, while memory lives.

I give you as a sentiment ; —

May the Records of your Lodge continue in the future, as in the past, to testify prosperity, unity, and the practice of all the Masonic virtues.

———•◦¦•¦◦•———

SPEECH OF THE R. W. SENIOR GRAND WARDEN, JOHN T. HEARD.

I return my thanks for the kindness that has prompted the flattering compliment contained in the toast just pronounced, — allegorically expressed, — in my honor as Senior Grand Warden. I had intended to present a few facts in relation to the history of Freemasonry in this country, which, owing to the lateness of the hour, I will omit, except the following, which have more especial relation to the interesting Centennial occasion we are celebrating.

The number of private Lodges erected in the American colonies by the Grand Lodge of Scotland were only five, viz : —

Lodge of St. Andrew, Boston,	. .	No. 81, in 1756
Blandford, Virginia, . . .	.	No. 82, in 1756
Union, Charleston, S. C.,	. .	No. 98, in 1760
Saint John, Norfolk, Virginia,	. . .	No. 117, in 1763
Saint John, Philadelphia,	. . . .	No. 177, in 1773

This list is compiled from the " Roll of Lodges holding under the Grand Lodge of Scotland," as presented in connection with the published " laws and constitutions " of that Institution. It will be noticed that the number of your Lodge as here given, is eighty-one, and not eighty-two as usually stated. I will observe, however, that in the critically prepared historical portion of the oration, to which we have listened this evening, the speaker has adopted the enumeration which I have here given.

The Grand Lodge of Scotland also established two Provincial Grand Lodges in the colonies, — one in Boston, and within one hundred miles of the same," in 1769; the other in North Carolina, in 1771. The former constituted subordinate Lodges in Massachusetts, New Hampshire, Connecticut, Vermont and New York : but to what extent the latter issued charters within its jurisdiction, I have not the means of showing. Without trespassing further upon precious time for these festivities, I will, with your permission, propose this toast : —

THE GRAND LODGE OF SCOTLAND AND THE LODGE OF ST. ANDREW, PARENT AND CHILD, — BRIGHT JEWELS IN THE DIADEM OF FREEMASONRY.

R. W. Junior Grand Warden, Hon. CHAS. R. TRAIN, responded eloquently to a felicitous sentiment offered in his honor by Bro. BROWNE, the Toast Master of the banquet. Bro. TRAIN, extending the thoughts of the sentiment which called him up, went on in mention of the distinguished men who passed the meridian of their lives in devotion to Freemasonry ; then, after graceful allusion to the famous names borne upon the roll of the Lodge of St. Andrew, he closed with this toast : —

The memory of our Brothers, WARREN, FRANKLIN, and HANCOCK, — LAFAYETTE, MARSHALL, and CLINTON, with the host of other true and faithful Masons, — a galaxy of stars, which adorned the Masonic hemisphere ! Although set in the western horizon of this terrestrial sphere, they will rise in the bright and glorious East of the Celestial.

SPEECH OF THE R. W. GRAND SECRETARY.

In response to the toast, —

"THE ANTIQUITY AND UNIVERSALITY OF MASONRY,"

Bro. MOORE spoke as follows, —

Worshipful Master —

I suppose it to be entirely true, — in view of the great accessions that have been made to its members within the last two or three years, — that there are many persons present who entertain, at best, but a very general and indefinite idea of the antiquity, extent, and magnitude of our Institution. And it is equally true that many even of our most intelligent and active young Brethren, not having their attention drawn to the subject, overlook its history and the extent of its influence, and naturally come to regard it in much the same light that they do the ordinary associations of the day ; and this as naturally leads to indifference. Masonry, like every other science, whether moral or physical, to be rightly estimated, must be understood in all its relations and conditions. The intelligent Mason values it in the exact ratio that he has investigated its history and studied its philosophy.

But my immediate purpose is not to discuss the importance of the study of Masonry as a science, but to show its universality as a fraternity. This will necessarily involve to some extent the history of its rise and progress.

In the beginning of the fifteenth century, HENRY the Sixth of England, asked of our Brethren of that day — " *Where did Masonry begin ?* " And being told that it began in the East, his next inquiry was — " *Who did bring it Westerly?* " — and he received for answer — that it was brought Westerly by "the *Phœnicians.*" These answers were predicated, not on archæological investigations, for the archæology of Masonry had not then been opened — but on the traditions of the Order, as they had been transmitted from generation to generation, and from a period running so far back along the stream of time that it had been lost in the mists and obscurity of the mythological ages. Recent investigations, guided by more certain lights and more extensive and clearer developments of historical truth, have shown that these Brethren were not misled by their traditions, and that their answers indicated, with remarkable precision, what the most learned of our Brethren, in this country and in Europe, at the present time believe to be the true origin of their Institution.

Freemasonry was originally a fraternity of practical builders — architects and artificers. This is conceded by all who are to any extent acquainted with its history or its traditions. The Phœnicians, whose capital cities were Tyre and Sidon, were the early patrons of that semi-religious mystic fraternity or society of builders, known in history as the "Dionysian Architects." That this fraternity were employed by the Tyrians and Sidonians in the erection of costly temples to unknown Deities, in the building of rich and gorgeous palaces, and in strengthening and beautifying their cities, is universally admitted. That they were the "cunning workmen" sent by Hiram, King of Tyre, to aid King Solomon in the erection of the Temple on Mount Moriah, is scarcely less certain. Their presence in that city at the time of the building of the Temple, is the evidence of history ; and Hiram, the widow's son, to whom Solomon intrusted the superintendence of the workmen, as an inhabitant of Tyre, and as a skilled architect and cunning and curious workman, was doubtless one of their number. Hence, we are scarcely claiming too much for our Order, when we suppose that the Dionysians were sent by Hiram, King of Tyre, to assist King Solomon in the construction of the house he was about to dedicate to Jehovah, and that *they* communicated to their Jewish fellow-laborers, a knowledge of the advantages of their fraternity, and invited *them* to a participation in its mysteries and privileges. The Jews were neither architects nor artificers. By Solomon's own admission, they were not even skilled enough in the art of building to cut and prepare the timber in the forests of Lebanon ; and hence he was compelled to employ the Sidonians to do that work for him. "The Tyrians," says a learned foreign Brother, "were celebrated artists ; Solomon, therefore, unable to find builders of superior skill, for the execution of his plans, in his own dominions, engaged Tyrians, who, with the assistance of the zealous Jews, *who contented themselves in performing the inferior labor*, finished that stupendous edifice." And we are told on the authority of Josephus, that "the Temple at Jerusalem was built on the same plan, in the same style, and by the same architects, as the temples of Hercules and Astarte at Tyre." They were doubtless all three built by one of the companies of "Dionysian Architects," who at that time were numerous throughout Asia Minor, where they possessed the exclusive privilege of erecting temples, theatres, and other public buildings.

Dionysius arrived in Greece from Egypt during the reign of Amphictyon, about 1500 years before Christ, and there instituted, or introduced, the Dionysian mysteries. The Ionic migration occurred about 300 years afterwards, or 1200 years B. C.—the emigrants carrying with them from Greece to Asia Minor, the mysteries of Dionysius, before they had been corrupted by the Athenians. " In a short time," says Mr. Lawrie, " the Asiatic colonies surpassed the mother country in prosperity and science. Sculpture in marble, and the Doric and Ionic Orders were the result of their ingenuity." " We know," says a learned encyclopedist, " that the Dionysiacs of Ionia " (which place has, according to Herodotus, always been celebrated for the genius of its inhabitants), " were a great corporation of architects and engineers, who undertook, and even *monopolized*, the building of temples, stadiums and theatres, *precisely as the fraternity of Masons are known to have, in the middle ages, monopolized* the building of cathedrals and conventual churches. Indeed, the Dionysiacs resembled the mystical fraternity, now called Freemasons, in many important particulars. *They allowed no strangers to interfere in their employment;* recognized each other by signs and tokens ; they professed certain mysterious doctrines, under the tuition and tutelage of Bacchus ; and they called all other men profane , because not admitted to these mysteries."

The testimony of history is, that they supplied Ionia and the surrounding country, as far as the Hellespont, with theatrical apparatus, by contract. They also practised their art in Syria, Persia, and India ; and about three hundred years before the birth of Christ, a considerable number of them were incorporated by command of the Kings of Pergamus, who assigned to them Teos as a settlement. It was this fraternity, whether called Greeks, Tyrians, or Phœnicians, who built the Temple at Jerusalem. That stupendous work, under God, was the result of their genius and scientific skill. And this being true, from them are we, as a fraternity, lineally descended, or our antiquity is a myth and our traditions a fable. Hence the answer of our English Brethren of the 15th century, to the inquiry of Henry the 6th, that Masonry was brought Westerly by the Phœnicians, indicated with great accuracy the probable origin of the Institution.

They might indeed have said to him, that long anterior to the advent of Christianity, the mountains of Judea and the plains of Syria, the deserts of India and the valley of the Nile, were cheered by its presence and enlivened by its song; — that more than a thousand years before the coming of the " Son of Man," a little company of " cunning workmen," from the neighboring city of Tyre, were assembled on the pleasant Mount of Moriah, at the call of the wise King of Israel, and there erected out of their great skill, a mighty edifice, whose splendid and unrivalled perfection, and whose grandeur and sublimity have been the admiration and theme of all succeeding ages. They might have said to him, that this was the craft-work of a fraternity to whose genius and discoveries, and to whose matchless skill and ability, the wisest of men in all ages have bowed with respect. They might have said to him, that having finished that great work, and filled all Judea with temples and palaces and walled cities — having enriched and beautified Azor, Gozarra, and Palmyra, with the results of their genius — these " cunning workmen," in after times, passing through the Essenian associations, and finally issuing out of the mystic halls of the " Collegia Artificium " of Rome, burst upon the " dark ages " of the world, like a bright star peering through a black cloud, and, under the patronage of the church, produced those splendid monuments of genius, which set at defiance the highest attainments of modern art. And, if in addition to all this, they had said to him, that in the year A. D. 926, one of his predecessors on the throne of England, had invited them from all parts of the continent, to meet him in general assembly at his royal city of York, the answer to his inquiry — " *Who did bring it Westerly?* " — would have been complete.

Henceforward for eight centuries, Masonry continued an operative fraternity; producing, both in England and on the Continent, those grand and unapproachable specimens of art, which are the pride of Central Europe, and the admiration of the traveller. But it is no longer an operative association. We of this day, as Masons, set up no pretensions to extraordinary skill in the physical sciences. Very few of us — accomplished Masons as we may be — would willingly undertake to erect another Temple on Mount Moriah! Very certain we are that our own honored M. W. Grand Master, — *primus inter pares*, as all his Brethren acknowledge him to be, — would hesitate a long time before consenting to assume the duties of architect for another Westminster Abbey, or a new St. Pauls! No. At the reorganization of the Craft and the establishment of the present Grand Lodge of England in 1717, we laid aside our operative character, and with it all pretensions to extraordinary skill in architectural science. We then became a purely moral and benevolent association, whose great aim is the development and cultivation of the moral sentiment, the social principle, and the benevolent affections, — a higher reverence for God, and a warmer love for man. New laws and regulations, adapted to the changed condition of the Institution, were then made, — an entire revolution in its governmental policy took place, — order and system obtained where neither had previously existed — and England became the great central point of Masonry for the whole world.

From this source have Lodges. Grand and Subordinate, at various times, been established and still exist and flourish — in France and Switzerland — in all the German States, save Austria, (and there at different times, and for short seasons,) — all up and down the classic shores of the Rhine ; — in Prussia, Holland, Belgium, Saxony, Hanover, Sweden. Denmark, Russia, and even in fallen Poland. — in Italy and Spain, (under the cover of secrecy) — in various parts of Asia. — in Turkey, — in Syria, (as at Aleppo, where an English Lodge was established more than a century ago,) — in all the East India settlements, — in Bengal, Bombay, Madras, (in all of which Lodges are numerous,) — in China, where there is a Prov. Grand Master and several Lodges, — in various parts of Africa — as at the Cape of Good Hope and at Sierra Leone — on the Gambia and on the Nile, — in all the larger islands of the Pacific and Indian oceans — as at Ceylon, Sumatra, St. Helena, Mauritius, Madagascar — the Sandwich group, — in all the principal settlements of Australia — as at Adelaide, Melbourne, Parrametta, Sidney, New Zealand ; — in Greece, where there is a Grand Lodge, — in Algeria, in Tunis, in the empire of Morocco — and wherever else in the old world, the genius of civilization has obtained a stand-point, or Christianity has erected the Banner of the Cross.

In all the West India islands, and in various parts of South America — as in Peru, Venezuela, New Grenada, Guiana, Brazil, Chili, etc., — Masonry is prospering as never before. In the latter Republic, the Grand Lodge of this Commonwealth has a flourishing subordinate, and the Grand Master has just authorized the establishment of another Lodge there.

On our own Continent, the Order was never more widely diffused, or in a more healthy condition. In Mexico, even, respectable Lodges are maintained, in despite of the opposition of a bigoted Priesthood ; and in all British America, from Newfoundland, through Nova Scotia and the Canadas to the icy regions of

19

the North, Masonic Lodges and Masonic Brethren may be found, "to feed the
hungry, clothe the naked, and bind up the wounds of the afflicted."

On the condition of the Institution in our own country, I need not dwell. The
existence of *thirty-four* Grand Lodges, with hardly less than *four thousand*
subordinate Lodges on their rolls, and numbering at least a quarter of a million
of members, — and that number increasing with a rapidity unprecedented —
speaks in a voice louder and stronger than any words of mine could do, for its
extent and popularity. Every State and Territory — except the unorganized
territory of Washington — including even Kansas, has its Grand Lodge ; and
nearly every considerable town and village, its one or more subordinate Lodges.
If we add to these, the large number of Chapters, Councils, Encampments, and
other Masonic associations, which are spread all over the length and breadth of
the land, we have the evidence of a prosperity unparalleled in the annals of any
other human Institution, in any age of the world.

Masonry is indeed a universal Institution. History does not furnish its parallel. It exists where Christianity has not gone ; and its claims will be respected,
even where the superior claims of religion would fail. It is never obscured by
the darkness of night. The eye of day is always upon it. Its foot-prints are to
be traced in the most distant regions and in the remotest ages of the earth.
Among all civilized people, and in all Christianized lands, its existence is recognized. It came to our shores at an auspicious period ; and it was here rocked
in the Cradle of Liberty by a Washington, a Franklin, a Hancock, and a
Warren. Unaffected by the tempests of war, the storms of persecution, or the
denunciations of fanaticism, it still stands proudly erect in the sunshine and
clear light of heaven, with not a marble fractured — not a pillar fallen. It still
stands, like some patriarchal monarch of the forest, with its vigorous roots
riveted to the soil, and its broad limbs spread in bold outline against the sky ;
and in generations yet to come, as in ages past, the sunlight of honor and
renown will delight to linger and play amid its venerable branches. And if ever
in the Providence of God, lashed by the storm and riven by the lightning, it
shall totter to its fall, around its trunk will the ivy of filial affection, that has
so long clasped it, still cling, and mantle with greenness and verdure its ruin
and decay.

SPEECH OF REV. BRO. WM. ROUNSEVILLE ALGER.

In response to the toast : —

"MASONIC FELLOWSHIP IN THE PAST AND THE FUTURE."

Bro. ALGER spoke as follows : —

Worshipful Master, Brethren and Friends : —

To do justice to so rich and sweet a theme as you have proposed to me, I ought to have at command a long and leisurely hour, and a voice combining the flute and the bugle. But the brevity of our moments here, no less than the presence of other claims on our attention, will allow me to strike only a few hurried notes. As far then as the history of our society enables us to look back, we see groups of Brothers recognizing each other by mystic signs, associated in loving communion, alleviating toil with friendly fellowship, enriching life with helpful deeds. As far forward as our faith in the indestructible principles of the Order guides our vision, we see companies of our Brethren mingling hearts at the festive board, marching side by side in enterprises of utility and ornament ; or hand in hand dropping the sprig of Acacia and tear on the grave of a fallen comrade. In the meantime, between those two long processions of our mystic fraternity, the army of departed Masons receding in the shadow of the past, the army of unknown Masons advancing in the brightness of the future, we of the living present, are permitted, for precious moments now and then, to gather at the Altar, the Banquet and the Bier, bask in the sunlight of nature, reflect its lustre upon each other from our friendly eyes, quaff the cup, and sing the song of guiltless cheer, and blend immortal memories and hopes in our prayer.

The privileges thus secured to us Brethren, we can scarcely prize too highly. The bell whose solemn strokes toll the death of a hundred years of old " Saint Andrew's " to-night, reminds us how swiftly time, and love, and joy, and life all go by. Let us make the best use of the instants as they pass. And what better use can be made of them than to fill them with innocent enjoyment, the culture of our noblest attributes, the love of one another, and the hopes of all mankind !

Envy, suspicion, revenge, and remorse are the four vultures of the heart.

Such virtues as we are called on to practise within the embrace of Masonic Fellowship scare those horrid birds afar. Whatever takes a man out of himself, and plants him with others with sympathetic identification tends to bless and ennoble him. And every influence of Masonry tends to this result alike, when it calls its votaries to labor, and when it calls them to refreshment. It sends our thoughts out to distant ages and realms, laden with interest and curiosity, and brings them back enriched with fraternal love.

Let no Mason be a niggard of his heart. The more he gives the more he will receive. Nothing is more impoverishing than a contracted devotion to a selfish routine. To unbend and expand in affectionate fellowship is a blessed thing. Does not every man reap as he plants? There is a merry proverb, " Tickle the earth with a hoe and she will laugh with a harvest."

The returns are rightfully measured by the investments we make. Whoso would secure returns of social joy, health of mind and heart, contentment and peace cannot do a better thing than frequently to invest some leisure moments in occasions like that which is now making us all feel so happy and proud here under the Centennial rose and thistle of "St. Andrew's." And as I take my seat it shall be with the hope, that as century shall succeed century, nothing may ever lessen the glories or the joys of that "Masonic Fellowship in the Past and Future," which binds with one common bond the dead, the living and the immortal.

In response to the toast, — "THE M. W. GRAND LODGE OF SCOTLAND,"

Bro. SAML. G. CLARK, Representative of the Honored GRAND LODGE of Scotland, — spoke of the commission which he had received from the Scotch Grand Lodge, to the interesting Centennial of its former subordinate Lodge. And in the name of the Grand Lodge of Scotland, he tendered hearty congratulations to "St. Andrew's" in the jurisdiction of Massachusetts.'

Bro. CHAS. ALLEN BROWNE, Toast Master, in response to a call, gave the following sentiment: —

" PAST MASONIC DIGNITARIES: We cherish the memory of them all, — from Tubal Cain the great Iron Master, through Bezaleel, the Son of Uri, the curious Artificer of Gold, and Hiram, that cunning Artificer in Brass, — all through the middle ages, and down the line of honored names to the present time."

"WINSLOW LEWIS LODGE — OUR YOUNGEST BORN — THE COMELY DAUGHTER OF VENERABLE ST. JOHN'S — WE WELCOME HER TO THE SISTERHOOD OF LODGES."

In response to the above Toast, Worshipful Bro. CLEMENT A. WALKER spoke as follows : —

Worshipful Master : —

According to the ancient usages of our operative Order, the entered apprentices were hewers of wood and drawers of water for their brethren. While learning the mysteries of the art, they were the servants of the craftsmen. In modern and speculative Masonry, their position is none the less clearly defined, and on all occasions, private as well as public, the inferior rank of the class is strictly and properly maintained.

But on this great festal day, you have generously chosen to put aside the traditions and customs of the fraternity, and have gathered within the charmed circle of your distinctive family, the youngest and lowliest of the Order.

And who could do so courteous an act with a higher grace than St. Andrew's Lodge? None, it is said, can so well afford to ignore the distinctions of class as he whose own position is well assured. So it was in the olden time, when Solomon and Hiram of Tyre sat down in council with good Hiram Abiff, and so to-night, "St. Andrew's" bids Winslow Lewis Lodge, as yet unknown and nearly unheard of, take an equal seat among her sisters. Such is the spirit of Masonry. Cold indeed must be the heart, and poor the brain that cannot find words of acknowledgment for an act so unexpected and so gracious.

Less than a twelvemonth ago, a few of us, children of good old St. John's, seeing all the Lodges so crowded with members, and so burdened with work, that the social element, the charm of the association was utterly crushed out, and the ritual of necessity neglected, formed a compact to withdraw from the old, loved fire-side, and to "set up" for ourselves, to labor in whatever part of the Temple our hands might find work to do. The conditions of the compact were a limited number of workmen, actual proficiency in the ritual, and work and earnest cultivation of the social virtues. To this end we sought the consent and approval of the Grand Lodge.

Such a request had not been heard for fifty years ; and at the unwonted sound, wonder and comment were excited. Amid the confusion of tongues, the Grand Master's gavel fell, and the demand was heard, "What is the cause of that unusual commotion in the west?" The Deputy Grand Master for this District, — a member of your Lodge, — replied thereto, by presenting our petition. To the stern inquiry, which followed, "Are they properly avouched for?" St. Andrew's Lodge, in token of her sincerity, and as a pledge of her fidelity, laid her own right hand on our prayer and answered "I vouch for them." From that hour our request was granted. Since then, under the prestige of his name, whom all true Masons love and delight to honor — in honoring whom they ennoble themselves — we have been testing the question, in our feeble way, if numbers or wealth are essential to the highest success of a Lodge in this jurisdiction. You have observed our progress with unfeigned interest, and have heartily hoped for our success. Not content with endorsing our project, when others looked coldly and doubtingly away, you loaned us clothing and tools, with which to prosecute our work, and up to this hour, you have cheered us by your countenance and counsel.

You saw us struggling for a principle, and you bade us God-speed ; you saw us poor and penniless, and you gave us material aid ; you saw us obscure and unnoticed, and you have called us up hither, and bidden us sit down among the most honored of your guests.

For all this, as the representative of Winslow Lewis Lodge, I offer you the fervent thanks of a full heart.

But, Worshipful Master, I must not be unmindful that the hour is far spent, and the call to labor may surprise us in our joy, and that there are others to be heard whose voices are always music to our ears. Therefore, with your permission I will offer a sentiment : —

"The Lodge of St. Andrew — Winslow Lewis Lodge proposes for herself no higher aim than to be accounted worthy to walk by her side, *haud passibus æquis*. May each Centennial day find her heart as young, as loyal and as warm, as now." So mote it be.

Guests who were at the head of Masonic bodies, and others, were called up ; from these gentlemen, — in the grateful variety of address, which is ever an accustomed feature of the Banquets of our Fraternity, — came eloquent, hearty, anon, most humorous responses. It would be in vain to attempt to reproduce all the felicitous speeches which sped the congratulations of this St. Andrew's Eve, and it must suffice to record, that in delicious measure; there reigned supreme the true Spirit of Masonry.

Before " Low Twelve," the Worshipful Master's gavel "came down," and the brethren joined hands for the : —

PARTING SONG.

BY A MEMBER OF THE LODGE OF ST. ANDREW.

AIR — *Auld Lang Syne.*

Should auld acquaintance be forgot,
  And ne'er be brought to min' ;
The Brothers who have wavered not,
  In days of auld lang syne ?
      CHORUS. — For auld lang syne, my dear,
          For auld lang syne,
          Our trustie frien's we'll ne'er forget,
          For auld lang syne.

For many years, St. Andrew's men
  Have met in mystic halls,
And many whom we used to ken
  Respond not to our calls.
      CHORUS.— For auld lang syne, my dear,
          For auld lang syne,
          Nae frien's o' ours will we forget,
          For auld lang syne.

Green memory shall ever place
  Upon their hallow'd brows
The laurel chaplets of a race
  Who always kept their vows.
      CHORUS. — For auld lang syne, my dear,
          For auld lang syne,
          St. Andrew's sons canna forget,
          For auld lang syne.

The hours we've passed since first we met
  Beneath these friendly walls,
The social cheer we'll ne'er forget,
  Nor e'er forget these halls.
      CHORUS. — For auld lang syne, my dear,
          For auld lang syne ;
          O no, we never will forget,
          For auld lang syne.

Now ere we part, no more to meet
  Again as we meet here,
O let us all, dear friends, repeat
  A hearty, friendly cheer.
>> CHORUS. — For auld lang syne, my dear,
>>   For auld lang syne,
>>   Ae hearty, frien'ly cheer repeat,
>>   For auld lang syne.

And when we leave this festal board,
  This scene to all endeared,
O let us in our hearts record
  The memories we have reared.
>> CHORUS. — For auld lang syne, my dear,
>>   For auld lang syne,
>>   This festal board we'll ne'er forget,
>>   For auld lang syne.

Now let us give one fond adieu,
  Before we hence depart,
Where mind has interchanged with mind,
  And heart has linked with heart.
>> CHORUS. — For auld lang syne, my dear,
>>   For auld lang syne,
>>   We'll gie ane hearty, fond adieu,
>>   For auld lang syne.

The Secretary's record continues thus : —

The music and poetry were original for this occasion. The singing was by a double quartette choir, under the direction of Bro. C. Francis Chickering, and was of a high order of excellence.

During the banquet, interspersed at intervals, several of the most celebrated old English glees were given, among them were " The Winds Whistle Cold," " The Cough and Crow," " Hark, Apollo." An ancient convivial table custom was also reproduced at a proper moment of the entertainment, in sending around a dish of roast peacock, preceded by bag-pipes.

EXTRACTS FROM "ST. ANDREW'S" RECORDS AT NEXT QUARTERLY COMMUNICA-
TION.

On motion of R. W. Bro. J. R. BRADFORD, it was voted that : —

The thanks of the Lodge of St. Andrew are eminently due, and are hereby presented to Worshipful Bro. HAMILTON WILLIS, Past Master, for the very able and highly interesting Oration delivered by him on the occasion of the recent "Centennial Festival," and that this vote be communicated to Bro. Willis with a request for a copy of the same for the use of the Lodge.

It was also voted that : —

The thanks of the Lodge be given to Brothers HENRY G. CLARK, E. T. WILSON and NATHANIEL B. SHURTLEFF, for the Ode, Song, and Hymn written by them respectively, for this Festival : —

That the thanks of the Lodge be communicated to S. P. TUCKERMAN, Esq., and G. H. WILCOX, Esq., for their admirable musical compositions on the occasion of the recent "Centennial."

The thanks of the Lodge were also presented to Bro. CHARLES FRANCIS CHICKERING, for valuable services, especially in the musical arrangements ; and also to each member by name, of the CENTENNIAL COMMITTEE.

Bro. J. B. SMITH, the celebrated Boston caterer, was complimented by the record of a letter of thanks from the committee, in these words :

BOSTON, Dec. 8, 1856.

To MR. J. B. SMITH : —

The undersigned, a committee of Free and Accepted Masons of the Lodge of Saint Andrew, who had the arrangement of the Centennial Festival of the Lodge, held on the evening of the twenty-ninth day of November last, being not only satisfied, but also gratified with the excellent manner in which you performed your engagements in providing for the banquet, hereby, by vote of the whole committee, tender to you their thanks and their special expression of approval and esteem for your very successful efforts on that occasion.

JOHN R. BRADFORD,
THOS. W. PHILLIPS,
THOS. RESTIEAUX,
WILLIAM PARKMAN,   *Centennial Committee*
SAM'L. P. OLIVER,   *of the*
C. ALLEN BROWNE,   *Lodge of St. Andrew.*
CHAS. W. MOORE,
CHAS. J. F. SHERMAN.

Thus closed one of the most superb and complete celebrations of the kind, which has ever taken place in this country. The ample resources of the Lodge were put forth for the object under the direction of an able committee in generous measure, and nothing occurred to mar the utmost fraternal good will, from the beginning of the preparation, to the imposing final accomplishment ; neither was there anything found to have been omitted, which would have added to the taste, elegance, and grand purpose of the Festival.

As an interesting Masonic occasion, it was probably without a parallel in the annals of " The Order " in the United States. In explanation of this remark, something is attributable to the rarity of the occurrence of a Centennial era among the Lodges of this country ; but chiefly, congratulations on this auspicious epoch are due to the reminiscences called up, in the singularly eventful history of this ancient Lodge, together with its intimate connection with the introduction of Freemasonry into New England, its essential work in sustaining Grand Lodge jurisdiction during the struggle for the independence of the colonies, and finally to the sterling character and patriotic record of the early members of " THE LODGE OF ST. ANDREW."

CENTENNIAL CELEBRATION

OF THE PURCHASE

OF THE

GREEN DRAGON TAVERN ESTATE,

BY

THE LODGE OF ST. ANDREW,

MARCH 31, 1864.

GREEN DRAGON TAVERN: — FREEMASONS' ARMS.

THE GREEN DRAGON TAVERN,

FREEMASONS' ARMS.

Noted landmarks, which call to mind associations with the early history of a nation, always possess a peculiar interest to all lovers of their country, and the story belonging to them is awakening, as well as instructive. Among the famous places of Boston, in past days, was a widely known and celebrated building called The Green Dragon Tavern, situated on the border of a mill pond, in what is now Union street, and near the corner of Hanover street; "in its day," it was the best hostelry of the town. The celebrity of the "Green Dragon" however, is not now due to any remembered excellence of hospitable entertainment, but for the social and political public and private gatherings of the people, — with other interesting local incident, — for three fourths of a century, antecedent to the American Revolution ; and above all, for the stirring, patriotic, no less than timely consequential measures determined under its roof by the historic men of '76, who brought to pass that memorable Epoch. It was indeed the cradle of "Rebellion;" the chosen asylum, where the Revolutionary master spirits, — who organized successful resistance to British aggression on the liberties of the colonies, — took grave counsel together.

To the Masonic Fraternity of Massachusetts, the old "Green Dragon," — which, a century ago, began to be called also "Freemasons' Arms," — presents associations of especial significance. It was here within its walls, that the Freemasonry of this Commonwealth was preserved in Grand Lodge jurisdiction, bright and vigorous ; where its charities, its hospitalities, and its good tidings were kept up between the years 1775 and 1792, a period which witnessed the disruption, by reason of the war for Independence, of important branches of the Order in Massachusetts. Still further, this was the scene of WARREN's most intimate political and Masonic associations, with the patriots and Masons of his time.

To the members of the Lodge of St. Andrew, this estate, — their own magnificent possession for more than a hundred years, — is endeared by ties which run over a still longer period.

No picture of the Green Dragon Tavern of any description, is known to be in existence, save the one now presented in this " Memorial." This was engraved recently for the Lodge of St. Andrew, from a model which the Hon. N. B. Shurtleff prepared some years since, with his usual accurate and thorough knowledge of ancient noted Boston houses. From this model in wood, with much painstaking on the part of the " Lodge," in the way of exhibiting it for criticism to old inhabitants who were familiar with the look and details of this ancient structure — which was removed forty-two years ago, — the present picture has been made. It is believed to be a faithful representation, and it may also be affirmed that it is unanimously recognized as such by every one who is competent to judge.

FROM THE RECORDS OF THE LODGE.

At a Quarterly Communication, March 24, 1864, the Worshipful Master, EDWARD STEARNS, called the attention of the Lodge to the fact that the Green Dragon Tavern was purchased by this Lodge, March 31, 1764, and that Thursday next, the 31st instant, would complete a period of one hundred years from the date of the deed of that estate. Whereupon, on motion of Bro. Wellington, it was

Voted, That a committee of five be appointed, with full power to make arrangements for celebrating the Centennial Anniversary of the purchase of the Green Dragon Tavern.

The following brethren were appointed : — A. A. Wellington, Charles W. Moore, J. R. Bradford, Samuel P. Oliver, and Isaac Cary.

On motion of Bro. Palmer, it was

Voted, That the above committee be increased to eight, that being the number of the original committee appointed January 12, 1764, "to purchase a house for the benefit of the Lodge of St. Andrew."

The Worshipful Master, Bro. Wm. F. Davis, Senior Warden, and Bro. John P. Ober, were thereupon added to the committee.

THE FOLLOWING IS THE LODGE RECORD OF THE CELEBRATION.

A special meeting of the Lodge of St. Andrew was held in the new building on the " Green Dragon " estate, Union street, on Thursday evening, March 31, 1864, at 6 1-2 o'clock, for the purpose of celebrating the Centennial Anniversary of the purchase of the Green Dragon Tavern.

An apartment in the building was suitably decorated for the festival, and a bountiful dinner provided.

The Worshipful Master presided, and in a dignified, appropriate address, invoked the attention of the brethren to the ceremonies of the evening, and to the remarks of members whom he should call upon to speak upon the pleasant Masonic memories suggested by the spot whereon the Lodge was then assembled, and to the historical incidents connected with the "ancient Inn." After a proper allusion to the distinguished men who had held Masonic intercourse together in times past in the hall of the "Green Dragon," the Worshipful Master called up M. W. Bro. WM. PARKMAN : —

Who stated that on the 12th day of January, 1764, the Lodge resolved by vote to purchase a house ; accordingly Thomas Milliken, Samuel Barrett, Edward Foster, Caleb Hopkins, Moses Deshon, William Haskins, Joseph Webb, and John Jenkins were chosen a committee for that purpose. On the succeeding 31st of March, Catherine Kerr, by her deed of that date, conveyed in fee the premises known as the Green Dragon Tavern, unto the above named committee. The estate was managed by committees of the Lodge until 1832, when the estate was conveyed to Brothers Benjamin Smith, Henry Purkett, Zephaniah Sampson, David Parker, Thomas W. Phillips, John Suter, and Ezekiel Bates, to be held by them as trustees for the use and benefit of the Lodge of St. Andrew. In January 1852, Bros. Smith, Purkett, and Suter being deceased, a new board of trustees, consisting of Bros. David Parker, E. Bates, T. W. Phillips, Z. Sampson, J. P. Ober, Thomas Resticaux, and William Parkman were chosen, to whom the premises were conveyed for the use and benefit of the Lodge. Bro. David Parker was chosen chairman, Bro. T. W. Phillips, treasurer, and Bro. Wm. Parkman, secretary. In 1855 Bro. Parker having removed from the city, resigned as chairman, and Bro. John P. Ober was elected to fill the vacancy. In 1859 Bro. Phillips died, and Bro. Resticaux was elected treasurer.

THE MOST WORSHIPFUL WINSLOW LEWIS then addressed the Lodge, and said that : —

By the dispensation of the Supreme Grand Master, a severe domestic affliction has deprived us all of the presence of Bro. Charles W. Moore, from whom we should have received the fullest information of those memorials of the past, which are so hallowed to the memories of every member of the Lodge of St. Andrew, who are now assembled to commemorate, on this spot, the associations connected with a locality dear to every Masonic heart, to every patriot's breast ! But, Worshipful Master, our Brother Moore, though absent, and stricken by bereavement, was not willing to let this Centennial occasion pass by, without communicating such interesting facts relating to the Green Dragon Tavern as he had from time to time preserved. And I therefore shall, with your permission sir, read a communication on this subject, which my Brother Moore has handed me, to be presented to the Lodge at this festival.

REMINISCENCES
OF
THE GREEN DRAGON TAVERN.

—᠅᠅—

With perhaps the single exception of Faneuil Hall, there was no public building in Boston at the close of the last century, which had acquired a more extensive notoriety or filled a larger place in the local history of the town, than the old " GREEN DRAGON TAVERN." I need not trouble you with any particular description of it, for that will be given by one who is pre-eminently distinguished for his extensive and accurate knowledge of all the interesting historical localities of the city.

We have no record or other authentic evidence of the fact, but there can be little doubt that St. Andrew's Lodge, which was, in its incipiency, composed largely of North-End men, originated and was informally organized in the " LONG ROOM," so-called, in the northerly end of this Tavern, in the year 1752. It is nevertheless proper to say, that this inference is predicated on the known fact, that it was in this Hall that in 1756 it was re-organized and commenced work under a Charter from the Grand Lodge of Scotland, — a circumstance that would not have probably occurred, had not the Hall been previously occupied by it, and was then in a condition suited to its purposes. And this hypothesis is strengthened by the additional fact, that it continued to hold its regular monthly meetings here until the year 1818, when it was removed to the Exchange Coffee House.

It was in this " Long Room," also, where so much of our Revolutionary history was made, that the MASSACHUSETTS GRAND LODGE — an offshoot of St. Andrew's Lodge — with JOSEPH WARREN for its Grand Master, was organized on the 27th of December, 1769, and continued to hold its meetings until its union with the St. John's Grand Lodge in 1792.

In 1697 the tavern was kept by John Cary, and was at that early day, and perhaps earlier, known as the Green Dragon Tavern.

In 1764 the property was purchased by St. Andrew's Lodge, when it took the name of " FREEMASONS' ARMS," — the new proprietors having placed a large

SQUARE and COMPASS on the front of the building. It however soon after dropped this title, and was more popularly known as "MASONS' HALL;" by which name it continued to be masonically designated until the removal of the Lodge, when it resumed its ancient title of "Green Dragon Tavern."

On the 24th of June, 1772, the festival of St. John the Baptist, was celebrated by the Massachusetts Grand Lodge, by a public procession, formed at Concert Hall, the brethren marching in full regalia to Christ Church in Salem street, where "a very suitable and pertinent discourse was preached by the Rev. Samuel Fayerweather, of Narragansett;" after which they returned to MASONS' HALL, and "dined together in the GARDEN, under a long Tent erected for that purpose; and the remainder of the day was dedicated to mirth and social festivity."

The GARDEN here spoken of, was in the rear of the house, and extended northerly to the water, covering the ground now occupied by Mr. Riddle as a salesroom. Our late Bro. Sampson has said to me that he was accustomed in his boyhood days, to fish for flounders at the lower end of this Garden; which, in early times, extended to what was then known as the "Mill Pond,"—a large basin of salt water, cut off from Charles river by dykes, and used for Mill and other purposes. It was here that in the winter-time the "North-End Boys" and the "West Enders" used to fight their mimic, and not always bloodless, sectional battles, until, after the occurrence of several serious mishaps, they were interfered with and their sports forbidden by the Selectmen of the town. It is hardly necessary to say that the area formerly occupied by this pond is now an extensive business section of the city.

There were present at the above celebration. M. W. JOSEPH WARREN, Grand Master; R. W. JOSEPH WEBB, D. G. M.; PAUL REVERE, S. G. W. *pro tem.*; THOMAS CRAFTS, J. G. W. *pro tem.*; SAMUEL BARRETT, G. Treasurer; WM. PALFREY, G. Secretary; and the Masters, Wardens, and Brethren of St. Andrew's, Tyrian, Massachusetts, and St. Peter's Lodges, together with a sufficient number of visitors to make a company of ninety-seven brethren, which at that early day was a very large and full attendance.

Public Masonic Processions were at this time of rare occurrence. One of the earliest of which we have any record, took place on St. John's Day, Dec. 27, 1749, and was the occasion of unusual curiosity and interest in the community. It called forth from a learned wit a short poem, in which the circumstance is treated

21

with much satirical humor and ridicule. The author of this poem was *Joseph Green*, a merchant of the town, and undoubtedly an Anti-Mason, though it would be difficult to tell from what motive, unless it was that he had failed to obtain admission into "the LODGE." But whatever the motive may have been, the poem is so well done and so keen in its satire, that I do not hesitate to quote a few passages for your amusement. The marching of the Procession is thus described : —

> "See ! *Buck* before the apron'd throng,
> Marches with sword and book along ;
> The stately ram, with courage bold,
> So stalks before the fleecy fold,
> And so the gander, on the brink
> Of river, leads his geese to drink."

The keeper of the Royal Exchange Tavern, where masonic meetings were at one time held, is taken notice of in this wise : —

> "Where's honest *Luke*? that cook from London ;
> For without Luke the LODGE is undone.
> 'Twas he who oft dispell'd their sadness,
> And filled the *Brethren's* hearts with gladness.
> *Luke* in return is made a *Brother*,
> As good and true as any other,
> And still, though broke with age and wine,
> Preserves the *token* and the *sign*."

In another place *Luke* comes in with less credit : —

> "The high, the low, the great and small,
> *James Perkins* short, and *Aston* tall ;
> *Johnson* as bulky as a house,
> And *Wethered* smaller than a louse.
> We all agree, both wet and dry,
> From drunken *Luke* to sober I."

The poet designates Lewis Turner as "Pump *Turner*," probably from his occupation. Dr. Thomas Aston figures as "Aston tall." Francis Johonnet is called "laughing Frank," and is thus nicely introduced : —

> " But still I see a numerous train :
> Shall they, alas ! unsung remain ?
> Sage *Hallowell*, of public soul,
> And laughing Frank, friend to the bowl ;
> Meek *Rea*, half smother'd in the crowd,
> And *Rowe*, who sings at church so loud."

Aston was an apothecary and grocer ; *Hallowell*, here referred to, was probably Captain Benjamin Hallowell, an active and influential Mason ; *John Rea* was a ship-chandler, and kept in Butler's Row ; *John Rowe*, afterwards Grand Master, was a distinguished merchant and importer, and lived in Essex street, and was the owner of Rowe's pasture, through which Rowe street now runs ; *Buck*, probably means Buckley, a member of the First Lodge, as were also *Henry Wethered* and *Henry Johnson.*

Our brethren, in these early days of the Institution in the colonies, were more particular in the observance of the winter and summer festivals of the Order (Dec. 27th and June 24th) than their successors have been. These celebrations, however, were not always public. On the contrary, I believe that of the 24th of June, 1772, was an exceptional case in the history of the Massachusetts Grand Lodge ; and, consequently, in that of our own Lodge ; for the two bodies, on all such occasions, moved as a unit, and held their festivals together at the Green Dragon. I will not occupy your time by referring to them in the order in which they took place, but that of 1773, being the *last* with which Gen. Warren's name is connected as being present, I deem it worthy of special notice in this connection ; and this cannot be done more satisfactorily than in the words of the record. The annual communication of the Grand Lodge was held this year, on the 3d of December, and after the ordinary business had been disposed of, the record says : —

"The Most Worshipful Grand Master (Warren) then desired the opinion of the Grand Officers present, with respect to Celebrating the Feast of St. John the Evangelist, 27th Instant.

" Motioned and Seconded, The Feast be Celebrated the 27th Instant, at Masons' Hall (at the Green Dragon).

" *Voted*, The Stewards of the Grand Lodge of St. Andrew's, and the Massachusetts Lodges, agree for and provide the dinner, and that three Brethren be desired to join the Stewards.

" *Voted*, Brothers Bruce, Proctor [and] Love.

" *Voted*, The Festival be advertised in the Public Prints."

I accordingly find in the "Boston Evening Post," of December 20, 1773, the following advertisement :

"THE Brethren of the Honorable SOCIETY of FREE and ACCEPTED MASONS, are hereby notified, That the Most Worshipful JOSEPH WARREN, Esq., Grand Master of the Continent of America ; intends to Celebrate the Feast of St. JOHN the Evangelist, on Monday the 27th of December Inst. at FREE MASONS' HALL (at the Green Dragon), Boston, where the Brethren are requested to attend the Festival.

By Order of the Most Worshipful GRAND MASTER.

WM. HOSKISS, G. Sec'y.

"N. B. Tickets may be had of Mess. Nathaniel Coffin, junr., William Mollineaux, junr., and Mr. Daniel Bell.

"The Table will be furnished at Two o'clock."

This "Feast" was held in the Long Room of the Green Dragon on the 27th, and the record names as being present, "M. W. Joseph Warren, Esq., Grand Master ; Hon. Wm. Brattle, Esq. ; Rev. Dr. Samuel Mather ; Worshipful Joseph Webb, Esq. ; and thirty-eight others including the Grand Officers."

There had formerly been some degree of coldness between the two Grand Lodges in the Province ; as was natural enough in view of the causes which led to the organization of the younger body. It is therefore the more gratifying to find on the record such unmistakable evidence of the fraternal feeling existing between them at this time, as the following : —

"The Most Worshipful Grand Master was pleased to direct three Brethren, viz : Jona. Williams, Elisha Thatcher, and H. Hatch, to wait upon The Most Worshipful John Rowe, Esq., Gd. Master, the Grand Officers and Brethren at Their Feast, at Col. Ingersoll's (Bunch of Graves Tavern), to acquaint them, their Healths would be drank at half after 4 o'clock. The committee returned for answer, that Grand Master Rowe and the Brethren concerned would return the Compliment at that period."

I give the following summary of the "Reckoning" on this occasion as a matter of curious reminiscence : —

50 dinners *a* 3 *s*	.	.	7. 10 0
13 dbtle. Bowles Punch,	.	.	1. 14 8
12 Bottles Port *a* 3 *s*	.	.	1. 16 0
17 do. Medaira, *a* 4 *s*	.	.	3. 8 0
Advertising	.	.	8 0
			£14. 16 8
Collected — 40 Tickets *a* 6 *s*	.		12. 0 0
After Collection	.	.	2. 16 0
			£14. 16 0

"Punch" was a favorite beverage in the days of which we are speaking, and very large "double Punch Bowles" were a fashionable, if not a necessary appendage to the dinner table on all public occasions ; nor were they dispensed with until a much later date.

Our late Bro. JOHN J. LORING was initiated into Masonry at the Green Dragon, and used to describe, with quiet humor, the appearance of Bro. EBEN'R. OLIVER, — one of the old-school North-End mechanics, and the Closet Steward of the Lodge, — while in the discharge of what the brethren then doubtless held to be one of the most *important* of his official functions. He was a large, portly man, and without exaggeration, might exclaim with Falstaff,

> " I am in the waist two yards about."

He was

> —— " fat,
> Sleek-headed, and such as sleep
> o' nights —— "
>
> " In fair, round belly, with good capon lined."

But withal a most excellent, amiable, and faithful brother.

The Lodge having reached a convenient resting place in its " work," the brethren were called from labor to *refreshment*, — and refreshment in those days was what the word in its common acceptation implies. At this interesting period of the proceedings, Bro. Oliver never failed promptly to present himself at the door, in his best, " bib and tucker," bearing a huge *Punch Bowl!* — one half resting on his correspondingly huge abdominal protuberance, the other supported by his brawny arms. Thus prepared for the encounter, — the brethren being seated " in order," with their glasses in hand, — he, with dignified solemnity, and fully impressed with the magnitude of the business before him, slowly commenced his tour of duty, — paying his respects first to the Master in the " East," and then passing regularly around the hall, until the members were all supplied, or in the technical language of the day, " *all charged*," and waiting the order of the Master. He then slowly retired, with the benedictions of his brethren, and a consciousness of having faithfully performed his share in the " work " of the evening !

Such a scene would not commend itself to favor at the present time ; but it was one of a class common, not only in the Lodges, but with modifications, in the social, civil, literary and religious societies of that early day, when

> —— " The funeral baked meats
> Did coldly furnish forth the marriage tables."

It was in the "Long Room" of the Green Dragon that on the 28th of August, 1769, the present *St. Andrew's Chapter* was organized as a ROYAL ARCH LODGE, under the authority of the Charter of St. Andrew's Lodge. This degree was anciently given in Masters' Lodges ; which arrangement was subsequently changed, and it was conferred in Royal Arch Lodges, attached to and working under the authority of the Charters of Craft Lodges. The present Constitutions of the Grand Lodge of Ireland still retain a nearly analogous provision in the following words : "Every Warrant to hold Councils or Encampments, shall be granted to some warranted or acknowledged Lodge to which a *Royal Arch Chapter is attached;* and shall not only bear the same number, but shall be held in the *same place* in which the Lodge and Chapter usually hold their meetings."

General WARREN was a member of this Lodge, and being present in 1770, the year after its organization, the record says he "gave his opinion in favor of holding (continuing) the Royal Arch Lodge until he should receive instructions from Scotland. If then so directed, he will grant them a Charter therefor." There is no evidence that such a charter was required or issued, and the Lodge continued to hold its meetings at the same place, and under its original authority, until the 25th of November, 1790, at which date we find in the records the following vote : —

Voted, That Bro. Matthew Groves be a committee to return the thanks of this Lodge to St. Andrew's Lodge for their politeness in granting us the *use of their Charter.*

General Warren, as before stated, was a member of the Royal Arch Lodge, as were also Col. Joseph Webb, Col. Paul Revere, and other prominent members of St. Andrew's Lodge. Indeed, of the *twenty-one* members who composed the Royal Arch Lodge in 1769, *fourteen* of them were members of St. Andrew's Lodge. In 1794 this Lodge assumed the name of a "Royal Arch Chapter," and in 1798 it united with King Cyrus Chapter of Newburyport, and at MASONS' HALL, in the "Green Dragon Tavern," organized the GRAND ROYAL ARCH CHAPTER OF MASSACHUSETTS.

On the 17th of May, 1770, the petitioners for "the Massachusetts Lodge," which was a scion of St. Andrew's Lodge, met at "Masons' Arms," in the "Green Dragon Tavern," and organized that body. It held its second meeting at the same place on the following 4th of June, and was then removed to

"Concert Hall." And on the 10th of November, 1795, Columbian Lodge also held a meeting at the "Green Dragon." These were the only occasions when the "Long Room" was ever occupied by any other private Masonic Lodge than our own. Columbian Lodge was at this date located at Concert Hall, and its occupancy of the room on the occasion referred to, was probably a matter of accommodation to the proprietors of that establishment, which was then the popular resort for dancing parties and other social purposes.

But it is perhaps to the political associations which cluster around its name, that the Green Dragon Tavern is more particularly indebted for its historic celebrity. It was here that many of the most important and eventful of the political transactions preceding the Revolution were, if not positively inaugurated, discussed, matured and put in execution. That this was so, is undoubtedly in some measure to be accounted for by the fact, that the Hall in the building was the only room in the northern section of the town, excepting Deblois's Hall, on the corner of Queen and Hanover streets, which at that time was adapted to popular assemblies; and by the additional and perhaps more significant fact, that the principal leaders of the Revolution in Boston, were members of the Masonic Fraternity, and many of them of the Lodge which held its communications there, — a circumstance which would very naturally influence them in the selection of the place for their private consultations. It is not however, to be inferred from this, that they either met as Masons or used Masonry as a cover to their purposes; for others than Masons were associated with them. But be this as it may, it will not be irrelevant nor perhaps wholly uninteresting to the members of the Lodge, to refer briefly to some of the more popular purposes to which the Hall, in the early days of its history, was appropriated.

One of the largest, and perhaps one of the most efficient of the political clubs which sprung into existence during the troublous times of 1768, and onward, was that known as "The North-End Caucus." This body was composed almost exclusively of North-End mechanics, — distinguished for their daring and activity, — and held its meetings in the Hall of the "Green Dragon Tavern." Warren who, Frothingham says, "was idolized by the North-Enders," was an influential member of it, as were Revere and others of his personal friends.

The Hall was also used as a central and safe place for the meetings of private committees and rallying clubs, with which Warren, as chairman of the "Committee of Safety," was in frequent consultation, and directed their movements. Barry, in his History of Massachusetts, says : — " The town (Boston) was full of clubs and caucuses, which were used with effect to secure unity of action ; and the hardy mechanics who had done so much to promote the industrial prosperity of the metropolis, and who now acted as patrols, were the steady supporters of the patriot cause. In vain were the artifices of loyalists employed to seduce them to compliance with the wishes of his excellency ; and when their services were required at the barracks, 'all the carpenters of the town and country' left off work ; and British gold was powerless to tempt them, though 'hundreds were ruined, and thousands were half starved,' nay, they went further, and obstructed the works of the governor. His supplies of straw were set on fire ; his boats conveying bricks were sunk ; and his wagons laden with timbers were overturned."

The character and services of these important Clubs are well illustrated by our Brother Paul Revere, in his narrative of the events of 1775, when he says, about thirty persons, chiefly North-End mechanics, had agreed to watch the movements of the British soldiers and the Tories, in anticipation of their descent on Concord. These patriots met at the Green Dragon Tavern. " We were so careful," he says, " that our meetings should be kept secret, that every time we met, every person swore upon the Bible that they (he) would not discover any of our transactions, but to Messrs. Hancock, Drs. Warren and Church, and one or two more leaders. They took turns to watch the soldiers, two by two, by patrolling the streets all night."

In reference to this club, Elliott, in his history of New England, has the following : — " Among the most active of the Sons of Liberty was Paul Revere. In the Fall and Winter of 1774–5, some of the best Boston mechanics formed themselves into a club, to watch the doings of the British soldiers. They were 'High Sons of Liberty,' and men of action, who met at the Green Dragon Tavern ; and every man swore on the Bible that nothing should be revealed except to Samuel Adams, John Hancock, Dr. Warren, and Dr. Church " (the latter a traitor). Revere was a leading man in this club, and was sent by Warren on the night of the 18th of April, to notify Hancock and Adams of the movement of the British troops on Lexington and Concord, at the former of which places these two patriots were concealed.

Another of these Clubs which held their meetings at the Green Dragon

Tavern, was the " *Caucus — Pro Bono Publico,*" of which Warren was the leading spirit, and in which, says Elliott, " the plans of the Sons of Liberty were matured."

It is to be regretted that no authentic record of the names of the persons who composed the *Boston Tea Party* in 1774, has come down to us. " But," says Frothingham, "as Warren was presented to the Privy Council as one of the prominent actors in these proceedings, and was held up by his political opponents at home, as one of the *Mohawks,*" and as " he was not one to shrink from any post of duty, it is not more improbable that he was one of the band who threw the tea overboard, than that his friend John Hancock (captain of the Cadets) should have been one of the guard to protect the actors."

The tradition of the Lodge is, that all the preliminary measures in this affair were matured at the Green Dragon, and that the execution of them was committed mainly to the members of the *North-End Caucus,* — that stalwart and fearless band of North-End mechanics, whose directing genius was Warren, — having the co-operation of the more daring of the " Sons of Liberty." That Warren was present as a leader in the affair, does not admit of any serious doubt : nor is there any question that his personal friends Samuel Adams, John Hancock, Joseph Webb, Paul Revere, Thomas Melville, Adam Collson, Henry Purkett (who used modestly to say he was present only as a spectator, and in disobedience to the orders of his Master, who was actively present), and other patriots of the day, were cognizant of it, — and some of whom at least are known to have participated in its final consummation. It was the first act in the great drama, the conclusion of which was the independence of the country.

The " Master " referred to above, with whom our late Bro. Purkett served his apprenticeship, was *Samuel Peck,* a cooper by trade, and one of the leading and influential members of the " North-End Caucus." He was also an active member of St. Andrew's Lodge, — a connection which strengthens the tradition of the Lodge, that the *table* for the famous *Tea Party* was first spread in its " Long Room." Among the members of the Lodge, who are known to have taken an active part in the affair, were Adam Collson, Thomas Chase, Samuel Gore, Daniel Ingollson, Samuel Peck, Edward Proctor, Henry Purkitt, and Thomas Urann.

I have looked in vain for a copy of an old revolutionary song said to have been written and sung as a " rallying song" by the " tea party" at the Green

Dragon. The following fragment, though probably not in all respects an exact transcript of the original, will indicate its general character : —

> Rally, *Mohawks!* — bring out your axes !
> And tell King George we'll pay no taxes
>   *On his foreign tea !*
> His threats are vain — and vain to think
> To force our girls and wives to drink
>   *His vile Bohea !*
> Then rally boys, and hasten on
> To meet our *Chiefs* at the Green Dragon.
>
> Our WARREN's there, and bold REVERE,
> With hands to do and words to cheer
>   *For Liberty and Laws !*
> Our country's " Braves " and firm defenders,
> Shall ne'er be left by true North-Enders,
>   *Fighting Freedom's cause !*
> Then rally boys, and hasten on
> To meet our *Chiefs* at the Green Dragon.
>
> *   *   *   *   *   *   *   *

I regret not being able to give the balance of this song, but perhaps some curious antiquary may hereafter discover it, if it ever appeared in print.   I am inclined to think, however, that it was a doggerel made for the occasion, and passed away when it ceased to be of use, or appropriate. The two stanzas I have re-produced, are given as nearly as my memory serves, as they were often recited more than a third of a century ago, by the late Bro. BENJAMIN GLEASON, who, born near the time, was curious in gathering up interesting reminiscences of the revolutionary period of our history.

In January 1788, a meeting of the mechanics and artisans of Boston, was held at the Green Dragon Tavern, and there passed a series of resolutions urging the importance of adopting the Federal Constitution, then pending before a Convention of delegates from the different parts of the State.   Hon. DANIEL WEBSTER, in a speech delivered by him at Andover, in the autumn of 1843, referring to this meeting and these resolutions, holds the following language: "There was a particular set of resolutions, founded on this very idea of favoring home productions, full of energy and decision, passed by the mechanics of Boston. And where did the mechanics of Boston meet to pass them? Full of the influence of these feelings, they congregated at the HEAD-QUARTERS OF THE REVOLUTION. *I see, waving among the banners before me, that of the old* GREEN DRAGON. It was *there*, in Union street, that John Gray, Paul Revere." — both members of the Lodge. — "and others of their class, met for consultation. There, with earnestness and enthusiasm, they passed their resolutions. A committee carried them to the Boston delegation in the Convention," then in session. Paul Revere, whom Mr. Webster in a previous address, delivered on another occasion, says, was "a man of sense and character, and of high public spirit, whom the mechanics of Boston ought never to forget," was chairman of this committee. He placed them in the hands of Samuel Adams. "How many mechanics," said Mr. Adams, "were at the Green Dragon when these resolutions were passed?" "More, sir," was the reply, "than the Green Dragon could hold." "And where were the rest, Mr. Revere?" "In the streets, sir." "And how many were in the streets?" "More, sir, than there are stars in the sky."

The late Hon. EDWARD EVERETT, in an address on the Battle of Lexington, delivered at Lexington on the 19th of April, 1835, speaking of the patriot Samuel Adams, says : —

"He was among the earliest and ablest writers on the patriotic side. He caught the plain, downright style of the Commonwealth in Great Britain. More than most of his associates, he understood the efficacy of personal intercourse with the people. It was Samuel Adams, more than any other individual, who brought the question home to their bosoms and firesides ; not by profound disquisitions and elaborate reports, — though these in their place were not spared, — but in the caucuses, the club rooms, *at the Green Dragon*, in the ship-yards, in actual conference, man to man and heart to heart."

The Old South Church was, in these stirring times, called by the patriots, the *Sanctuary of Freedom ;* while, on the other hand, the Green Dragon Tavern was denounced by the Tories as a *Nest of Traitors !* The distinction in these appellations is more obvious than the difference ! The enemies of the tyrannical and oppressive measures of the government, were all either *patriots* or *traitors*, according to the standard by which they were tried.

I give these anecdotes as striking and forcible illustrations of the popular character of the Green Dragon, and of the important part which the mechanics of the North-End played in public affairs, at that day. It is not however, to be inferred that the mechanics residing in other sections of the town were inactive. That the former appear more prominently than others of their class, is probably owing to the circumstance that the North-End was then the business part of the town, and where most of the mechanical trades were carried on.

After the close of the Revolutionary War, and when the occasion for political clubs, and other secret political associations, had passed away, the hall was used for more pacific and social purposes ; and I have often heard our late Brother JAMES WASHBURN, a sterling North-End mechanic, felicitate himself that he was not only there initiated into Masonry, but that he was there also initiated into what he used facetiously to call the " *Terpsichorean Mysteries,*" or, in less classical language, that he there received his first lessons in dancing ! The fact shows that the hall was at the time used as a dancing academy. There were probably others among the old members of the Lodge who might have shared this honor with him, but I am not able to give their names.

About the year 1789. Mr. Benjamin Dearborn, long and favorably known to our citizens as an ingenious scientific mechanic, and manufacturer of scales, removed from Portsmouth, N. H., and occupied the " Long Room " as an academy. He subsequently purchased a part of what was then known as " Wakefield's garden lot," between Milk and Franklin streets, and there erected a building better suited to his purpose, and opened a large and popular school, which he continued for some years, when he gave it up and devoted his entire attention to scientific and mechanical pursuits.

On the 18th of October 1764, Mr. *Robert Sandeman,* a native of Perth, in Scotland, whose writings, as a religious reformer, had excited a deep interest among some of the people of the town, arrived here direct from Glasgow, and on the following Sunday preached his first sermon in America, at " Masons' Hall," in the Green Dragon Tavern. For some reason, not now known, he afterwards, for a short time, held his meetings at the house of Mr. Edward Foster in Black Horse Lane, near Prince Street ; but his followers becoming more numerous, he returned to the Green Dragon Tavern, where he remained until his society built a house for themselves near the " Mill Pond." This house was burned in 1773. The society however, continued to hold its meetings until 1823, when it was dissolved. The worshippers were denominationally known as the *Sandemanians.*

It is more than probable that the hall was frequently used for other similar purposes by the people residing in the section of the town where it was located, of which, however, there are no reliable data. Public halls were not so common then as now, in proportion to the population, or what should seem to have been the public requirements. Had the fact been otherwise, Mr. Sandeman, at the most exciting period of his mission, would not probably have been put to the necessity of holding his meetings at a private house. Enough however, has been preserved to indicate the purposes for which the hall, through a long and interesting series of years, was principally occupied, — enough to show that if Faneuil Hall was the " Cradle of Liberty," many of the children rocked in it were born at the Green Dragon !

It may, I think, be safely assumed, that from the year 1767, when the Townshend Revenue Acts were passed, imposing a Tax on Tea, creating a Board of Customs, and legalizing Writs of Assistance, to the close of the War of Independence, there was not another public house in the whole country, and assuredly not in Massachusetts, where so much of the "secret history" of the Revolutionary period was made, as at the old Green Dragon Tavern ; and it is to be deeply regretted that the subject was not attended to when that history could have been intelligently and reliably written. It is now too late. The patriotic men who alone could have furnished the material have passed away, — *and they have taken their* " SECRET " *with them.*

When Mr. Webster, who was perhaps better read in the early local history and events of the Revolutionary period than any other public man of his time, described the Green Dragon Tavern as the " HEAD-QUARTERS OF THE REVOLUTION," he wrote the title page, and opened a volume, which, if written as he alone could have written it, would have been an addition to the early political annals of the Commonwealth of surpassing interest and importance.

SPEECH OF DR. N. B. SHURTLEFF.

Brother Nathaniel B. Shurtleff was next called upon, and rising, spoke substantially as follows —

Worshipful Master: —

It is with much pleasure that I find myself in a meeting of the Lodge at this place. The site is not only dear to me for its association with the early days of this, our small band of brothers of the mystic rite, and also with the large fraternity of Massachusetts Freemasons; but its very intimate connection with remarkable events in the history of the municipality in which I was born, and where I have resided all my days, make it especially an object of peculiar interest to me, independent of all other considerations. Distinguished as it is, and ever will be, as one of the most noted landmarks of this ancient metropolis — a spot where, in the olden time, the fathers of the town were wont to meet in social gathering, and where the Sons of Liberty of the times that tried men's souls, held their secret meetings for consultation, and enkindled that flame of patriotism that gave birth to the confederation of the North American colonies, and consequently to the freest government that the world has ever known and acknowledged — the spot whereon we are now collected, has remembrances that hallow every inch of ground connected with this time-honored estate.

It is well, my brothers, that we are here to-day. It is well that we recognize in this social manner the provident forethought of the fathers of St. Andrew's Lodge. I think it will be better, however, if we emulate their example of thrift, patriotism and good-fellowship, and, as we partake of the bounties which their foresight has provided, and grateful for the benevolence, we resolve most sacredly to transmit to our successors an undiminished heritage, which shall produce for them, as it has for us and those who have preceeded us, rich harvests of comfort, pleasure, and charity.

Perhaps, brothers, you may be able to form a better idea of the length of time that this estate has been in the possession of the Lodge, if I call your attention to the old English elms that now skirt the street in front of the Granary Burial Ground, and tell you that those noble trees were but striplings of two years growth when this estate was purchased by our predecessors. I might also tell you that Boston, at the time of the purchase, was a small town of less than sixteen thousand inhabitants, scarcely enough for one of the present wards, whereas now it can count a population of nearly a quarter of a million of souls ; and that our now powerful country a hundred years ago was but a collection of small colonies owning allegiance to a foreign power, which it has since rejoiced over as a conqueror in two wars fought most bravely for liberty and for the freedom of the seas. What changes have taken place in America, and I may also say, throughout the whole world, during these eventful years ! What an example has our beloved country placed before the nations of the earth ! And who, may I ask, were the men that gave character and energy to the endeavors that produced the results that brought about these changes ? They were, I answer, our own brethren of St. Andrew's Lodge — the very men, who upon our altars consecrated themselves to noble works and high Christian charities, and who, with the best attributes of human nature, true patriotism and love of liberty, have by their words and heroic deeds made their names illustrious wherever the love of country and of the human race is known and appreciated.

Through all these years, when, perhaps, at times darkness and gloom were as well known and felt, as were the more happy days of peace and good fellowship enjoyed, the Lodge has remained true to itself and to Freemasonry. Humble in its origin — a North-End notion perchance — it was in its early days more known for its worth than for its wealth. Its members were the sturdy sons of the town, — industrious, honest, and given to good deeds of brotherly love, charity and hospitality. They have passed along in their unpretending ways of duty. They have fulfilled their obligations to Masonry, to their families and to their fellow-beings. They have not sought distinction nor honors, although these unbidden have fixed their everlasting marks upon many of them. May the sons emulate the virtues and good characteristics of the fathers ! And may they leave an inheritance of name as worthy of transmission, as that is estimable that they have received, and which they cherish so much, so honorably and so dearly !

Perhaps a brief sketch of the old Green Dragon Tavern estate, the heirloom of the Lodge, may not be inappropriate with the objects of this present celebration. If so, if you will bear with me a few minutes, I will give you some particulars which may not be generally known to the brethren.

Only a few steps from Hanover street, in that portion of Union street which leads towards the site of the old mill pond, formerly stood an ancient building of considerable notoriety, known in the olden time as the Green Dragon Tavern, and even until quite recently retaining this distinctive name.   It was early a noted landmark even in the first century of Boston's history; and, as time wore on, it became as famous as any private edifice — if such it could be called considering the public uses to which it was frequently put — that could be found upon the peninsula.   If its early occupancy and use brought it into notice, so also was new fame added to that which it had already acquired by the patriotic gatherings held within its sombre walls during the darkest days of the American Revolution, when Samuel Adams, James Otis, Joseph Warren, Paul Revere, and other true sons of liberty, in their secret councils planned the deliverance of their country from thraldom and the grievous oppressions of Great Britain.

This old relic of ancient times disappeared from its lot near the close of the last year of the mayoralty of the elder Quincy ; and its appearance is fast fading out of the remembrance even of those who in their early years were well acquainted with its most hidden recesses.   The estate on which it stood now belongs to St. Andrew's Lodge of Freemasons, and its history can be traced back to the first settlement of the town.   It is a portion of the three-quarters of an acre of marsh and upland originally granted to James Johnson, a glover, who settled in Boston as early as the year 1635, and who was distinguished among his contemporary townsmen as a deacon of the church, and as captain of the Artillery Company in 1656, — a company which by its age and ancient renown has acquired the designation of the " Ancient and Honorable Artillery Company." The property is first mentioned in 1643, in the Book of Possessions of the first settlers of the town, on the twentieth page, and is there described as " three-quarters of an acre of marsh & upland, bounded with the Cove on the North & the East, John Smith, West, & John Davies, South."   The Cove is elsewhere in the volume quoted, called the " Cove or Mill Pond ; " and the contiguous estate on the south, which separated Mr. Johnson's estate from the street (now Hanover street), was the original grant made to John Davies, a joiner, consisting of a house and garden.   Davies, on the twenty-eighth of June, 1645, conveyed his house and garden to John Trotman, whose wife Katherine, as the attorney of her husband, sold the same on the same day to Thomas Hawkins, of Boston, at that time a noted biscuit baker, but subsequently an innholder, and on this lot was a few years afterwards built the "Star Inn," probably kept in those early days successively by Mr. Hawkins and his goodwife Rebecca, John Howlet and his wife Susanna, and Andrew Neal and his wife Milicent. The Neals died in possession of the corner about 1709, having purchased it of Howlet's widow, who bought it of Hawkins; and the estate passed from their heirs by sale to John Borland, who in his turn passed it down to Francis Borland, Esq.

After Mr. Hawkins had come in possession of the Davies lot, he became desirous of obtaining the Johnson lot also; and subsequently purchased it of Mr. Johnson, through the intervention of his cordwainer, Thomas Marshall, on the tenth of October, 1662. Hawkins soon began keeping an inn upon his newly acquired estate, and probably put additional buildings on the lot, as he subsequently mortgaged it to Rev. Thomas Thacher, the future pastor of the Old South Church (just establishing), on the sixth of December, 1667; and, on the twenty-ninth of May, 1671, Thacher, who had married the widow of Jacob Sheafe, the most opulent Bostonian of his day, assigned the mortgage to Sampson Sheafe, Esq., who had married Elizabeth, one of the daughters of his wife. Mr. Hawkins put a second mortgage on his estate on the fifteenth of June, 1671, to secure money borrowed of Mr. Sheafe, and died in the latter part of the year 1671, and his widow Rebecca (his second wife) relinquished her right of dower on the sixteenth of January, 1671-2, the estates having been forfeited to Mr. Sheafe for non-fulfilment of the payments. Sometime previous to the fifteenth of June, 1676, the Green Dragon Tavern estate passed into the possession of William Stoughton, a man having excellent traits of character, although in a judicial capacity, which he held before his appointment as Lieutenant-Governor of the Province, he was most wickedly intolerant in the trials of the miscalled witches; for which cruelty and barbarism his gift of Stoughton Hall to Harvard College will not in the slightest degree compensate.

Lieutenant-Governor Stoughton, the son of Israel Stoughton, of Dorchester, was a person of considerable ability. He was educated at Harvard College, graduating in 1650, and he passed some time in studying for the ministry, but relinquished the design of becoming a preacher after having delivered the annual election sermon in 1668, preferring the field of politics to that of religion. In May, 1692, he entered upon the duties of Lieutenant-Governor, having been appointed to the position under the second Massachusetts Charter establishing the Province, at the same time that Sir William Phips was commissioned as

23

Governor. In November, 1694, on the return of Governor Phips to England, he became acting governor, performing the duties until the arrival of the Earl of Bellomont in May, 1699; and succeeding him in the same capacity in July, 1700, and so continuing until the seventh of July, 1701, when he died at the age of about seventy years. He died, possessed of a large landed property in Boston, comprising in part the Green Dragon Tavern estate, the Star Inn estate, and the old Blue Ball estate where the father of Franklin resided after the birth of the great Bostonian, — the last named estates being at the opposite corners of Hanover and Union streets. He devised this property to his nieces, the Green Dragon Tavern and Franklin corners falling to Mehitible, the wife of Captain Thomas Cooper, the father of Rev. William Cooper, one of the early pastors of Brattle Square Church. Mrs. Cooper was a very distinguished person. She was the daughter of James Minot, of Dorchester, by his wife Hannah, the sister of Lieutenant-Governor Stoughton, and was born in Dorchester on the seventeenth of September, 1668. Captain Cooper, her husband, died at sea in 1705, and she married for her second husband Peter Sargeant, Esq., he who built for his mansion house the old Province House. On the death of Mr. Sargeant on the eighth of February, 1714, she married her third husband, Simeon Stoddard, Esq., who died on the fifteenth of October, 1730, in his eightieth year, leaving her a third time a widow in her sixty-second year. Mrs. Mehitible Stoddard died, a widow, on the twenty-third of September, 1738. At the time of Mr. Cooper's death in 1705, the Green Dragon estate was valued at £650.

On the eighteenth of August, 1743, about five years after the decease of Mrs. Stoddard, her son, Rev. William Cooper, sold the Green Dragon Tavern estate to Dr. William Douglass, not only a noted physician, but also the author of the very celebrated "Summary" of New England History. Dr. William Douglass was born in Gifford, in the County of Haddington, a short distance from Edinburgh, Scotland, and died in Boston the twenty-first of October, 1752, aged, as nearly as can be ascertained, about sixty years. He came to Boston in 1716, but did not make a permanent settlement here until the year 1718. He first dwelt in Hanover street, near Mr. Welstead's meeting-house; but at his decease the house in Green Dragon Lane was styled his mansion house, and was the only one on the estate not let by him to tenants. His father George was a portioner (distributor of tithes) in Gifford, near Edinburgh, and the factor of

John. Marquis of Tweedale. His father's children were : Cornelius (a surgeon and portioner) who had a son Cornelius (a joiner) who removed to Boston after the decease of Dr. William Douglass ; Dr. William, the second child ; George, who died in youth ; and Catherine, who married a person named Kerr (sometimes written Carr), and who came to Boston with her nephew, and afterwards married a Mr. Robinson. Catherine Kerr, the sister, and Cornelius Douglass, the nephew of Dr. William Douglass, shared his property equally by a division made the twenty-seventh of September, 1754, and recorded with Suffolk deeds. Lib. 88, fol. 76. Dr. Douglass left about £3,185. Over twenty dozen gloves were bought for his funeral.

In this noted old house Dr. Douglass wrote his famous books, and in it he died. By an agreement of his heirs, made the twenty-seventh of September, 1754, and recorded with the Suffolk Records, the old mansion house fell to Catherine Kerr, and she, a widow, by deed dated the thirty-first of March, 1764, conveyed it, for the consideration of £466 13s. 4d, to Moses Deshon and others, members of St. Andrew's Lodge of Freemasons. Since this date the estate has been in the possession of the Lodge.

The old tavern stood on the left side of the street, formerly called Green Dragon Lane, now the northerly portion of Union street, leading from Hanover street to the old mill pond, now filled up and built upon. It was built of brick, and in its latter days was painted of a dingy color. In front it showed only two stories and an attic ; but in the rear, from the slope of the land and the peculiar shape of the roof, three stories, with a basement, were perceptible. It covered a piece of land fifty feet in front and thirty-four in depth, and had connected with it a large stable and other out-buildings. In recent times the lower story was used as the common rooms of a tavern, while in the second, on the street front, was a large hall used for public as well as for Masonic purposes. The attic story afforded ample accommodations for sleeping apartments. The chimneys were substantially built in the side walls, and were of the style usually found in houses built at the close of the seventeenth century. The attic windows on the front part of the roof, and the walk railed in on the upper part, added much to the appearance and comfort of the building, which, in its best days, must have been commodious, and comfortably arranged.

The whole estate comprised a large lot of land, the main portion being situated back of Green Dragon Lane, with other estates in front, and extending northerly to the Old Mill Pond. The extensive yard was much used by the boys who dwelt in the neighborhood as a playground ; and here it was, undoubtedly, that the youthful Franklin first essayed in his mechanical feat of building his stone wharf, alluded to in his autobiography. The old tavern stable became in its latter days a well-known convenience ; and served many years as a livery stable kept by men well acquainted with their business.

In front of the building there projected from the wall an iron crane, upon which was couched a Green Dragon. This peculiar mark of designation was very ancient, perhaps as old as the building itself. It was formed of thick sheet copper, and had a curled tail ; and from its mouth projected a fearful looking tongue, the wonder of all the boys who dwelt in the neighborhood. When the building was taken down, this curious relic of the handiwork of the ancient mechanics of the town disappeared, and has never since been found, although most searching inquiries and diligent examinations for it have been made among workmen and in the collections of the dealers in old material. In 1854, a committee of St. Andrew's Lodge was appointed to put in the new building, that stands upon the site of the old one, a memorial to commemorate the old house, and they inserted in the wall, on the first of November, 1855, a stone effigy, elaborately carved in sandstone in a most skilful and artistic manner, by a workman in the employ of Mr. Thomas J. Bailey, of this city ; and this magnificently sculptured emblem now proudly supplies the place of the old weather-beaten dragon, which had for nearly a century and a half withstood the storms and tempests of the hard New England seasons, and outlived the violence of political mobs and the rudeness of inimical soldiery in the time of the war — a fit object to perpetuate in some degree the remembrance of the old hall, in which the patriots of the American Revolution used to meet, and also to designate the Masons' Hall of by-gone days.

The old mansion-house must have been erected not far from the year 1680, when many substantial buildings of a similar kind were put up. In 1695, and perhaps earlier, it was used as an inn by Alexander Smith, who, and his widow also, died as its occupants in 1696. Hannah Bishop had a license in October, 1696, for keeping a tavern in it : and she was succeeded by John Cary, a brewer, in October of 1697, who certainly was its occupant as late as 1705, although Samuel Tyley appears to have been the tenant of Lieut.-Gov. Stoughton, at the time of his decease in July, 1701. In 1734, Joseph Kidder, who came from the

Three Cranes in Charlestown, was the keeper. It would not be surprising if Thomas Milliken, a member of St. Andrew's Lodge, was also a landlord at some time of the Green Dragon Tavern ; for he was a victualler by occupation, and was mainly instrumental in its purchase for the Lodge, being Chairman of the Committee authorized on the eleventh of January, 1764, to buy it. On the thirty-first of the month, of the same year, the deed was passed by Mrs. Catherine Kerr to Moses Deshon and others ; and on the thirteenth of April the Lodge held for the first time a monthly meeting in the hall. On the fourteenth of June, 1764, the hall was formally named " Freemasons' Hall," and from that time, for a long series of years, was the regular place of meeting of the Lodge. It would be useless, were it even possible, to name the various persons who carried on this famous tavern ; suffice it to say, that at times it was the most popular of the old houses of " entertainment for man and beast " in the town, and was noted for being a favorite hall for festive as well as political occasions. Undoubtedly the famous " Tea Party " of 1773 had its origin within the walls of this old mansion ; for it is known that several of the most active spirits engaged in it were members of the Masonic Lodge that held its meetings there monthly. A Lodge meeting called for the thirtieth of November, 1773, being St. Andrew's day, was closed without the transaction of business in consequence of the fewness of the brethren present, and the following words in a distinct hand were entered on the page with the record, "(N. B. Consignees of Tea took up the Brethren's time.)" The meeting which was to have been held on the sixteenth of December — the day of the destruction of the tea — was also given up for the same reason.

From the following document, signed by the Lieutenant-Governor, it appears that in the Revolutionary war the building was sometimes used for other purposes :

BOSTON, Feb. 24th, 1776.

To the Rev'd Doc'r Caner, Col. Snelling, Maj Paddock, Cap Gore, & Cap Gay.

Gentlemen — Having occasion for a large commodious House for the Purpose of a Hospital in which the poor — Infirm and Aged can be lodged upon the Charity in which you are appointed Stewards — and having the Consent of the Proprietors in Town of the House Commonly called the Green Dragon to apply that to this Purpose, you are hereby required to take possession of said House and prepare it as a Hospital for the Reception of such objects as shall require immediate Relief, for which this shall be your authority.   THOS. OLIVER.

In October, 1828, as the travel from Charlestown had much increased, and as the filling up the Mill Pond had given room for many buildings, and therefore required the widening of Green Dragon Lane, the old building was taken down by order of the city authorities, and a considerable part of its site taken for the proposed widening; and, then passed almost from remembrance the appearance of one of the most noted and interesting landmarks of the early days of the town. On its site, and covering the whole estate, a large warehouse has been erected by the Lodge, which is now occupied as a carriage depository. Although the old house, that had stood the effects of time and the destroying elements for more than a century and a half, was quietly removed to give way for much needed improvements, no authentic picture of its appearance was preserved. Nevertheless, from my own personal recollections, I have made a drawing and model of this old landmark, which has been most critically examined by many persons who have had the best opportunities for knowing and remembering it; and they have sanctioned my efforts and pronounced the reproduction a good representation.

Thus, brethren, I have given you an outline history of our old Green Dragon Tavern estate. I have purposely avoided noticing many things that would perhaps have been interesting to the Lodge. But you have not time to hear more on this occasion; nor would it be desirable that so dull a theme should occupy too much of the time that should be given to social enjoyment, and the recollections of a more personal character, with which, I am sure, the older members of the Lodge can enlighten and delight you. I, therefore, thank you for your attention and patience, and give way for others, that I may be able to enjoy with you what I know so many are able and prepared to say.

After the conclusion of Bro. Shurtleff's speech, several capital songs and glees were sung. And in pleasant commemoration of the old time hospitality of the ancient Inn and Freemasons' Arms, a few popular ballads of a hundred years ago, were reproduced by the brethren and guests. Short speeches interspersed in pleasing variety the above performances.

In the course of the Festival, Bro. Shurtleff presented to the Lodge a bottle of Madeira wine, which was put up in 1784 by Mungo Mackay, who was made a member of "St. Andrew's" in 1780. The bottle was opened and the wine proved of excellent quality. This bottle of wine was handed to Bro. Shurtleff for the purpose of a gift to the Lodge by Joseph Richardson, Esq., who married a grand-daughter of Bro. Wm. Burbeck, one of the earliest and most valued members of "St. Andrew's," and whose name is in the Charter of the Lodge.

THE NEW BUILDING ON THE GREEN DRAGON TAVERN ESTATE.

The growth of Boston, and the increasing demand for large warehouses, determined the Lodge of St. Andrew, to cover the Green Dragon Tavern Estate with a modern commodious building. In 1854-5, the present structure of brick was erected. The custom of putting some name, or designative inscription conspicuously upon the front of large warehouses, being a fashion of the day, it was at once suggested to the members of the Lodge, that a design in the similitude of the noted Copper Sign representing a Dragon, — which had been the sign of the famous Inn itself for a century and a half of its existence, — should be placed on the new building.

This suggestion met the hearty concurrence of every member of St. Andrew's but here a question arose, namely: What had become of the old Copper Dragon itself? This question baffled all recollection or enquiry. Venerable Lodge members, neighbors and citizens generally, — who were old enough inhabitants. —all remembered the Green Dragon Sign perfectly well; every feature of the copper figure of the monster was plain before their eyes, but the original sign itself could not be laid hands on. It had no doubt been removed in October, 1828, when the old building was taken down for the purpose of widening Union street, and this was then and there the sum and substance of all knowledge of its whereabouts. The Lodge however, were not content thus to part with the "old Green Dragon," whereupon a select committee consisting of old members of St. Andrew's, each of whom were familiar with the looks of the ancient sign, was chosen on the 12th of January, 1854, and their Report made at the regular meeting of the Lodge. November 8, 1855, will explain the purpose of their appointment, and the final result. This Report is here introduced as an appropriate close of this division of the "Memorial."

REPORT ON GREEN DRAGON.

The committee appointed to make diligent search for the Old Green Dragon sign, and in case of failure in finding the same, to procure a model of one as like the original as possible, have attended to the duty assigned to them, and respectfully

REPORT.

That after having made enquiries of all persons, whom they thought might in any degree be likely to know anything of the old figure, or of its whereabouts, and also made very diligent search in all places where it might be supposed to be laid away or concealed, and having entirely failed of obtaining the slightest clue to its present condition, and despairing of ever being able to discover what had become of the original sign, and after spending more than eighteen months in enquiries and fruitless search, have prepared a model which they have caused to be carved in a truly artistic and workmanlike manner, in durable sandstone, by a skilful person in the employ of Mr. Thomas J. Bailey, of this city. They have also caused the same to be inserted in the front wall (near Hanover street) of the brick building lately erected on the site of the Green Dragon estate on Union street.

The sculpture was placed in situation on the first of the present month, Nov. 1855. In general features it resembles the copper sign, as far as the memory of those who retained any knowledge of it could point out. The artist has, however, with commendable pride, made it a very sightly and creditable production, and wherein memory failed, he has supplied the defect from a very beautiful and costly work of art, representing the patron saint of England, St. George, and his usual accompaniment, the Dragon, designed and executed by an eminent member of the Royal Academy of Great Britain, by direction of his Royal Highness, Prince Albert.

The monster represented is entirely fabulous, and is variously delineated by artists. The Dragon of Heraldry assumed one form, and its varieties others. The Old English Dragon, which is constantly associated with St. George, is seldom depicted in the same manner. Our Dragon, as it now appears, is undoubtedly one of the finest models of the monster now to be seen ; and in the opinion of the committee marks a spot which should never be forgotten as one of the early meeting places of St. Andrew's Lodge, and as memorable for its connection with many of the events of the American Revolution, and which they trust will not derogate from the interest which we entertain for the estate.

Respectfully submitted.

JOHN RAYNER,
EZEKIEL BATES,   } *Committee.*
SMITH W. NICHOLS. |

LODGE OF ST. ANDREW,
BOSTON, November 8, A. L. 5855.

24

CENTENNIAL OBSERVANCE

OF THE

INAUGURATION

OF

JOSEPH WARREN

AS GRAND MASTER OF

THE MASSACHUSETTS GRAND LODGE,

DECEMBER 28, 1869.

"EAST" OF THE GRAND LODGE ROOM OF MASSACHUSETTS.

Introduction

At the annual meeting of the GRAND LODGE OF MASSACHUSETTS held at Boston, on the eighth day of December 1869, the M. W. GRAND MASTER, W. S. GARDNER in his report remarked : —

" It is well known that our history embraces the so-called ST. JOHN'S GRAND LODGE which was established in 1733, and the so-called MASSACHUSETTS GRAND LODGE which originated in 1769. One hundred years ago, on the 27th of this December, JOSEPH WARREN, the Revolutionary Patriot, was installed as first Grand Master of the Massachusetts Grand Lodge. Since the union in 1792, we have followed the forms and customs of this Grand Lodge with singular fidelity. It was the first Grand Lodge upon this continent, which declared its independence. I would recommend that the approaching Festival be celebrated in a manner becoming the recurrence of such an anniversary, and that a committee charged with the matter be appointed."

In accordance with the recommendation of the Grand Master, a committee on the Festival of St. John the Evangelist was appointed, consisting of

R. W. Brother JOHN T. HEARD,
         "   "   SERENO D. NICKERSON,
         "   "   CHARLES W. MOORE,
   W.   "   SAMUEL C. LAWRENCE,
   R. W.   "   CHARLES LEVI WOODBURY.

This committee made arrangement for the Feast, upon a scale somewhat more extended than usual. Notices were sent to all the Lodges, inviting them to be present, and unite in celebrating the Centennial. Invitations were also sent to the M. W. Grand Masters of Maine, New Hampshire, Vermont, Rhode Island, Connecticut and New York, and to Past Grand Master Josiah H. Drummond of Maine.

By a provision of the constitution of the Grand Lodge, when the Festival of St. John the Evangelist "shall happen on a Saturday, Sunday or Monday," it shall be celebrated on the following Tuesday; the 27th of December coming this year — 1869 — on Monday, the Grand Lodge was held on Tuesday the 28th of December. A large number of Brethren convened in Sutton Hall, in the Masonic Temple at half past five o'clock, P. M., when the M. W. Grand Lodge was opened in ample form, — and the installation of the Grand Officers proceeded. At the conclusion of the ceremonies the following stanzas on the death of WARREN were recited : —

> "His countrymen mourned for the hero brave,
>   Who inspired each bosom with trust ;
> While MASONRY knelt by the blood-hallow'd grave,
>   And wept o'er the slumbering dust.
> She wept for the light from her temples withdrawn,
>   The BROTHER so honored and brave,
> That even the *forman's* proud arm was upthrown
>   So noble a spirit to save ;
> The Patriot GRAND MASTER, who fell in his might,
>   The *second of three* — in defence of the right !
>
> "A soldier — the brightest of laurels were twined,
>   Unfading around his fair name —
> While his mem'ry in thousands of hearts is enshrined,
>   The rarest and purest of fame.
> A Mason — his life was unselfish and pure,
>   Made true by the compass and square ;
> An ashlar of beauty that long will endure,
>   Which LIGHT proves both perfect and fair.
> The *world* may forget him ; but while there's a stone
>   In Masonry's Temple still *there*,
> The name of our WARREN will not be unknown,
>   But cherished with reverence and care.
> Peace, peace to thy memory, brave WARREN, for aye ;
>   The LIGHT from thy life shall fade never away ! "

After which M. W. WM. S. GARDNER, Grand Master, delivered his address.

Address

— ❧ —

The feast which we this day celebrate derives additional attraction from the fact that it is the Centennial of the inauguration of the so-called "Massachusetts Grand Lodge." In 1717, the London Grand Lodge was established under the title of "Grand Lodge of England." It proved to be a cause of great dissension among the English Masons; so much so that, about the year 1738, an open revolt against its authority broke out, which resulted in another Grand Lodge, which assumed the name of "Ancient Masons," and "Ancient York Masons," and gave to the members of the London Grand Lodge the title of "Modern Masons." These dissensions spread to Scotland, Ireland, and to the Colonies of Great Britain. In 1733, the London Grand Lodge commissioned Henry Price, Grand Master of Masons in North America, and under this authority Lodges were chartered in Massachusetts, the East of the Provincial Grand Lodge being here at Boston. This Grand Body acquired strength and influence, and conducted its affairs with great pomp and parade. Its officers and members were, many of them, men of dignity and character in the Province, and in the management of the affairs of the Grand Lodge they exhibited much of that exclusiveness which existed in the civil government.

Prior to 1756, the schism which originated in England had spread to this Province. Some persons who had applied to the regular Lodges in Boston, and who had been rejected, obtained their degrees in the Lodges of Ancient Masons attached to the Royal

Regiments stationed here, or were made Masons after the ancient system in some irregular way, and attempted afterwards to visit the Boston Lodges, but were denied admission. They, as well as others who had not been rejected, but who were Ancient Masons, and had also been driven from the doors of the Lodges, feeling aggrieved at the course pursued by the Grand Lodge towards them, petitioned the Grand Lodge of Scotland for a charter to hold a Lodge under its auspices in Boston. This request was granted, and November 30, 1756, St. Andrew's Lodge, No. 81, was chartered, under which the Brethren commenced their labors.

Immediately after its organization, the members of St. Andrew's attempted to place themselves on friendly terms with the Brethren of the Grand and subordinate Lodges then existing here. The records show that an extensive correspondence between St. Andrew's and the Grand Lodge took place, and that the latter refused to recognize the members of the former as Masons.

Under the Grand Mastership of Jeremy Gridley, the Grand Lodge passed a vote forbidding the Lodges under its jurisdiction, upon any consideration, to admit the visits of any of the members of St. Andrew's Lodge. In January, 1766, St. Andrew's raised a committee, of which Joseph Warren was a member, to wait on the Grand Lodge the following Friday night with a complimentary address, desiring them to visit St. Andrew's whenever they may think proper, "and that for the future there may be a happy coalition."

This committee visited the Grand Lodge and received an answer in writing, which, when reported to St. Andrew's, was declared to be "by no means satisfactory, as it is ill-grounded."

The same committee were directed to prepare an address, in answer to the Grand Lodge, and in June, 1766, a committee, of which Joseph Warren was chairman, was raised to transmit all that had passed between St. Andrew's and the Grand Lodge in Boston to the Grand Master of Scotland.

In September, 1767, was announced in the Grand Lodge the decease of " M. W. Jeremy Gridley, Esq., Grand Master of Masons over all North America, Attorney General for the Province of Massachusetts Bay, a member of the Great and General Court of said Province, and a Justice throughout the same, Colonel of the First Regiment of Militia, and President of the Marine Society," etc.

At this meeting, says the record, " Mr. Joseph Webb, Mr. Samuel Barrett, and Doctor Joseph Warren, a committee from St. Andrew's Lodge, waiting below, sent up word that they desired to be admitted into the Lodge to present a message from said St. Andrew's Lodge."

It was voted unanimously to admit them. "When they came up, they informed the Deputy Grand Master that it was the Lodge's desire that they may attend the Grand Master's funeral as Masons."

The Grand Lodge unanimously granted their request. In the order of the funeral procession, which is most carefully set out in the Grand Lodge records, after the officers of the Grand Master's Regiment, and members of the Marine Society, came —

" The Tyler of St. Andrew's Lodge with the sword."

" The Stewards of said Lodge with their wands."

" The members of said Lodge two by two, all properly clothed."

After which came the subordinate Lodges and the Grand Lodge.

The Deputy Grand Master Rowe, required of the Master of St. Andrew's a list of the members and others who joined with them, and ordered it to be entered in the Grand Lodge Book, which was done. The whole number in attendance was sixty-four, Joseph Warren being Senior Warden.

The Brethren of St. Andrew's had performed their duty in a noble and fraternal manner, and the Grand Lodge, in the hour of its deep distress over the lifeless remains of its distinguished Grand Master, forgot for the moment its animosity, and they mingled their tears together.

The Deputy Grand Master, John Rowe, had probably encouraged the Brethren of St. Andrew's in the step they took. He had contributed generously to the fund of charity of St. Andrew's, and December 1, 1766, was unanimously made a member of the Lodge, and a committee was appointed to communicate to him the votes passed.

After every generous effort on the part of St. Andrew's had completely failed, and when it was evident that no "happy coalition" could be made, the Brethren changed their ground. St. Andrew's was composed of some of the most active, prominent, and distinguished men of Boston; men who, like Warren, Revere, Hancock, and others of illustrious name, young, ardent, brave, could not calmly and patiently permit themselves and their associates to be denounced as illegitimatists, clandestine Masons, and impostors. The spirit of manliness, as well as of patriotism, glowed in their bosoms, and prompted them to vindicate their own characters as Masons, and to stand forth in defence of the Lodge which made them. On St. Andrew's Day, 1767 (Nov. 30), they voted unanimously, —

"*Whereas*, The Grand Lodge holden in Boston, whereof the late Jeremy Gridley was Grand Master, passed a vote that the Master or Masters of the Lodge or Lodges under his jurisdiction, more especially in Boston, should not, on any condition, admit of the visits of any of the members of St. Andrew's Lodge, which vote is disadvantageous to this Lodge, inasmuch as divers gentlemen here have been thereby prevented from offering themselves to be made here ; "

"*Therefore, Voted,* That this Lodge will not from henceforth admit of the visits of the members of any of the Lodges in this town, or any person that shall be made therein, until the said vote of said Grand Lodge shall be reconsidered and made void, except they are members of this Lodge, or have been raised Master here."

The following year, 1768, the Lodge voted in December to keep the Feast of St. John the Evangelist, and "that none vulgarly called Modern Masons be admitted to the Feast."

The political affairs of the Province of Massachusetts were such in 1768 that the Crown determined to quarter a standing army upon Boston. About the first of October in that year, a fleet of British men-of-war arrived in the harbor, having on board the Fourteenth and Twenty-Ninth, and a portion of the Fifty-Ninth Regiments, with a train of artillery ; and a short time after, the

Sixty-Fourth and Sixty-Fifth Regiments, direct from Ireland, landed in town and garrisoned Boston.

In the Sixty-Fourth Regiment was the Duke of York's Lodge, No. 106, Registry of Scotland ; in the Fourteenth Regiment was Lodge No. 58, Registry of England ; and in the Twenty-Ninth Regiment was Lodge No. 322, Registry of Ireland, all working under the " Ancient System."

The presence of these Regiments in Boston created an intense excitement among the citizens, and the members of St. Andrew's, particularly Joseph Warren, participated in the universal feeling of opposition to the continuance of this strong force in Boston. Warren was a member of a committee which, in March, 1769, drew up a petition to the king for the removal of the troops. Notwithstanding this strong feeling in the community, the members of St. Andrew's saw the opportunity before them of forming a Grand Lodge under the authority of the Grand Master of Scotland, and did not scruple to join with their Brethren of the obnoxious regiments.

On St. Andrew's Day (Nov. 30), 1768, Joseph Warren being Master, the Lodge appointed a committee to consider the expediency of applying to the Grand Lodge of Scotland for a Grand Master of Ancient Masons in America, and to confer with such committees as " shall be appointed by the other Ancient Lodges now in town." The committee was composed of Joseph Warren, Moses Deshon, William Burbeck, Ezra Collins, William Collins, William Palfrey, Paul Revere, and Samuel Danforth.

At the same meeting, the Lodge granted the use of their hall to the Regimental Lodges in the Twenty-Ninth and Sixty-Fourth Regiments.

Early in December following, eight days after the committee was empowered, they reported that agreeable to appointment with the committees of the Ancient Lodges then in Boston, and after mature deliberation, they agreed that it was necessary to have a Grand Master of Ancient Masons in America. They proposed as officers of the Grand Lodge : Br. Joseph Warren, of St. Andrew's Lodge, No. 81, for Grand Master; Br. Jeremiah French of the jurisdiction of Ireland, No. 322, for a Grand Senior Warden, and Br. Thomas Musgrave, of the Duke of York's Lodge, No. 106, for Junior Grand Warden.

The Lodge adopted the report of the committee, and the petition was prepared accordingly, being signed by the four Lodges of Ancient Masons : " St. Andrew's, 81, Registry of Scotland ;" "Duke of York's, 106, Registry of Scotland, held in 64th Regiment of Foot ;" " Lodge No. 58, Registry of England, held in 14th Regiment ;" "Lodge No. 322, Registry of Ireland, held in 29th Regiment ;" "An. F. & Ac. Masons, resident in Boston, Mass." Thus executed, it was forthwith transmitted to Scotland.

Before an answer was returned, in June, 1769, the Sixty-Fourth and Sixty-Ninth Regiments were removed from Boston.

On the 30th of May, 1769, the Earl of Dalhousie, Grand Master of Masons in Scotland, appointed "Joseph Warren, Esq., Grand Master of Masons in Boston, New England, and within one hundred miles of the same," and sent the commission by Captain Lawrence Frazier to Warren.

It was received in Boston prior to September 19, 1769, for on that evening St. Andrew's voted to provide the necessary articles to be used by the Grand Lodge, and "that the Grand Master be installed on the 27th of December next."   •

Little notice was taken of the Regimental Lodges in the preparation of the installation by St. Andrew's. The only notice of them appears in the proceedings of the Lodge held December 14, 1769, at which meeting Warren was present, when the committee appointed to conduct the instalment, reported " That it is their opinion that an information be given to the Lodges in 14th Regiment and 29th, that the instalment of a Grand Master will be on Wednesday, the 27th, at Masons' Hall."

On the 27th of December, 1769, the Grand Lodge was formally inaugurated, the record of which is in full as follows : —

" At the Assembly and Feast held at Boston, New England, at Masons' Hall, on Wednesday, December 27, 5769 —

The Most Worshipful Joseph Warren, Esq., Grand Master elect.

The Master, Wardens, and Brethren of St. Andrew's Lodge.

The Master and Wardens of Lodge No. 58, of the Registry of England.

The Master and Wardens of Lodge No. 322, of the Registry of Ireland.

A commission from the Right Honorable and Most Worshipful George, Earl of Dalhousie, Grand Master of Masons in Scotland, bearing date the 13th day of May, A. L. 5769, appointing the Most Worshipful Joseph Warren, Esq., to be Grand Master of Masons in Boston, New England, and within one hundred miles of the same, was read.

The Brethren then proceeded in ample form to install the Most Worshipful Joseph Warren, Grand Master of Ancient Free and Accepted Masons in Boston, &c.

After which the following Brethren were nominated by the Most Worshipful Grand Master, and unanimously elected as Grand Officers for the year ensuing, viz :—

Jeremiah French, Esq., Capt. in 29th Regt. .	Senior Grand Warden.
Ponsonby Molesworth, Esq., " " .	Junior Grand Warden.
William Palfrey, (by Proxy)	Grand Secretary.
Thomas Crafts . .	Grand Treasurer.
Joseph Webb . . .	Grand Marshal.
Paul Revere . . .	Senior Grand Deacon.
Samuel Danforth . .	Junior Grand Deacon.
Thomas Urann, } Caleb Hopkins, }	Grand Sentinels.
Edward Proctor	Grand Sword-Bearer.

The above is the full recorded history of this first meeting of "The Grand Lodge," as it was then called, for it did not take the name of "Massachusetts Grand Lodge" until December 6, 1782.

The records of St. Andrew's devote a page to this important meeting, stating that the Feast was holden, and giving the name of each brother who attended. By this it appears that sixty-two were present.

The Boston *Gazette* of January 1, 1770, a weekly paper published by Edes and Gill, contained this notice :—

"By virtue of a commission lately received from the Right Honorable and Most Worshipful the Earl of Dalhousie, Grand Master of Ancient Free and Accepted Masons in Scotland, on Wednesday, was solemnized at a Grand Lodge of Ancient Free and Ac-

cepted Masons in this town, held at Masons' Hall, the instalment of the Most Worshipful Joseph Warren, Esq., Provincial Grand Master of Ancient Free and Accepted
Masons in North America. On the occasion there was an elegant oration. After the
instalment there was a grand entertainment."

Although little credit can be given to newspaper notices of masonic meetings, yet in this instance as the publishers of the *Gazette*
were strong political friends of Warren, it is more than probable
that they were correct in stating that an oration was delivered.
If so, Warren, who afterwards distinguished himself as an orator,
undoubtedly pronounced the oration.

On the same day that the " Massachusetts Grand Lodge " was
organized at the Green Dragon Tavern, forty brethren of the St.
John's Grand Lodge celebrated the Feast at the Bunch of Grapes
Tavern, John Rowe presiding as Grand Master.

Joseph Warren, who was thus installed Grand Master one hundred years ago, at this Feast of St. John the Evangelist, was born
at Roxbury, Massachusetts, June 11, 1741. At the age of fourteen
he entered Harvard College, and was there graduated in 1759,
aged nineteen. He was proposed to St. Andrew's Lodge by Br.
William Palfrey, September 10, 1761, and was then initiated, being
twenty years and three months old. On the 2d of the following
November, he was "passed a Fellow Craft." It is uncertain at
what time he was made a Master Mason, but on the 14th of November, 1765, the Lodge voted unanimously that Dr. Joseph
Warren be re-admitted a member of the Lodge. After this time
he appears to have been zealous and active in his masonic labors.
He was chosen Senior Warden in November, 1766, and served his
year, and was Master of St. Andrew's from November, 1768, to
November, 1769.

During his Grand Mastership there were thirty-seven meetings
of the Grand Lodge, thirty-four of which he attended and presided
over.

From the time of his first installation until the last quarterly
meeting held during his life, he was engaged in public affairs of the
greatest importance. His practice as a physician was very large ;

he was a member of various political clubs ; was one of the Committee of Safety of Boston, and of the same Committee of Massachusetts, a member of the Committee on Correspondence, and was a representative to the Provincial Congress, and at the time of his death its presiding officer. His correspondence with public men, not only in Massachusetts but in all the colonies, was voluminous, and yet he found time amid all these cares, perplexities and labors, to earnestly attend to his duties as Grand Master.

On the 26th of April, 1773, he lost his beloved wife, but the following week found him at the Grand Lodge, called "upon an especial occasion."

I have compared the dates of many of the meetings of the Grand Lodge, when he was present, with the well-known public services of Warren, and it is surprising that he was able to devote any time to his Grand Master's duties.

On the 5th of March, 1773, the annual commemoration of the Massacre was held. Dr. Church delivered the oration, and Warren was on the committee that matured the business. Yet he found time to attend the Grand Lodge that day, and the record reads that " the Grand Master was pleased to adjourn this Grand Lodge to Monday, the 8th instant."

June 4th, of the same year, the record states : "The Grand Lodge being opened, the Grand Master observing but few Grand Officers present, was acquainted of their necessary engagement in another society."

Warren was absent from three meetings of the Grand Lodge — June 16, 1773 ; June 3, 1774 ; and September 2, 1774.

It is uncertain what detained him from the meeting of June 16, 1773 ; but June 2, 1774, he was engaged on a committee to draft "a solemn league and covenant," as also upon other important committees, and at the same time he was writing vigorous articles for the *Gazette.*

On the 2d of September, 1774, he was absent for the last time. This was the occasion of the " Powder alarm." The day before, he was called to Cambridge to prevent a collision with the troops, spent the day there, and the next day, the 3d, was engaged with a committee in corresponding with the towns.

His last attendance at the Grand Lodge was March 3, 1775. On the 6th, which was Monday, he delivered his famous oration upon the anniversary of the Massacre, and his mind must necessarily have been preoccupied with the great subject upon which he was to speak, and of the personal danger to himself which he was thereby incurring. Notwithstanding, he was at his post of duty, and for the last time presided over the Craft.

The following entry is made at the end of the record of this meeting : —

"Mema. 19th April, 1775. Hostility commenced between the troops of Great Britain and America in Lexington Battle. In consequence of which the Town was blockaded, and no Lodge held until December, 1776."

On the 17th of June following, Warren breathed out his heroic spirit on Charlestown Heights, and the Grand Lodge was left without a Grand Master.

At the meeting held on the 6th of December, 1771, the Grand Master acquainted the Grand Lodge that he appointed R. Worshipful Joseph Webb, Deputy Grand Master, and on the 27th of the same month he was installed into office.

At the Feast held December 27, 1773, was read a communication from the Right Honorable and Most Worshipful Earl of Dumfries, Grand Master of Masons in Scotland, dated March 3, 1772, appointing the Most Worshipful Joseph Warren Grand Master of Masons for the Continent of America. The Grand Master was in ample form installed.

"Then the Most Worshipful Grand Master, by virtue of the authority granted him in the foregoing commission, ordered the Grand Secretary to read a commission dated at Boston, New England, 1773, appointing Joseph Webb, Esq., D. G. Master, under him the said Joseph Warren, Esq., Grand Master, who was accordingly installed."

Although the record states that the Grand Lodge did not assemble until December, 1776, yet the Deputy Grand Master convened the Grand Body and held one of the most interesting and important meetings in the history of the "Massachusetts Grand Lodge" before that date.

After Warren was shot, it is uncertain by whom he was buried. The *Gazette*, published at Watertown, June 26, 1775, says : "Warren was among the slain, and was buried by his friends at Charlestown." All accounts concur in this, that his body was recognized and that he was buried on the field.

March 17, 1776, the British troops evacuated Boston, but it was not until the 4th of April following that his body was found and identified. It was buried about three feet below the surface of the ground, and was much disfigured, but was identified by two artificial teeth set for him a few days before his death.

On the same day that his body was discovered, the Provincial Congress of Massachusetts accepted the report of a committee appointed to take under consideration the erecting a monument to the memory of the " Honorable Major-General Joseph Warren," in which the committee say they " find that the place where his body was buried is discovered, and that the Lodge of Freemasons in this Colony, whereof he was late Grand Master, are desirous of taking up the deceased's remains, and, in the usual funeral solemnities of that society, to decently inter the same, and that his friends are consenting thereto." The committee "are of opinion that the said Lodge have leave to put their said intentions into execution."

The next day, April 5, the Deputy Grand Master, Joseph Webb, wrote to Bro. Perez Morton, at Watertown, then a member of the Provincial Congress, and who was also a member of St. Andrew's Lodge, and an intimate personal friend of Warren, saying, that he was requested by the Brethren of the Grand Lodge to beg the favor of him " to pronounce an oration on Monday next at the re-interment of our late Grand Master, Joseph Warren, Esq." The next day, April 6, " Brother Morton " replied by letter, modestly accepting the task assigned him.

26

In the *Gazette* of April 8, 1776, was published the following notice : —

" Notice is hereby given to all the Brethren of the Ancient and Honorable Society of Free and Accepted Masons that this day will be re-interred the remains of the late Most Worshipful Joseph Warren, Esq., Grand Master of Ancient Masonry for North America, who was slain at the Battle on Bunker's Hill, June 17, 1775.

" The Procession will be from the State House, in Boston, at four o'clock, P. M., at which time the Brethren are requested to attend with their Clothing and Jewels. By order of the Right Worshipful Joseph Webb, Esquire, Deputy Grand Master.

WILLIAM HOSKINS, *Grand Secretary.*"

The New England *Chronicle,* of Boston, published that week, contains a description of the procession, which was composed of a detachment of the Continental forces ; a numerous body of the Honorable Society of Free and Accepted Masons, the mourners ; members of the two houses of the General Assembly, &c., &c. The body was carried to King's Chapel, where, after prayer, by the Rev. Dr. Cooper, Br. Perez Morton delivered the oration, from which I take the following extract : —

" Into this Fraternity he was early initiated, and after having given repeated proofs of a rapid proficiency in the arts, and after evidencing by his life the profession of his lips, finally, as the reward of his merit, he was commissioned the Most Worshipful Grand Master of all the Ancient Masons through North America ; and you, Brethren, are living testimonies with how much honor to himself, and benefit to the Craft universal, he discharged the duties of his elevated trust ; with what sweetened accents he courted your attention, while with *wisdom, strength, and beauty,* he instructed his Lodges in the secret arts of *Freemasonry ;* what perfect order and decorum he preserved in the government of them ; and in all his conduct what a bright example he set us, *to live within compass and act upon the square.* With what pleasure did he silence the wants of poor and penniless brethren ; yea, the necessitous everywhere, though ignorant of the mysteries of the Craft, from his benefactions felt the happy effects of that institution which is founded on *Faith, Hope, and Charity,* and the world may cease to wonder that he so readily offered up his life on the altar of his country when they are told that the main pillar of *Masonry* is the *love of Mankind.*

" The fates, as if they would reveal, in the person of our *Grand Master,* those mysteries which have so long lain hid from the world, have suffered him, like the great master builder in the temple of old, to fall by the hands of ruffians, and be again raised in honor and authority. We searched in the field for the murdered son of a widow," — the day before his death he parted from his widowed mother at Boston, and said to her that they would never meet again, — "and we found him *by the turf and the twig,* buried under the brow of a hill, though not in a decent grave. And though we must again commit his body to the tomb, yet our breasts shall be the burying spot of his masonic virtues, and there —

> "' An adamantine monument we'll rear
> With this inscription, "Masonry lies here." ' "

This beautiful and touching allusion by the eulogist must have deeply impressed the brethren whom he addressed. No higher praise can be awarded to it than this, that every masonic writer who, since that time, has alluded to the death of Warren, has copied the idea, if not the exact language, of the distinguished Morton in his oration; and it is to be regretted that the name of Morton has never been connected with it.

Governor Gore, in an oration delivered in 1783, says: "The rosemary and cassia adorned and discovered his hallowed grave."

And Josiah Bartlett, Esq., afterwards our Grand Master, in an address delivered on Saint John the Baptist's Day, 1790, which is recorded at length in the records of the Massachusetts Grand Lodge, remarks: —

"The political events of the year 5775 produced important changes in the state of Masonry. These were no other than the heroic death of the Grand Master on the celebrated heights of Charlestown, and a temporary dispersion of the Grand Officers who, soon after the evacuation of Boston by the British army on the following year, influenced by a pious regard to the merits and memory of their departed patron, were induced to make search for his body, which was rudely and indiscriminately buried on the field of slaughter."

"They accordingly repaired to the brow of the hill, and, by the direction of a person who had been on the ground about the time of his burial, a spot was found where the earth had been recently turned up, and was distinguished by a small cluster of sprigs."

"Having removed the turf and opened the grave, the remains were easily ascertained, by means of an artificial tooth, and being decently raised, were conveyed to the State House, in this metropolis, whence, on the 8th of April, 5776, after every mark of respect, and the just tribute of patriotick and affectionate applause, they were committed to the silent tomb; but as the whole earth is the sepulchre of illustrious men, his fame, his glorious actions, are deposited in universal remembrance, and will be transmitted to the latest ages."

After the oration in King's Chapel, the procession was reformed and proceeded to the Granary Burying Ground, on Tremont street, where the remains of Grand Master Warren, agreeably to the solemn ceremony of Freemasonry, and in all probability according to a ritual which, before this time, Saint Andrew's Lodge had perfected, were re-interred in the tomb of George Richard Minot, a friend of the family. There they laid in peaceful repose until 1825, when, says Frothingham, "they were identified by the nephew of the general, Dr. John C. Warren, by the eye-tooth, and the mark of the fatal bullet behind the left ear." They were then carefully placed in a box of hard wood, bearing a silver plate with the inscription "In this tomb are deposited the earthly remains of Major-General Joseph Warren, who was killed in the battle of Bunker Hill, on June 17, 1775," and were removed to the Warren Tomb, in Saint Paul's Church, Boston. August 3, 1855, these precious ashes were carefully deposited in an imperishable urn, and placed in the family vault at Forest Hills Cemetery, where they now repose.

After the re-interment in the Granary Burying Ground, the procession reformed, and the Grand Lodge returned to the State House. The following record was made up, and was printed with the oration of Morton : —

COUNCIL CHAMBER, Boston, April 8, 1776.

At a meeting of the Grand Lodge, and a numerous body of Free and Accepted Masons, after the re-interment of our Most Worshipful Grand Master, Joseph Warren, Esq., who was slain in the battle of Bunker Hill, June 17, 1775,

" In the chair, the Right Worshipful Joseph Webb, D. G. M.

" *Voted,* That our Brothers, Paul Revere, Edward Proctor, and Stephen Bruce, be a committee to wait on our Brother Perez Morton, Esq., and present our cordial thanks for his oration delivered this afternoon, and request a copy thereof for the press.

Attest, WILLIAM HOSKINS, *Grand Secretary.*"

During the Grand Mastership of Warren, three charters for Lodges were granted, viz.: March 2, 1770, Tyrian Lodge at Gloucester; May 13, 1770, Massachusetts Lodge at Boston; March 6, 1772, Saint Peter's Lodge at Newburyport.

With the exception of Saint Peter's, these Lodges are now in flourishing existence, and with their mother, Saint Andrew's, are here this evening to participate in the Centennial of the Grand Lodge, whose subordinates they were, and still are.

At the fourth meeting of the Grand Lodge, held May 11, 5770, it was —

"*Voted.* Unanimously, as the opinion of this Lodge, that whenever summons are issued for convening a Grand Lodge, and in consequence thereof is congregated, the same is to all intents and purposes a legal Grand Lodge, however few in number, and as such may, with the strictest propriety, proceed to business."

The doctrine contained in this vote, as I understand, is peculiar to Massachusetts, and has been substantially followed as regards a quorum from that day to this. Other Grand Lodges require the presence of the representatives of a certain number of its subordinates to constitute a quorum, while Massachusetts and the Grand Lodges of the other New England States, are not restricted by any such rule.

There are many interesting matters in the Records of the Massachusetts Grand Lodge which I should be pleased to refer to did time permit, especially the history of its independence. This was the first Grand Lodge upon the continent which declared its independence of all other Grand Lodges, and which followed the destiny of its country at a time when even this humble support was most gratefully received by every patriotic heart.

At some other time I may trace its history through succeeding years down to March, 1792, when the Massachusetts Grand Lodge and Saint John's Grand Lodge mingled together in fraternal union, and buried forever in the peaceful waters of oblivion the animosities of nearly half a century. In that union disappeared forever the name of Modern Masons, but there was reserved that other name,

"Ancient" as well as "Honorable," which was dear to the Brethren of Saint Andrew's and their associates, and which we are still proud to retain in our title.

Brethren, — We stop for a moment in the busy turmoil of life to contemplate him whom the Craft, one hundred years ago, saluted as their Grand Master. We view him during all those trying scenes through which he passed, until he offered up his life upon the altar of Patriotism, and was consigned by loving hands to the silent tomb. We again open the grave of our lamented Grand Master, and over his mangled remains drop the fraternal tear of affection, and again plant there the acacia, fit emblem of his earthly immortality.

When the Centennial again comes round upon the dial of time, his fame will be as world-wide as now, and the Craft, as they gather to celebrate the Feast, and pay their homage to the memory of Warren, may turn to the record of this Festival, and read that the magic spell of his influence was upon us, and that the "young, brave, blooming, generous, self-devoted martyr" awakened in our breasts the purifying emotions of tenderness and admiration.

FROM THE GRAND LODGE RECORDS.

At the conclusion of the address of the Grand Master, the Grand Lodge was called from "labor to refreshment."

The Grand Marshal formed a procession of the brethren with the Three Great Lights and representatives of the Three Lesser Lights in their proper places, with the members of SAINT ANDREW'S, TYRIAN and MASSACHUSETTS LODGES, immediately after the Grand Officers, and proceeded to the Banquet Hall, where the Feast of St. John the Evangelist was celebrated after the manner of Masons.

The first toast — To the memory of our lamented Grand Master, General JOSEPH WARREN — was drank standing, and in silence.

R. W. Bro. Past Grand Master JOHN T. HEARD responded to a sentiment complimentary to the "Massachusetts Grand Lodge."

R. W. Bro. Past Grand Master WINSLOW LEWIS, to "Saint John's Grand Lodge."

For Saint Andrew's Lodge, R. W. Bro. Past Grand Master WILLIAM PARKMAN, R. W. P. D. G. Master C. W. MOORE, and Bro. HAMILTON WILLIS responded.

The M. W. Bro. AMOS E. COBB answered for the Grand Lodge of Connecticut.

Letters were read from Grand Masters JOHN H. LYNDE, of Maine, A. M. WINN, of New Hampshire, JAMES GIBSON, of New York, and from R. W. Bro. DRUMMOND, of Maine, excusing and regretting their absence.

For the Grand Lodge of England, and the Grand Master, the Earl of Zetland, W. Bro. ALFRED F. CHAPMAN, Master of Zetland Lodge, responded.

W. Bro. JOHN A. GOODWIN spoke for Tyrian Lodge.

R. W. Bro. MARSHALL P. WILDER spoke for Massachusetts Lodge.

R. W. Bro. Past Grand Master CHARLES C. DAME, answered for Saint Peter's Lodge, formerly of Newburyport.

The Grand Chaplain, W. Bro. JAMES A. BOLLES, responded to a sentiment relating to St. John the Evangelist.

At the Feast, ninety-seven brethren sat down, and their names are entered upon the Record of the Communication. The speeches were eloquent, and full of interesting historic matter.

The Grand Lodge was called from "refreshment to labor."

At Low Twelve the R. W. Deputy Grand Master closed the M. W. Grand Lodge of Massachusetts in DUE FORM.

SOLON THORNTON, *Rec. Grand Secretary.*

THE BANQUET AND SPEECHES.

The tables were spread in the Grand Banquetting Hall of the Temple. The M. W. Wm. S. Gardner, Grand Master, presided, and after the removal of the cloth, lead off in the more intellectual part of the Feast, in a brief, eloquent speech, and then felicitously called upon the brethren as set down in the record above.

SPEECH OF R. W. JOHN T. HEARD, P. G. M.

Most Worshipful: —

Since last evening, when you honored me with the request that I would respond to the toast which has just been announced, I have gathered together a few facts suggested by the toast and pertinent to the occasion we are celebrating.

A century ago yesterday, a number of young men met in Masons' Hall, in the Green Dragon Tavern, on the corner of Hanover and Union streets, in the town of Boston, the metropolis of the Province of Massachusetts and of New England. The gleam of joy which animated their countenances, the hearty congratulations which passed between them, and their air of triumph, denoted that the occasion of their assembling gave them great satisfaction and pleasure. They were fellow-townsmen, friends and brother masons; and it was in the latter of these relations that they were then about to act. Among them were Joseph Warren, he who gave his life a sacrifice to his country; Paul Revere, the skilful, intelligent and patriotic mechanic; Joseph Webb, a colonel in the war of the revolution; Dr. John Warren, the eminent surgeon; Christopher Gore and Perez Morton; Jeremiah French, P. Molesworth, Thomas Crafts, William Palfrey, Moses Deshon, Ezra Collins, Samuel Barrett, Joseph Tyler, Dr. Samuel Danforth, Thomas Urann and Edward Proctor.

The meeting having been called to order, Bro. Warren announced that he had received a commission from the Right Honorable and Most Worshipful George, Earl of Dalhousie, Grand Master of Masons in Scotland, bearing date the 30th day of May, 5769, appointing him to be Grand Master of Masons in Boston, New England, and within one hundred miles of the same. Whereupon, Bro. Warren was installed and proclaimed as Right Worshipful Grand Master. He afterwards appointed and invested the other Grand Officers, namely : —

R. W. Jeremiah French, Senior G. Warden ; R. W. P. Molesworth, Junior G. Warden ; Thomas Crafts, G. Treasurer ; and William Palfrey, G. Secretary. Bro. Webb was subsequently appointed Deputy G. Master. The Grand Feast was then celebrated "after the manner of Masons."

At that time the town of Boston embraced about four thousand houses, and twenty thousand inhabitants. The population chiefly resided on the outer end of the then narrow tongue of land connected with the main land at Roxbury. The Green Dragon Tavern was nearly in the centre of this population.

Freemasonry had been established in Boston thirty-six years before, by the Saint John's Grand Lodge, who derived their Charter or warrant from the G. Lodge of England. In 1756, Saint Andrew's Lodge received a Charter from Lord Aberdour, then G. Master of Scotland. The members of the latter claimed to be *ancient*, while those of the former were denominated *modern* Masons. A Grand Lodge of *ancient* Masons being desired by St. Andrew's Lodge and other ancient Masons, they petitioned the Grand Master of Scotland for the commission, the acts under which this occasion is intended, more particularly, to commemorate.

At the quarterly communication of the Massachusetts G. Lodge, held Dec. 27, 5775, was read a commission from the Right Honorable and Most Worshipful Patrick, Earl of Dumfries, Grand Master of Masons in Scotland, bearing date the third of March, 5772, appointing R. W. Joseph Warren, Esq., Grand Master of Masons for the continent of America. It will be observed that the jurisdiction assigned to Bro. Warren in the first commission was Boston and one hundred miles of the same, while that last given was for the continent of America.

Bro. Warren remained at the head of the Massachusetts G. Lodge to the time of his death, June 17, 1775. The last communication over which he presided was that of March 3, 1775.

Boston being in possession of the British army until March 18, 1776, no meetings of the G. Lodge could of course be held during that time. It was not long after that occurrence, but previous to any regular *communication*, that the brethren caused the remains of their G. Master to be removed with appropriate ceremonies from Bunker Hill, to the Granary Burying Ground. Afterwards they were placed in a tomb under Saint Paul's Church in Boston, by his relatives.

On the 8th of March, 1777, an Independent Grand Lodge was formed "with powers and prerogatives, to be exercised on principles consistent with and subordinate to the regulations pointed out in the '*Constitutions of Ancient Masonry.*'" This, it is believed, was the first G. Lodge established, independently of European authority, in the United States, late Provinces of England.

Under this organization the Grand Lodge elected Col. Joseph Webb as Grand Master. He was elected annually to the office until 1783, when, on account of Col. W.'s military duties calling him out of the State, Dr. John Warren was chosen G. Master for 1783.

Again, in 1784, Bro. Webb became G. Master, in which capacity he acted until the time of his death in 1786.

Dr. John Warren succeeded him in 1787.

In 1788, Bro. Moses M. Hayes became Grand Master. He held the office until the union with the St. John G. Lodge, March 5, 1792.

Of the Lodges to whom the Massachusetts G. Lodge granted Charters in this Commonwealth, there now exist only —

Tyrian, Gloucester, chartered March 2, 1770.
Massachusetts, Boston, chartered May 13, 1770.
Essex, Salem, chartered March 9, 1779.
King Solomon's, Charlestown, chartered Sept. 5, 1783.

With the exception of about two years succeeding the death of Warren, which includes the period in which Boston was garrisoned by British troops, the Grand Lodge of Massachusetts met with great regularity for nearly a quarter of a century. while the Saint John's G. Lodge held no communication from January 27, 1775, until 1787.

The union of the two Grand Lodges, March 5, 1792, was a hearty co-operation of brethren whose ritualistic differences, in themselves puerile, were happily ended. This unity has given efficiency to the acts of the Fraternity, designed to promote its usefulness and influence, and has carried us through good and evil to a condition of influence and prosperity which, through divided counsels, would never have been attained.

SPEECH OF R. W. WM. PARKMAN, P. G. M.

Most Worshipful Grand Master: —

In response to your call, I rise, though my call was entirely unexpected, and I am therefore unprepared to speak ; but, sir, permit me to thank you for your very flattering and kind introduction, and if in any way I have ever contributed anything by way of steadfast devotion to this Institution, which has aided in its prosperity, thereby meriting the commendation of my brethren, no higher award of praise could be desired. But on this occasion all who have been called up, were previously notified, and amply prepared ; and upon all occasions my excellent Brother Moore is expected to answer from the storehouse of his prolific mind for any call that may be made upon St. Andrew's Lodge, — of whose history he is the Royal bound Edition, having been present when the foundation of our history was laid. But as you all know, he don't like to talk, but he prefers to think and write. But, sir, for and in behalf of the good old Lodge of St. Andrew, permit me to return you our united thanks for the very able and beautiful address to which we have this day listened. An address beautiful in its diction, fair in its treatment of historic fact wherever found, and so truthful in the relation of incidents now a century old, that all who have to-day listened to it, have silently resolved to dedicate themselves anew with more and renewed devotion to the upholding of the Grand Lodge of Massachusetts, whose whole history was so gloriously begun by men pre-eminent in every good work and word.

Sir, while you was to-day speaking of the moral beauty of Warren's life, I could but compare his life with the beautiful tenets of our Institution, — Brotherly Love, Relief, and Truth, — and every time we hear the virtues of the illustrious dead repeated, they shine with greater lustre. Our tenets are like the harp, whose strings, when swept by a master hand, bring out the diviner melodies of sweetest music which stimulate us all anew, leading us all to strive to see " who best can work and best agree." In common with all, we owe our love to the immortal Warren ; but with us there is another bond. He was of our Lodge, — of us, — of our family. The moment a member enters there, among his earliest instructions are reminiscences of Warren, Burbeck, Revere,

Sigourney, Purkett, and a host of others who carried on the Lodge in the old Green Dragon Tavern, a building which stood in Union street, in the time of the Revolution, and was then and is now the property of St. Andrew's Lodge. The traditions, the instructions of these prominent men, are so often talked of, that every member of St. Andrew's Lodge feels additional pride, when they know of anything to the glory of one who was of us, and of our own Lodge. In the memory of him whom we have to-day met to celebrate, we are all personally interested, and we certainly thank the Grand Lodge for allowing us the privilege of being present and having the great pleasure of participating in these interesting ceremonies.

Again thanking you for the privilege of speaking, I will, with your permission offer as a sentiment :

The memory of Past Grand Master Joseph Warren, — a gem of purest lustre, which this Centennial Day has reset with added splendor.

SPEECH OF BRO. HAMILTON WILLIS,

In reply to a sentiment given in honor of THE LODGE OF ST. ANDREW.

Most Worshipful Grand Master: —

By reason of the unavoidable absence of Doctor Ezra Palmer, the accomplished Master of the Lodge of St. Andrew, — an absence which is to be regretted exceedingly, — it is made my duty first to say to you, Sir, on his behalf, that nothing less than an engagement professionally, would have kept the Worshipful Master of St. Andrew's away from a scene here to-night of so much interest to him, and which you, Most Worshipful, have by your graceful line of remark made an occasion of so much honor to the ancient Lodge of St. Andrew. In behalf of that Lodge then, I thank you for having given official recognition of this Centennial Day, — the hundredth anniversary of the Second or " Massachusetts Grand Lodge," and still more significantly the commemoration of a century since General Joseph Warren, the first great martyr of the Revolution, was saluted in ample form as Grand Master in this Commonwealth, then a colony of Great Britain.

St. Andrew's thanks you, Sir, for remembering that Warren came from that Lodge, and also for the eloquent language and historic judgment by which you were pleased to estimate the part that Lodge took in maintaining Freemasonry through the trying events which betided the change from colonial dependence to National independence.

St. Andrew's however, must not take too much merit to itself, without attributing something to circumstances. It was the good fortune, Sir, of that Lodge, — alone in the whole Order, — to be the owner of a House of its own, from the very beginning of the series of memorable acts, which culminated in the supreme act of the American Revolution. The same noted estate has remained the property of this Lodge ever since. On this estate was the building known as the Green Dragon Tavern; yes, a century ago it was known as the "Old Green Dragon." Here, the idea of the Massachusetts Grand Lodge was conceived; here, its purpose and organization were matured; from this house its petition for "erection" went forth to Scotland; here, WARREN was first saluted as GRAND MASTER; here he passed his whole Masonic life with St. Andrew's; it was here that he held secret counsel together with the patriots; and it was here in the "Green Dragon," in the Lodge room of St. Andrew's, that the communications of Massachusetts Grand Lodge were held, from first to last, without interruption during the Revolution, save while the British army occupied the town. For the whole period of thirteen years, next succeeding the event we are this night celebrating, the Grand Lodge and St. Andrew's were nearly identical in persons. At the commencement in 1769, the Grand Master of the one, and the Master of the other, were the same individual Brother, — JOSEPH WARREN! In 1777, on an occasion which is sometimes reckoned as the era of the independence of the Grand Lodge over which you now preside, every member of that distinguished body, but one, were members of the Lodge of St. Andrew. But there came a change over the spirit of these close relations; parent and child were sundered! And I am not agoing to tell the story of that domestic jar; no, no, not to-night, not a word more either of "ancient and modern" family parting. You, Most Worshipful, with your familiar acquaintance with Massachusetts Masonic history for a century and a quarter past, can tenderly appreciate this claim for St. Andrew's of thus much of intimate connection with regular Grand Lodge jurisdiction in Massachusetts. Sir, the long years of utter isolation from any affiliation whatsoever with Grand Lodge or Brethren, endured by my beloved Lodge, may pleasantly now suggest a likeness to the parable of that prodigal son of Scripture. — St. Andrew's, 'tis true, can't be said to have eaten many husks, owning a famous Inn all the while as it did, but surely that fond parent, this Grand Lodge, when we came home in 1809, did welcome us even when "afar off, and did bring hither the fatted calf and kill it, saying let us eat and be merry," declaring also to the rest of the household, "thy Brother was dead, and is alive again, was lost and is found."

St. Andrew's nevertheless, must be proud of its record, proud too, of its return to this Grand Lodge, — her parent by lawful adoption; and Brethren, it is owing to the courtesy and good will invoked by occasions like this, in days gone by, that the way has been smoothed out of the bitterness of old controversies, towards bringing into one fold the entire Masonic Fraternity of Massachusetts. Sir, the Grand Lodge of. this State was pre-eminent in its good offices for this noble accomplishment. Before the sands of the eighteenth century had run out, the welcome note of harmony, the harbinger of Masonic union went forth from this jurisdiction.

Well met then to honor the Epoch of 1769, well met always at the call to refreshment of our venerable Grand Lodge, to contemplate in social interchange, the bright heritage which century by century shall bequeath our Order, and to refresh the duties of the present, with the life-current of the past.

I give you as a sentiment:

The Most Worshipful Grand Lodge of Massachusetts, — erected in 1733; co-eval with the modern organization of Freemasonry; re-inforced in 1792, by harmoniously concentrating within itself all Massachusetts Masonic jurisdiction; perfected in 1809, by the honorable and complete affiliation of the Brethren throughout her borders; — the Grand Lodge stands to-day, consecrated in the obedience, veneration, and love of all Free and Accepted Masons! May she abide in the roll of centuries to come, a perpetual benediction, and her Centennial Days be grateful re-unions in general thanksgiving!

SPEECH OF THE REV. BRO. JAMES A. BOLLES, D.D., GRAND CHAPLAIN.

Most Worshipful Grand Master: —

In response to the toast just read, and your kind remarks, I wish in the first place to thank you for your appointment of me to the office which I hold in this

Grand Lodge — a most distinguished honor which I shall always remember with gratitude and affection. When I first received the notice of this Centennial Celebration of the Inauguration of the Immortal Warren, as Grand Master, and saw that it was to be on this day, as the Feast of St. John the Evangelist, my first thought was, that our Fraternity had made a change in the Christian Calendar, or had mistaken the day for that of the Holy Innocents — the former of which is on the 27th, and the latter, the 28th, the day on which we are assembled. But upon examination I found from the notice that no mistake had been made, and that God in His providence had so arranged the Ecclesiastical year, as that we could with propriety combine in one celebration the whole galaxy of suns and stars, which must forever usher in, and follow after, and shine around, that most blessed and glorious of all events, the Festival of Christmas — the central sun of the firmament from which all others derive their radiancy and their glory. Then it seemed to me, a special blessing that both the Festivals of St. John the Evangelist, and of the Holy Innocents, should be combined in our celebration to-day ; for in many remarkable respects, both are illustrative, not only of the principles, but of the history of our Order.

Who was St. John ? Not only an apostle, not only an Evangelist, but of all the apostles, and of all Evangelists, the most wonderful exponent and defender of the three cardinal virtues, upon which our Institution is based, — *Faith, Hope and Charity*. Then as St. John the Divine, in his Book of Revelations, we have all the mystical signs, symbols, emblems, mementos, tokens, and outward representations which, in all ages, have especially distinguished the Institution to which we belong, and for the maintenance and protection of which in the world, our Order has accomplished almost more than any branch of the Christian Church.

Who were the Holy Innocents ? Unconscious martyrs for the truth. It was the design of Herod by the massacre of these Holy Innocents, to crush and destroy the Infant Saviour, and in the pride and pomp of his worldly power, he vainly imagined that the object was accomplished. But how impotent the effort ! The Infant Saviour rose again, with renewed energy and power, and at all times, and in every place, no bars of death or of hell have been able to confine Him in the grave. So it has been, I say it with reverence, and so it must ever be with the great principles of our Order. Many have been the seasons of trial and persecution when our enemies have imagined that the Brotherhood, which we represent, was destroyed, and many have been the unconscious martyrs who have suffered and died in its defence. I say unconscious, because they were as ignorant almost as the new-born babe of the glorious results of their fidelity, nor can there be any doubt that over and above all temporal considerations, they simply surrendered themselves to the necessity of the occasion, as sheep led to the slaughter. The tendency of all such persecutions has been simply to reproduce a new generation of men, ready to act as unconscious martyrs, stronger and more indestructible than before.

Let me propose to you, as a sentiment,

The Types and Emblems of St. John the Divine, and of The Holy Innocents.

SPEECH OF R. W. CHARLES LEVI WOODBURY, D. G. M.

The M. W. Grand Master here resigned the Gavel to the R. W. Deputy Grand Master CHARLES LEVI WOODBURY, who assumed the chair, and said —

Brethren : —

The Grand Master, unwilling that this feast of reason and flow of soul should be retarded, has directed me to perform the functions of my station by presiding over this Grand Lodge during his absence.

A Centennial celebration of an important event transitorily arising in the history of a voluntary and charitable society is a rare thing in this land of change and progress. As I have listened to the interesting facts of a hundred years ago, thrown in life-like images on our attention, by the eloquent orators of the evening, my imagination has gone back to that era, and I am impressed with the great part which the Free Masons of this continent played in the struggle for Independence and self-government. How notable was the share that the children of the widow's son had in noble deeds and generous devotion to their country! Their country do I say. At first it only existed in the deep recesses of their souls, where the hidden light alone illuminates. Reason and justice approved the thought. Their strong wills said "so mote it be," and they bent their willing hearts and brawny arms to create that concrete and living fact — *our* country. I cannot name all those who stood on the lower spokes of fortune's wheel, nor even all the heroes and statesmen who issued from our Lodges to build this new Temple in the West, where in equity and justice, in equality and fraternity, the pursuit of happiness was to go on. Washington and Franklin, LaFayette and Warren, — that Grand Master whom we mourn to-night — are not they enough to name on this occasion ? Warren baptizing with his martyr blood the cause of liberty. The four, building like Nehemiah of old, with his sword in one hand, his trowel in the other. What more poetic and heroic picture does history shadow in modern or ancient times ? Massachusetts mourned her young hero with acute grief; did she think then that his name would be immortal in the history of men and Masons ? Yet it is men like these who link the present and the past in fraternal sympathy. Our reverential hero-worship and the spirit-moved self-abnegation of the hero make us one. From his immolation of mean pleasures and low ambitions on the altar of his high purposes comes a legacy of good which we repay by our gratitude. Amid this perpetual war of Ormuzd and Ahriman, of good and evil, faith aids us to cling to the past, and hope guides us trustfully towards the unknown future. A hundred years ago in our good city, Freemasonry was the lofty school for bold devoted men, both of humble and conspicuous positions in society. The triangle told its mystic lesson of heaven, and the square taught the rule of honest and correct life. The sentinel Tyler did his duty without, and the Worshipful Master governed within. The like ritual taught the like lessons of duty and benevolence. That well of spiritual truth, the holy Bible, was reverentially consulted. Freemasonry has learned no new lessons of duty to man or God since. The rule of unchanging right was taught then ; time has not improved upon it. A hundred years ago to-night, and Warren stood before St. Andrew's Lodge, clothed in the insignia of his high station, eloquently addressing the members on the antiquity of the Craft, the stern purity of its morals, and the liberality of its benevolence ; perhaps some veiled thoughts radiant with the spirit-light of a dawning liberty, giving passion's roseate hue to the youthful lips of the fervid orator. When this century has passed away, from this chair, some other Grand Master more eloquent than myself, may repeat the like thoughts. Thus two centuries ago in China, the first Grand Master of the Hung League invoked the three Grand Masters who met in the Peach Garden fifteen centuries before to organize the mystic Heaven and Earth League. So also the serene countenance of the Granite Memnon for thrice a thousand years has defied unmoved the storms and heat of Egypt, and thus in calm and awful grandeur the veiled truths of Freemasonry unscathed by revolutions, uncankered by the calm of peace, still reflect the same serene light.

28

Brethren, we are responsible for all time for the light entrusted to our care ; and let Warren's example teach us that manifested in the upright lives of the fraternity are the fruits of those mysteries, which it is the glory of God and of the faithful spirit to conceal.

In response to the toast, FREEDOM and FREEMASONRY,

R. W. JOHN H. SHEPPARD spoke as follows : —

The connection between Freedom and Freemasonry was a remarkable trait in the early history of our institution, and has been conspicuous at all periods since. The illustrious Warren, whose installation as the first Grand Master of the Grand Lodge one hundred years ago this evening is celebrated, lived and died in the cause of Freedom. The brief notice, therefore, of Pythagoras, the Friend of Wisdom, who left Samos, his native country, because he was disgusted with the tyranny of Polycrates, and who afterwards exerted a vast influence in promoting free institutions in Magna Græcia, will not be inappropriate, as the antiquity of Masonry has ever been associated with his name.

Pythagoras was one of the most extraordinary and renowned men in any age or country. He was the first who assumed the name of philosopher. He was born about 588, and died 500 years before Christ. His father Mnesarchus was a person of distinction, who gave him a fine education. At eighteen he won the crown at the Olympic Games, where the elegance of his person and the courteousness of his address attracted much attention. In pursuit of knowledge he travelled to Egypt, Chaldæa and Persia, and according to Cicero, who called him *vir præstanti sapientia*, he visited many countries on foot. In the island of Crete, he was initiated into the Eleusinian Mysteries of Greece, and in Egypt, into the priesthood, and ceremonies of Isis. It was Isis who said, *I am all that has been, that shall be, and none among mortals has hitherto taken off my veil.*

At the age of forty he selected Crotona for his residence and opened his famous school. Crotona (now Cortona) in the kingdom of Naples, lies near the mouth of the river Æsarus, which enters the Ionian sea ; a walled city with a strong citadel and about five thousand inhabitants, though anciently thirty thousand, when it was one of the richest and most powerful cities in Magna Græcia ; now it is a decayed and abject place.

He was skilled in music, medicine and geometry ; and such was his advance in astronomy, that he placed the sun in the centre of the solar system and the planets revolving in their orbits around it; and more than twenty centuries passed before this fact was established and believed. He added strings to the harp and increased the scale of music. Dr. Burnet says he invented the harmonical canon or monochord. His discoveries in geometry were very great; many of them were found in Euclid, particularly the celebrated 47th Proposition, of such infinite value, the demonstration of which is one of the most beautiful pieces of scientific logic which are known.

In addition to his school he instituted a college in his house, where the more abstruse sciences were taught. Jamblicus, who wrote his life in Latin — I have seen no English translation of this work — speaks of his college, where a brotherhood used to assemble in secret meetings, using mysterious symbols and peculiar signs of recognition. Whence many learned writers have derived the rudiments of Masonry, and therefore from time immemorial he has been claimed by Masons as a brother, and his celebrated Square of the Hypotenuse recognized as a symbol. The late Law-professor Simon Greenleaf, L.L. D., of Cambridge, a distinguished civilian and formerly G. M. of Maine, was a firm believer in the Masonic School of Pythagoras, and in his work on Freemasonry refers to it.

The aspect of the Samian sage was noble and his presence dignified. His life was devout in religious duties and exemplary in morals; and such was his habit of abstemiousness, that he avoided animal food. The influence which he exerted in Crotona was so powerful, that it is said, he reformed the voluptuous and vicious habits of the young men, and his eloquent lectures were listened to by large crowds. From Pythagoras emanated the maxim, "*My friend is my better half*." In the midst of an idolatrous people, he worshipped one God — the Supreme Intelligence. His "Golden Verses" have come down to us in Greek; they were translated by Dr. Watts, and may be found in his "Improvement of the Mind" — a book deserving a place in every young man's library.

> How sweet the home of this good man;
> His "Golden Verses" led the way;
> With orison the morn began,
> With vesper hymn he closed the day.

Such was Pythagoras, one of the purest and greatest men that ever lived one who should be endeared to every Mason.

Crotona, once so beautiful,
　The glory of the Ionian sea,
Lives but in memory of the school
　Whose light illumin'd Italy.
No more the watchman from the tower
　Espies the Adriatic fleet ;
Like moonbeams in their waning hour,
　The past glooms o'er the grass-grown street.

Yet, there Pythagoras foretold
　Truths, which for ages none could solve ;
He saw the planets, as they roll'd,
　Around a central sun revolve.
He swept the harp of ancient time ;
　Chords then unknown his spirit stirr'd ;
Till, listening in his soul sublime,
　THE MUSIC OF THE SPHERES he heard.

He solv'd that geometric Gem,
　No Ariadne could explore,
The pearl in Euclid's diadem,
　The symbol of Masonic lore.
The glory of that grand old school,
　Alas ! no vestige leaves behind ;
All nature there is beautiful ;
　But where's the freedom of the mind ?

Oh ! for a spirit hand to trace
　This eve, a hundred years ago —
The youthful form — the noble face
　Of WARREN, e'er he braved the foe.
He gave his life at Freedom's call,
　The holiest sacrifice on earth ;
St. Andrew's Lodge, who wept his fall,
　Saw in his death a Nation's birth.

" IN MEMORIAM" of the Centennial occasion, several capital short recitations were given during the Feast; and Worshipful Bro. Hon. John A. Goodwin, of Lowell, in a very humorous manner illustrated some amusing characteristics of the mode of conducting Lodges in the olden time. Past Grand Master Hon. Charles C. Dame, although responding for a single Lodge, extended his remarks to a general survey of the consequences resulting from the erection of " Massachusetts Grand Lodge." The R. W. Hon. Marshall P. Wilder also, in a happy vein of reminiscence, called up associations of the trying ordeal which the order endured at the time of the building of the first Masonic Temple in Boston. As the record of Grand Lodge states, all the exercises of the celebration were of a high order of excellence, and a variety of interesting Masonic historical matter was freshly presented.

LODGE OF ST. ANDREW.

MEMBERS' BADGE.

OFFICERS

OF

THE LODGE OF ST. ANDREW,

A. D. 1869 — 70.

——➤❧≼❀◆——

WORSHIPFUL EZRA PALMER, M. D., Master.

THOMAS E. CHAMBERLIN,	Senior Warden.
WILLIAM PARKMAN, JR.,	Junior Warden.
SAMUEL H. GREGORY,	Treasurer.
ALFRED A. WELLINGTON,	Secretary.
HASKET DERBY, M. D.,	Senior Deacon.
EDWARD B. W. RESTIEAUX,	Junior Deacon.
WILLIAM PARKMAN,	Chaplain.
WILLIAM F. DAVIS,	Marshal.
GEORGE C. STEARNS,	Senior Steward.
HALES W. SUTER,	Junior Steward.
JOHN REED,	Inside Sentinel.
EBENEZER C. LEMAN,	Tyler.

THE LODGE OF ST. ANDREW.

FROM 1756 TO 1870.

THE RECORD LOST from 1752 to 1756.
ISAAC DE COSTER, from April 10, 1756, to July 10, 1760.
WILLIAM BURBECK, from 1760 to 1765.
JOSEPH WEBB, from 1765 to 1766.
WILLIAM BURBECK, from 1766 to 1767.
MOSES DESHON, from 1767 to 1768.
JOSEPH WARREN, from 1768 to 1769.
SAMUEL BARRETT, from 1769 to 1770.
PAUL REVERE, from 1770 to 1771.
JONATHAN SNELLING, from 1771 to 1772.
THOMAS URANN, from 1772 to 1773.
JOHN LOWELL, from 1773 to 1774.
EDWARD PROCTOR, from 1774 to 1776.
JOHN SYMMES, from 1776 to 1777.
PAUL REVERE, from 1777 to 1779.
WILLIAM HOSKINS, from 1779 to 1780.
PAUL REVERE, from 1780 to 1782.
WILLIAM BURBECK, from 1782 to 1784.
JAMES CARTER, from 1784 to 1786.
THOMAS DAKIN, from 1786 to 1789.
SAMUEL MOORE, from 1789 to 1792.
THOMAS DAKIN, from 1792 to 1794.

BENJAMIN HURD, JR., from 1794 to 1795.
JOSHUA EATON, from 1795 to 1801.
ANDREW SIGOURNEY, from 1801 to 1803.
WILLIAM WILLIAMS, from 1803 to 1804.
HENRY PURKITT, from 1804 to 1806.
JAMES FARRAR, from 1806 to 1809.
JAMES GREEN, from 1809 to 1810.
HENRY FOWLE, from 1810 to 1817.
JOHN JAMES LORING, from 1817 to 1818.
HENRY FOWLE, from 1818 to 1820.
DAVID PARKER, from 1820 to 1823.
BELA LINCOLN, from 1823 to 1825.
ALEXANDER H. JENNINGS, from 1825 to 1827.
DAVID PARKER, from 1827 to 1828.
ABEL P. BAKER, from 1828 to 1832.
CHARLES W. MOORE, from 1832 to 1833.
EZEKIEL BATES, from 1833 to 1835.
DAVID PARKER, from 1835 to 1836.
JOHN R. BRADFORD, from 1836 to 1839.
EDWIN BARNES, from 1839 to 1841.
HUGH H. TUTTLE, from 1841 to 1844.
SMITH W. NICHOLS, from 1844 to 1847.
HAMILTON WILLIS, from 1847 to 1850.
JOHN R. BRADFORD, from 1850 to 1852.
SAMUEL P. OLIVER, from 1852 to 1857.
WILLIAM PARKMAN, from 1857 to 1860.
CHARLES J. F. SHERMAN, from 1860 to 1863.
EDWARD STEARNS, from 1863 to 1865.
WILLIAM F. DAVIS, from 1865 to 1868.
EZRA PALMER, from 1868 to ——

PRESENT MEMBERS,

AND DATE OF ADMISSION.

CHARLES W. MOORE,	Oct. 10, 1822.
EZEKIEL BATES,	Nov. 8, 1827.
EBENEZER C. LEMAN,	Feb. 9, 1832.
SMITH W. NICHOLS.	March 10, 1836.
EDWIN BARNES,	March 10, 1836.
ROBERT N. TULLOCK,	Jan. 14, 1841.
HAMILTON WILLIS,	Nov. 9, 1843.
EDWARD STEARNS,	Dec. 14, 1843.
ALBERT H. KELSEY,	April 11, 1844.
THOMAS RESTIEAUX,	June 13, 1844.
C. ALLEN BROWNE,	June 13, 1844.
JOHN MEARS, JR.,	June 13, 1844.
B. FRANKLIN BAYLEY,	June 13, 1844.
GEORGE C. STEARNS,	June 13, 1844.
WILLIAM PARKMAN,	Dec. 12, 1844.

William H. Johonnot,	Dec. 12, 1844.
Amos Bates,	Feb. 13, 1845.
Henry G. Clark,	Dec. 10, 1846.
John P. Ober,	Dec. 10, 1846.
Henry Davis,	Dec. 10, 1846.
James Perkins,	May 11, 1848.
Samuel P. Oliver,	March 8, 1849.
Alfred A. Wellington, .	Jan. 9, 1851.
Samuel H. Gregory,	Jan. 9, 1851.
C. J. F. Sherman,	Nov. 10, 1853.
Peter Wainwright,	Nov. 10, 1853.
Hales W. Suter,	Sept. 22, 1854.
David Pulsifer, .	Sept. 22, 1854.
Charles F. Chickering,	Sept. 22, 1854.
John Reed, Jr., .	Dec. 28, 1854.
Nathaniel B. Shurtleff,	June 29, 1855.
William F. Davis,	March 22, 1860.
Henry L. Dalton, . .	Sept. 27, 1860.
Edward B. W. Restieaux,	Sept. 27, 1860.
Ezra Palmer,	Sept. 27, 1860.
Thomas E. Chamberlin,	Dec. 26, 1862.
Hasket Derby,	Dec. 26, 1862.
John P. Ober, Jr., .	Dec. 26, 1862.
William Parkman, Jr., .	Dec. 26, 1862.
William L. Wainwright,	Dec. 26, 1862.

•

1756.

Kimbal Bass.
George Bray.
Peter Blin.
William Burbeck.
Ezra Collins.
Isaac De Coster.
Henry Emms.
David Flagg.
James Graham.
George Graham.
William Hallowell.

George Hodge.
William Hodge.
Alexander Inglish.
John Jenkins.
George Louttil.
Thomas Milliken.
Samuel Peck.
James Tourner.
Robert Whalley.
Joseph Webb, Jr.

1757.

Daniel Bridge.
Shubael Cook.
James Dickey.
James Dennie.
William Davis.

William Hinkling.
Phillip Lewis.
Thomas Stevenson.
Edward Stone.
Elisha Thacher.

1758.

Samuel Harris.
Benjamin Holden.
James Jackson.

John Robinson.
John Willard.
Francis Yates.

1760.

Samuel Barrett.

Thomas Urann.

1761.

Increase Blake, Jr.
Hugh Brown.
Moses Deshon.
Josiah Flagg.
Wait Gray.
William Gould.
Nathaniel Hitchborn.
John Hoffain.
William Ham.
George Jefferds.
Edward Jarvis.
Walter Kerr.
William McAlpine.

Alexander Mackay.
James Nicholas.
Israel Obear.
William Palfrey.
Edward Potter.
John Phillips.
Richard Pulling.
Paul Revere.
Ambrose Sloper.
Henry Stanbridge.
John Whitten.
Joseph Warren.
Henry Wells.

1762.

Edward Burbeck.
Thomas Crafts, Jr.
Elisha Callender.
Caleb Hopkins.
Philip Marett.
James Seaward.

Phillip Taber.
Joseph Tyler.
Francis Tree.
William Wingfield.
Thomas Webster.

1763.

Gilbert Ash.
William Bell.
John Ball.
Edward Cailleteau.
Adam Collson.
Seth Chipman.

Ambrose Farrell.
William Larkin.
Henry Leahy.
John Marlton.
Samuel Moody.
Thomas Metcalf.

Peter Doyle.
Benjamin Frothingham.
Edward Foster.

Jonathan Snelling.
John Tyler.

1764.

Thomas Carey.
Thomas Knox.

John Lowell.
Ebenezer Symmes.

1765.

Joseph Cordis.
Samuel Danforth.
Friend Dole.
Thomas Emmons.

Thomas Paine.
Edward Proctor.
Asa Stodder.
Jeremiah Webb.

1766.

William Darracott.
Nathaniel Howland.
John Jeffries, Jr.
Thomas Knox.

Peter Nogues, Jr.
John Symmes.
Andrew Sigourney.

1767.

Stephen Bruce.
John Edwards, Jr.

Winthrop Gray.
William Roberts.

1768.

Samuel Allen.
Richard Bradford.
Nathaniel Cudworth.
Moses Dorran.
John De Costa.

Nathaniel Fellows.
John Hill.
Joshua Loring.
Ebenezer Williams.

1769.

Samuel Andrews.
James Carter.

John Grant, Jr.
Charles Haynes.

Thomas Chase.
Phenix Frazier.
Alexander Gray.
John Gray. .

Frederick Moth.
Benjamin Mayhew.
Samuel Webb.
Christopher White.

1770.

Josiah Waters, Jr.

1772.

William Hoskins.

Thomas Newell, Jr.

1773.

Gibbons Bouve.
Nathaniel Cook.

Nehemiah Webb.
Eliphar Weston.

1774.

Joseph Bryant.
Thomas Clement.
Shubael Downes.
Jonathan W. Edes.

David Ford.
John Fulford.
Thomas Frazier.
Nathaniel Mills.

1776.

Joseph Dunckerly.
Thomas Farrington.
Jeremiah Hill.

Perez Morton.
Nathaniel Pierce.

1777.

Isaiah Audibert.
Robert Allen.
David Bradlee.
Henry Burbeck.
Edward Compston.
Samuel Cutter.
Joseph Cunningham.

Amos Lincoln.
William Miller.
Andrew Newell.
Enoch Putnam.
James Swan.
Thomas Snoden.
John Sprague.

Robert Davis.
Isaiah Doane.
Nathaniel Goodwin.
Lazarus Goodwin.
Abraham Hunt.
Benjamin Hitchborn.
John Hopkins.
Thomas Loring.

John Swift.
William Shattuck.
William Storey.
Edward Tuckerman.
Alexander Thomas.
Joseph Tilden.
Joseph Whittemore.
Benjamin White.

1778.

John Adams.
Jacob Brown.
William Billings.
Joseph Balch.
Benjamin Coolidge.
John Doak.
Joshua Davis.
Thomas Fosdick.
Samuel Gore.
Benjamin Hurd, Jr.
James McGee.
Robert McElroy.
Eliphalet Newell.

Michael Newell.
Jonathan Oakes.
Jeremiah Obrien.
Daniel Parker.
Thomas Russell.
Joseph Ruggles.
Elisha Sigourney.
George Stillman.
Thomas Smart.
Joseph Swasey.
John Savage.
James N. Shannon.

1779.

Daniel Adams.
Joseph Bush.
John Coolidge.
Silas Devol.
Zaccheus Dunnels.
Abraham Eustis.
Patrick Fletcher.
Cornelius Fellows.
Nicholas Gardner.
Timothy Green.
Israel Loring.
Thomas Leverett.

David Newell.
Thomas Nottage.
Enoch Pond.
Freeman Pulsifer.
St. De Mertino Pry
Edward Rumney.
Daniel Rea, Jr.
Jonathan Stodder.
Elias Thomas.
Joseph Webber.
Nathaniel Willis.

1780.

John Boit.
Joseph Bradford.
Andrew Brown.
John Cade.
J. J. Carnes.
Joshua Cheever.
Jacob Dunells.
D. Eustis.
Matthew Groves.

David Howe.
Simon Hall.
George Miles.
Samuel Moore.
Mungo Mackay, Jr.
Simon Mansir.
Thomas Prince.
Moses Ring.
John Rand.

1781.

Norton Brailsford.
Manasseh Marston.
Elias Parkman.

William Peak.
Richard Whellen.

1782.

Thomas Beals.
John Connor.
George De France.
Levi Hearsey.
Micah Hammond.

Daniel Ingersoll.
John T. Morgan.
James Oliver.
Thomas Powars.
Eleazer Wheelwright.

1783.

William Cordwell.
Thomas Dakin.
Thomas P. Low.

Edward Proctor, Jr.
Isaac Snow.
Thomas Wells.

1785.

Jonathan Fowle.
William Harris.

Joseph Spear, Jr.
James Smith.

1786.

James Green.

1787.

Ebenezer Smith.

1788.

Timothy Healey.

1790.

Joshua Eaton.   William Williams.

1792.

Phillip Wentworth.

1793.

Thomas Bentley.   John Hayward.
Nahum Fay.   Robert Molineux.
Henry Fowle.   Benjamin Smith, Jr.
Ebenezer Herring

1794.

William Blake.   Matthew Parkes.
Matthew Clark.   Andrew Sigourney.
Hezekiah Hudson.   Joseph Whitney.
Benjamin James.

1795.

Edward Bell.   Caleb Loring. Jr.
William Eustis.   William Woart.

1796.

Joab Hunt.   Joseph Smith.
Jonathan Loring, Jr.   Seth Sweetser.
Anthony Otheman.

1799.

Henry Purkitt.   Elijah Swift, Jr.

'1800.

Hezekiah Chadwick.   Adam French.
James Farrar.   Joseph Gleason.

1801.

Antoine Dumernill.   William Farmer.
Jonathan Fletcher.   Henry Murphy.

1802.

Seth Lothrop.

1803.

Martin Burr.   Henry Hutchinson.

1804.

Elijah Knowles.

1805.

Henry Morgan.   Zephaniah Sampson.

1806.

Benjamin Ingols.   John Smith.
Nathaniel Patten.

1808.

James Washburn.

1809.

Thomas Fobes.   Joseph Grammar.

1811.

Edward Harvey.   John J. Loring.

1813.

Daniel Rhodes.   Seth Webber. '

1814.

Seth Johnson.   Thomas B. Kendall.

1815.

Alexander Bowers.

1816.

David Parker.   William Smith.

1817.

Daniel G. Dawes.

1818.

Thomas K. Williams.

1819.

Lucius Q. C. Bowles.

1820.

Benjamin D. Baldwin.   Alexander H. Jennings.

1821.

Richard Bruce.

1822.

Leonard Battelle.   Ebenezer C. Preston.
Jonas Chickering.   Thomas W. Phillips.
Bela Lincoln.   Augustus Reed.
Calvin Lane.   Joshua Stone.
Moses Morse.

1823.

Elisha Dwelle.   Reuben D. Weston.
Nathan Hale.   William Weir, Jr.
Charles Newman.

1824.

Henry Daggett.   Daniel Prowse.
Andrew Garvin.

1825.

Abel P. Baker.   John Rayner.
Jeremiah Foster.   John Suter.

1826.

Frederick Lecain.   George Strong.
John Phillips.

1831.

Thomas J. Stone.

1836.

John R. Bradford.

1837.

Hugh H. Tuttle.

1843.

Aaron Leman.

1844.

William B. Oliver.

1851.

Isaac Carey.

1862.

Henry Jordan.

FAC SIMILE

AUTOGRAPHS

of early Members of the

Lodge of St. Andrew

Joseph Warren — Richard Bradford,

William Burbeck John De Costa

Jos Webb John Jeffries jur

Thos Milliken Benj:a Frothingham —

Wm Palfrey William Loskin

George Bray Adam Collson

John Jenkins Thomas Crafts

Paul Revere Caleb Hopkins

Samd Barrett Thomas Paine

Ph: Marett Edwd Pruthumun

Nathl Fellows

Moses Deshon Jno Carter

Ezra Collins Edwd Tofter

Perez Morton Samuel Danforth

Asa Stodder —   Thomas Bentley

Jeremiah Webb   Jon.ᵃ Snelling

Edward Jarvis   Jon.ᵃ W. Edes

Andrew Sigourney

Ben.ⁿ Guppett   Jonas Chickering

B. Smith   John R Bradford

Joseph Dunckerley   John J. Loring

David Bradlee —

                       Mungo Mackay
Alexander Mackey   Tho.ˢ Dakin

William Story   Nath.ˡ Willis

Freeman Pulsifer   Seth Webber

Henry Burbeck   Joab Hunt,

Elisha Sigourney   James Farrar

Wm Cordwell   David Parker

Zephaniah Sampson   Thomas W. Phillips

Jam Swan   Henry Fowle

A LIST OF MEMBERS

OF THE

LODGE OF ST. ANDREW,

WITH THEIR OCCUPATIONS AND RESIDENCES.

MADE AT COMMUNICATION HELD IN ROYAL EXCHANGE
TAVERN, KING STREET, BOSTON, THE 2d
THURSDAY OF JANUARY, 1762.

George Bray,	Baker,	Williams' Court, Corn-hill.
William Burbeck,	Carver,	New Salutation Alley.
James Graham,	Chairmaker,	Head of Clark's Wharf.
Samuel Peck,	Glazier,	By Hallowell's Ship Yard.
Thomas Milliken,	Bricklayer,	Fish Street.
John Jenkins,	Baker,	Near Mill Bridge.
Moses Deshon,	Auctioneer,	Dock Square.
Joseph Webb, Jr.,	Ship Chandler,	Head of Oliver's Dock.
Samuel Barrett,	Sailmaker,	Pulling's Wharf.
Ambrose Sloper,	Shipwright,	Battery March.
Paul Revere,	Gold Smith & Engraver,	Fish Street.
Thomas Crann,	Ship Joiner,	By Hallowell's Ship Yard.
Phillip Lewis,	Merchant.	Middle Street.
George Jefferds,	Sugar Refiner,	Atkinson Street.
Nathaniel Hitchborn,	Boat Builder,	Near Draw Bridge.
Increase Blake,	Tin Plate Worker,	West End Faneuil Hall.
William Palfrey,	Merchant,	Town Dock.
Samuel Moody,	Merchant,	Old York.
Edward Potter,	Cooper,	Milk Street.
John Whitten,	Gun Smith,	By Hallowell's Ship Yard.
William McAlpine,	Stationer & Bookbinder,	Marlboro' Street.

James Nicolls,	House-wright,	Atkinson Street.
Josiah Flagg,	Jeweller,	Fish Street.
John Hoffins,	Sugar Refiner,	New Boston.
Richard Pulling.	Merchant,	Fish Street.
Thomas Crafts,	Japanner & Painter,	Opposite the Great Tree.
Joseph Warren,	Physician,	Corn-hill.
William Gould,	Merchant,	King Street.
Elisha Callender,	Sail Maker,	New Boston.
William Ham,	Merchant,	West Indies.
John Marlton,	Merchant,	West Indies.
Henry Stanbridge,	Painter,	Cross Street.
Edward Burbeck,	Carver,	New Salutation Street.
James Seward,	Gun Smith,	Fish Street.
Ezra Collins,	Hat Maker,	Fish Street.

SEAFARING MEMBERS.

Capt. Edward Jarvis.	Capt. Wait Gray.
" Henry Wells.	" Walter Kerr.
" Seth Chipman.	" Ambrose Ferrell.
" Phillip Marett.	" Edw'd Cailleteau.
" Peter Doyle.	" Philip Tabor.
" William Wingfield.	" Gilbert Ash.
" Israel Obear.	" Alexander Inglish.
" John Phillips.	" Thomas Webster.
" Hugh Brown.	" William Bell.

NOTE.

Williams' Court, under the arch near Herald Office. Salutation Alley, took the name of Salutation Street in 1825. Clark's Wharf, subsequently called Hancock's Wharf, now included in Lewis' Wharf. Hallowell's Ship Yard, near the foot of Milk Street. Fish Street, part of North Street, between Cross and Fleet Streets. Mill Bridge, over the creek in Hanover Street, near the Green Dragon Tavern. Dock Square, the same as now. Oliver's Dock, from Lindall Street and Hawes Street, between Central and Water Streets, to the water. Pulling's Wharf led from Cross Street to the water. Battery March, from Liberty Square to Broad Street, now Batterymarch Street. Middle Street, part of Hanover Street between Blackstone and Prince Streets. Atkinson Street, now the part of Congress Street, between Milk and Broad Streets. Draw Bridge, a bridge formerly over the creek in what is now North Street. West End Faneuil Hall, now Market Square. Town Dock, north of Faneuil Hall. Old York, means York in Maine. Milk Street, same as now. Marlboro' Street, part of Washington Street from School to Summer Streets. New Boston, west part of town. The Great Tree, stood opposite Boylston Street; after the 14th of August 1765, it was called The Liberty Tree. Corn-hill, Washington Street between School Street and Dock Square. King Street, present State Street. Cross Street, same as now. New Salutation Street, same as present Salutation Street.

RECORD OF A. D. 1784.

Record of members of St. Andrew's Lodge in 1784, who voted to continue under the Grand Lodge of Scotland; and of those who voted to place themselves under the jurisdiction of " Massachusetts Grand Lodge." The minority at once proceeded to form the RISING STATES LODGE : —

FOR GRAND LODGE OF SCOTLAND.

Samuel Barrett.
Wm. Burbeck.
Thomas Urann.
Asa Stodder.
James Carter.
William Bell.
John Symmes.
Elisha Sigourney.
Elias Thomas.
Edward Rumney.
Alexander Thomas.
Manassah Marston.
Samuel Moore.
James Graham.
Isaac Snow.
Jacob Dunnels.
Thomas Wells.
Timothy Green.
Thomas Dakin.
Joseph Bush.
Wm. Peak.
Benj. White.
Jona. W. Edes.
Thomas Knox.
John Whitten.
John Rand.
Gibbons Bouve.
Moses Dorran.
Samuel Gore.
Freeman Pulsifer.
(total 30.)

FOR MASSACHUSETTS GRAND LODGE.

Nathaniel Fellows.
Paul Revere.
Jona. Stodder.
John Boit.
Cornelius Fellows.
Benj. Coolidge.
David Howe.
J. Dunckerly.
John T. Morgan.
Robert McElroy.
R. Hichborn.
Amos Lincoln.
Levi Hearsey.
Simon Hall.
Daniel Rea.
Enoch Pond.
Joshua Davis.
Joseph Webber.
Daniel Ingersoll.
Thomas Russell.
Thomas P. Low.
Norton Brailsford.
Nathaniel Willis.
(total 23.)

————◦◦;◦◦————

The Grand Lodge of Scotland in account current with St. Andrew's Lodge, No. 81.

DR.

CR.

1763.	1807.
June. To cash remitted the Grand Lodge of Scotland as per receipt of the Treasurer.	1807. By fees of Initiation of 827 Candidates from Sept. 1760 to Nov., 1807, as per record at 2·6 each, £103. 7s. 6d.
£7. 7s. 0d.	
1769.	
May. To cash remitted do. as per receipt,	
£9. 0. 5.	
To cash paid Grand Lodge in Boston from 1770 to 1783, £23. 8. 0.	
1807.	
Nov. 30. Balance due G'd Lodge 63. 12. 1.	
£103. 7. 6.	£103. 7. 6.

1808.

Jan. 12. To cash remitted the Grand Lodge of Scotland, in Bill of Exchange on Sam. Williams, Esq., London, for £90. per Brig William, Capt Benj. Willis, via: Liverpool.

The excess of £26. 7. 11. over and above balance of £63. 12. 1. is meant to cover the amount of dues which St. Andrew's paid to Provincial Grand Lodge at Boston, between 1769 and 1783, and which St. Andrew's believes were never paid to Grand Lodge of Scotland

ANDREW SIGOURNEY, Treasurer, St. Andrew's Lodge.

The Grand Lodge of Scotland failing at the time to acknowledge the receipt of the above remittance, the Treasurer of "St. Andrew's," under date Dec. 30, 1808, asks S. Williams, Banker, London, if the Bill had been paid. The following is in answer :—

LONDON, 8th March, 1809.

Mr. Andrew Sigourney, Treasurer, St. Andrew's Lodge, Boston,

Sir, In reply to yours of 30th of December, I duly received yours of 12th of January, 1808, and forwarded the enclosure, addressed to the Grand Lodge of Scotland. I know that the letter got safe to the hands of the Grand Master, having on the 5th of April, accepted Messrs. T. C. Amory's Bill to your order for £90.

I am your obedient servant,

(Signed) S. WILLIAMS.

R. W. BRO. JAMES LOGAN.

The name of Bro. James Logan of Falkirk. Scotland, is one of the most conspicuous in the early history of " St. Andrews" for his valuable services, and he was the first Brother, and the only Mason outside the roll of members, who is recorded to have received a gift in testimony of the esteem and gratitude of the Lodge. He was also for a number of years the representative of "St. Andrew's" in the Grand Lodge of Scotland.

The great services of Bro. Logan to this Lodge, are duly authenticated in its record; but beyond this, besides the fact that he was a Scotchman of influence and character, as a citizen and a Mason, but little is now known. He appears to have been a frequent visitor at what was styled a "Masters Lodge," which was formed in Boston. A. D. 1737. His payments of the usual fees are recorded up to 1751. At this period the erection of an ANCIENT LODGE was considered, and Brothers who sympathized in the new movement met together under the old system of assemblage, and made a Lodge which in 1756 became the Lodge of St. Andrew, chartered by the Grand Lodge of Scotland. Bro. Logan was one of these Brothers. In 1754, he was the bearer to Scotland of a petition for this charter, and for six years he was the sole agent and friend of the Lodge, in all concerns consequent upon its grant, and final dispatch to America.

In memory of this early steadfast friend, the Lodge of St. Andrew have placed here the Signature of James Logan, in FAC-SIMILE, from his letter accompanying the transmission of its CHARTER.

DECLARATION

OF

THE FREEMASONS OF BOSTON

AND VICINITY.

PRESENTED TO THE PUBLIC,

DECEMBER 31, A. D. 1831.

WHILE the popular mind remained in the high state of excitement to which it had been carried by the prejudiced and inflammatory representations of certain offences, alleged to have been committed by a few misguided members of the MASONIC INSTITUTION, in a sister State ; it seemed to the undersigned, residents of Boston and vicinity, to be expedient to refrain from any public declaration of their principles or engagements as MASONS. But, believing the time now to be fully come, when their fellow-citizens will receive with candor, if not with satisfaction, A SOLEMN AND UNEQUIVOCAL DENIAL OF THE SCANDALOUS ALLEGATIONS which, during the last five years, have, in consequence of their connection with the MASONIC FRATERNITY, been reiterated against them, they respectfully invite attention to the following

DECLARATION.

WHEREAS, it has been repeatedly asserted and published to the world, that in the several degrees of FREEMASONRY, as they are conferred in the United States, the candidate, on his initiation and subsequent advancement, binds himself, by oath, to sustain his Masonic brethren in acts which are at variance with the fundamental principles of morality, and incompatible with his duty as a good and faithful citizen : in justice therefore to themselves, and with a view to establish TRUTH and expose IMPOSITION, the undersigned, many of us the recipients of every degree of FREEMASONRY known and acknowledged in this country, do most SOLEMNLY DENY the existence of any such obligations in the INSTITUTION, so far as our knowledge respectively extends. And we as SOLEMNLY AVER, that no person is admitted to it, without first being made acquainted with the *nature of the obligations* he will be required to incur and assume.

FREEMASONRY secures its members in the freedom of thought and of speech, and permits each and every one to act according to the dictates of his own conscience in matters of RELIGION, and of his personal preferences in matters of POLITICS. It neither knows, nor does it assume to inflict upon its erring members, however wide their aberrations from duty, any penalties or punishments, other than ADMONITION, SUSPENSION, and EXPULSION.

THE obligations of the Institution require of its members a strict obedience to the laws of GOD and of Man. So far from being bound by any engagements inconsistent with the happiness and prosperity of the Nation, every citizen who becomes a MASON, is doubly bound to be true to his GOD, to his COUNTRY, and to his FELLOW-MEN. In the language of the "Ancient Constitutions" of the Order, which are printed and open for public inspection, and which are used as text-books in all the Lodges, he is "required to keep and obey the MORAL LAW; to be a quiet and peaceable citizen; true to his government and just to his country."

MASONRY disdains the making of PROSELYTES. She opens the portals of her asylums to those only who seek admission, with the recommendation of a character unspotted by immorality and vice. She simply requires of the candidate, his assent to one great fundamental religious truth — THE EXISTENCE AND PROVIDENCE OF GOD; and a practical acknowledgment of those infallible doctrines for the government of life, which are written by the finger of God on the heart of man.

IN view of the foregoing expositions, and of the solemn declarations here voluntarily made as MASONS, as CITIZENS, as MORAL MEN, and CHRISTIANS; and being deeply impressed with the conviction that our INSTITUTION has been, and may continue to be, productive of great good to our fellow-men : and having received the laws of the society, and its accumulated funds, the latter in sacred trust for CHARITABLE USES, the undersigned *can neither renounce nor abandon it;* and do therefore, most cordially unite in the fervent declaration and hope, that should the people of this country become so infatuated as to deprive Freemasons of their civil rights, in violation of their written constitutions, and the wholesome spirit of just laws and free governments, a vast majority of the Fraternity will still remain firm, confiding in GOD and the rectitude of their intentions, for consolation under the trials to which they may be exposed.

This Declaration was signed by several thousand Freemasons in Massachusetts, and in other States ; such however, was the relentless virulence of the Anti-Masonic party, and so severe was the persecution, upon the social and business relations of Masons, especially in the Cities and large Towns, that many Brothers who by no means renounced the Order, shrank from appearing upon so public a manifesto as this Declaration. It should be also stated, that no general effort was made to get signatures ; and further, by reason of absence, old age, sickness, as well as other causes, many of the most faithful and outspoken members of the Fraternity had not the opportunity to place their names on this Record. Now it has come to pass, that those Brothers who did thus boldly proclaim their loyalty to the Order, in the face of the trying ordeal of 1826-34, have since enjoyed a full measure of gratitude from all Freemasons.

The following, out of a roll of membership numbering but Thirty, are the members of the Lodge of St. Andrew, who attached their names to the Declaration of 1831. The four with a star prefixed to their names, were not at the time members of the Lodge, but have been admitted since.

John J. Loring,
John Suter,
Charles Newman,
Benjamin D. Baldwin,
Alexander H. Jennings.
Abel P. Baker,
Henry Daggett,
Thomas J. Stone,
Leonard Battelle,
Charles W. Moore,
Augustus Reed,
Zephaniah Sampson,
James Washburn,
*Hugh H. Tuttle,
*Ebenezer C. Leman,

Jonas Chickering,
David Parker,
Henry Purkitt,
Benjamin Smith,
Ebenezer Oliver,
Frederick Lecain,
Ezekiel Bates,
Jeremiah Forster,
Thomas W. Phillips,
John Rayner,
Martin Burr,
Henry Fowle.
*John R. Bradford,
*Edwin Barnes.

— 1870. —

In the above list there are but four LIVING MEMBERS left, namely : Bros. MOORE, LEMAN, BATES and BARNES.

MEMORIAL

SURRENDERING TO THE GENERAL COURT,

THE

ACT OF INCORPORATION

OF THE

M. W. GRAND LODGE OF MASSACHUSETTS.

JANUARY, 1834.

To the Honorable Senate
            and House of Representatives, in General Court Assembled:

The Memorial of the undersigned, the Master and Wardens of the Grand Lodge of Freemasons, within the Commonwealth of Massachusetts, respectfully represents : —

That the said Grand Lodge was established and organized in the then town of Boston, in said Commonwealth, as a voluntary association, on the 30th of July, A. D. 1733 — assuming and exercising all the powers, rights, and privileges which, by the ancient laws and usages recognized by the Fraternity of Freemasons, in their consociated capacity, it was empowered so to assume and exercise : That, in the legitimate exercise of those powers and privileges, and in its official capacity, as the head of a prosperous and growing BENEVOLENT ASSOCIATION, by the liberal donations of individual Freemasons, and by the usual contributions of the subordinate Lodges, it was, in time, enabled to create and establish the Fund known as the "CHARITY FUND OF THE GRAND LODGE OF MASSACHUSETTS ;" subject to the provision that the income thereof should be held in sacred trust for, and faithfully applied to, charitable purposes — to the relief of the distressed and suffering. And your memorialists have the gratification to believe that the letter and spirit of this provision have ever been, and they trust will long continue to be, scrupulously observed and performed.

Your memorialists further represent : that from the period of its establishment until the year 1817, this Fund was held by, and under the control and direction of the said Grand Lodge, acting as a voluntary association. This tenure was not only thought to be insecure, but the management of the Fund was found to be attended with the various and unavoidable difficulties which are always incident to the conduct of property thus situated. Under these circumstances, and in the belief that an act of incorporation would increase the security of the Fund, and facilitate the distribution of its charities, FRANCIS J. OLIVER, Esq., and others, members of the said Grand Lodge, petitioned and obtained of the Hon. Legislature, on the 16th June, 1817, an act, by which the Master, Wardens and Members of the Grand Lodge were incorporated and made a body politic, authorized and empowered to take by purchase, gift, grant or otherwise, and hold real estate, not exceeding the value of twenty thousand dollars, and personal estate not exceeding the value of sixty thousand dollars; and to have and exercise all the privileges usually given by acts of incorporation, to charitable societies. And so far as the knowledge of your memorialists extends, or their experience enables them to judge, they most confidently believe and affirm : That all the transactions of the said Grand Lodge (with the single exception hereafter noted,) have been conducted with a scrupulous regard to the original purposes of its Institution, and with an honorable endeavor to preserve the inviolability of the corporate powers with which it was invested by the Hon. Legislature of the Commonwealth : That in performance of the interesting duties pertaining to this connection, its members have conducted as honest and peaceable citizens, recognizing in the following "Ancient Changes" of their Order, unexceptionable rules of duty in all their social and political relations : — that they have "agreed to be good men and true, and strictly to obey the moral law; to be peaceable subjects, and cheerfully to conform to the laws of the country in which they reside; not to be concerned in plots or conspiracies against government, but patiently to submit to the decisions of the supreme Legislature; to pay a proper respect to the civil magistrate, to work diligently, live creditably, and act honorably with all men." And that, confidently relying on the protection guaranteed alike to all classes of citizens, by their written constitutions, they have rested quietly under their own vine and fig-tree, giving just cause of offence to none, and willing to believe they had none to molest or make them afraid.

Such was the condition of the affairs of the said Grand Lodge, prior to the summer of the year 1830, when, having previously been under the necessity of vacating the commodious apartments which it had for a long term of years occupied in one of the public buildings of the city, and experiencing much inconvenience from the want of suitable permanent accommodations for the transaction of Masonic business, it was proposed and determined, by a unanimous vote of its members, to erect an edifice, which, while it afforded ample accommodations for the Fraternity, should also be an ornament to the city, and a public convenience. Your memorialists would not disguise the fact, that considerations of revenue contributed to produce this determination on the part of the Grand Lodge. As the depository and guardian of a Charitable Fund, the Grand Lodge held itself morally responsible to the indigent recipients of the charities accruing from it, and felt bound to see that it was rendered as productive as a proper regard to its security would allow.

Under these circumstances, and not entertaining a suspicion that the Hon. Legislature would refuse, or that the most unyielding among the opponents of Freemasonry could object to such a modification of its act of incorporation, as would enable it to hold a greater amount of real estate, and proportionally less of personal estate, than it was then empowered to do, — the said Grand Lodge, in the autumn of 1830, laid the corner-stone of the building known as the " MASONIC TEMPLE," in the city of Boston.

The original purchase of this estate was far within the amount which the act of incorporation authorized the Grand Lodge to hold ; but foreseeing that the augmenting value of the rising structure would exceed this amount, a petition was presented to the Hon. Legislature, at the winter session of 1831, praying for such a modification of its corporate powers as would enable it to hold real estate, not exceeding the value of sixty thousand dollars, and personal estate, not exceeding the value of twenty thousand dollars. The petitioners did not ask for an extension of their corporate powers, nor to be invested with any additional ones ; but simply for such a modification of the rights and powers which they already enjoyed, as the Hon. Legislature has always shown itself willing to make for the accommodation of other corporate associations, — a modification which, your memorialists humbly conceive, was calculated to lessen, rather than to increase the power of the corporation, and by which no principle of law or policy was to be surrendered or prejudicially affected. For reasons which impartial history will doubtless exhibit, but the pertinence of which the wisdom of the historian may not easily recognize, the prayer of these petitioners was not granted.

The embarrassment in which this unexpected result involved the Corporation will readily occur to your Hon. body. The land on which the contemplated building was to be erected had been purchased, the foundation laid, and the contracts made for its erection. Your memorialists respectfully submit that there can be no difference of opinion among the ingenuous and unprejudiced portion of your Honorable body, in respect to the course it was proper, under these circumstances, for the Grand Lodge to pursue. It determined to go on with the erection of the building it had commenced, and either to trust to the magnanimity and justice of a future Legislature, for the necessary modification of its act of incorporation, or to dispose of the property, as circumstances might dictate, when it should become saleable. For reasons, with which it is unnecessary to trouble the Legislature, the Grand Lodge have adopted the latter alternative.

Although your Memorialists had observed in the proceedings of a former Legislature that certain citizens, professing to be jealous of the powers conferred by our act of incorporation, or of the manner in which they were exercised, had applied for a repeal of it, we had received no formal notice of any measure for that purpose until a few days ago, when a Circular, purporting to be a copy of a Memorial to your Honorable Body, was addressed and handed to all the principal officers of the said Grand Lodge, by a sheriff. The ultimate object of this petition seems to be a revocation of the act of incorporation of the Grand Lodge. On the face of it, however, is spread out a series of direct charges and scandalous insinuations against the principles and practices of that corporation. But, as they are true or supposable, only as a faithful representation of the spirit and proceedings of those who originated them, a due regard to the blamelessness and respectability of the said Grand Lodge, as well as a personal sense of self-respect, alike admonish your memorialists to refrain from any more particular notice of them. The Grand Lodge can enter into no discussion of the principles of Freemasonry with prejudiced and abusive partizans ; but especially would it avoid the indecorum of obtruding such a controversy into the presence of the Legislature of the Commonwealth. All controversy which may be honorably avoided is inconsistent with the conciliatory precepts and beneficent designs of our association. We are required rather to suffer undeserved persecution and injury.

than unnecessarily to maintain strife and bitterness. And although as citizens of a government of laws we can submit to nothing that is clearly wrong, as the friends of peace and order we can persist in nothing that is not clearly right. Actuated by these sentiments, and by a sincere desire to spare the Legislature the annoyance and unprofitable consumption of time, which the political party interested in the petition may otherwise occasion, the Grand Lodge has determined to make a voluntary surrender of its civil Charter; and the undersigned, the present memorialists, have been duly appointed to inform the Honorable Legislature that by a vote, passed at a regular meeting of that Corporation, on the evening of December 27th, 1833, (a copy of which is hereunto annexed,) its corporate powers were relinquished, its act of incorporation vacated, and your memorialists instructed to return it to the Honorable Legislature, from whom it was derived.

Finally, that there may be no misunderstanding of this matter, either in the Legislature or among our fellow-citizens, we beg leave to represent precisely the nature and extent of the surrender contained in this Memorial. By divesting itself of its corporate powers, the Grand Lodge has relinquished none of its Masonic attributes or prerogatives. These it claims to hold and exercise independently alike of popular will and Legislative permission — not of toleration, but of right. Its members are intelligent freemen, and although willing to restore any gift or advantage derived from the government, whenever it becomes an object of jealousy, however unfounded, nothing is further from their intentions, or from their convictions of duty, than to sacrifice a private institution, for social and benevolent purposes — the interests of which have been entrusted to them — in order to appease a popular excitement, of which that Institution may have been the innocent occasion.

> JOHN ABBOT, *Master.*
> ELIAS HASKELL, | *Wardens of the G. L. of*
> Attest, BENJ. B. APPLETON, } *Massachusetts.*

CHARLES W. MOORE,
    Grand Secretary.

CENTENNIAL ODE.

Counter Tenor. *mf*   *p*   Music by S. P. TUCKERMAN, Mus. Doc.

1. Saint Andrew's Eve! From yonder tow'r As tolls the bell the passing hour; As si - lent

First Tenor.

Second Tenor.

1. Saint Andrew's Eve! From yonder tow'r As tolls the bell the passing hour; As si - lent

Bass.   *mf*   *p*   *f*

dim. p   *mf*   *f*

glide time's eb - bing sands A cen - tu - ry com - pleted stands, A cen - tury completed stands!

glide time's eb - bing sands A cen - tu - ry com - pleted stands, A cen - tury completed stands!

dim. p   *mf*   *f*

This Unison passage, if too high for the Alto, may be sung an Octave lower.

2. Saint Andrew's Eve! Well met to-night! To Cel - e - brate the century's flight, And gather,

2. Saint Andrew's Eve! Well met to-night! To Cel - e - brate the century's flight, And gather,

ere it dis - ap - pears, The harvest of a hundred years, The harvest of a hundred years!

ere it dis - ap - pears, The harvest of a hundred years, The harvest of a hundred years!

3. A mem'ry and a tear, for those who lie in dreamless death's re-pose! Let green A-ca-cia deck each grave, And solemn cy-press o'er it wave, And solemn cypress o'er it wave.

4. Grey moss creeps o'er the cas - tle walls Of A - ber - dour's an - ces - tral halls; But still our char - ter stands as fair As when the Douglas sealed it there, As when the Douglas sealed it there.

5. So fades the past! The pres - ent yields Its fruits and flowers from fair - er fields ; For beauty's

6. The crescent moon her sil - ver shield Has lift - ed o'er the golden field ; Come, let us

radiance lights the east, And loving friends will grace our feast, And loving friends will grace our feast!

bind our ripened sheaves, And garland them with Autumn leaves, And garland them with Autumn leaves!

A SONG FOR THE LODGE.

The following Song, selected and adapted for the celebration in 1856, came too late for the occasion. The Lodge will be glad to find it preserved here.

TUNE, — *The Brave Old Oak.*

A song for the Lodge — the old St. Andrew Lodge !
 That has lived in the light so long !
On the LEVEL and SQUARE, we all repair,
 To join in the feast and song !
In the days gone by, there was joy in each eye,
 When the CHARTER gave birth to her name,
On this festal night, in Masonic light,
 Let us join in one acclaim,

   In a song for the Lodge — the old St. Andrew Lodge !
    That lives not in light alone !
   But doth honor and cheer the Grand Lodge here,
    Though a hundred years are gone.

To the Lodges all that are here at the call !
 By name as by number " Free,"
By St. Andrew's Cross, a bumper we'll toss,
 With " Masonic" cheers by " three,"
If brotherhood claim any more than a name.
 Let us build on the corner stone;
And a Temple raise, that will draw the gaze,
 When a hundred years are gone !

   Then a song for the Lodge — the old St Andrew Lodge !
    That has lived not in light alone !
   But doth honor and cheer the Grand Lodge here.
    Though a hundred years are gone.

A Song for the Lodge — the old St. Andrew Lodge !
 For by that sainted name,
To each Mason here will be more dear,
 His Lodge's honor and fame.
May ABERDOUR's name with Masonic fame,
 Descend on sculptured stone !
Be his memory bright on St. Andrew's night,
 When a hundred years are gone !

   Then a song for the Lodge — the old St. Andrew Lodge !
    That has lived not in light alone !
   But doth honor and cheer the Grand Lodge here.
    Though a hundred years are gone.

CENTENNIAL

OF

MASSACHUSETTS LODGE, BOSTON,

MAY 12, 1870.

While the last pages of this Memorial were passing through the press, the "Centennial" of an honored sister Lodge has been duly celebrated. In fraternal courtesy let a mention of the interesting Festival of our Brothers of "Massachusetts" be handed down on the page, and with the record of the Lodge of St. Andrew: —

MASSACHUSETTS LODGE, Boston, No. 2 on the roll of the Second, or Provincial Grand Lodge in the Colony of Massachusetts, and the third in age in the city, was chartered by Grand Master JOSEPH WARREN, May 12, 1770, and its one hundredth anniversary was celebrated in an elegant manner, at the Masonic Temple. The entire structure was placed at the disposal of this occasion ; and the principal services were a voluntary on the organ, the reception of the M. W. Grand Master of the Grand Lodge of Massachusetts, music by the choir, address of welcome by W. Bro. George Emerson, Master of the Lodge, prayer by Rev. Bro. John P. Robinson, reading of the Charter by R. W. A. A. Dame, Senior Member, and the singing of an ode by the choir, written by W. Bro. W. S. Adams. After which an oration was delivered by W. Bro. Chas. W. Slack. This production was finely written ; the topics were presented with admirable perspicuity, and it was replete with interesting historical matter.

From this Oration, the following incidents in the history of Massachusetts Lodge are gathered.

The first and second meetings of the Lodge were held at the Green Dragon, when it was voted to hold future meetings at Concert Hall, on Queen, now Court Street. On the 3d of January, 1774, the M. W. G. M. JOSEPH WARREN visited the Lodge in Due Form, his last official and personal visit. From October, 1774, to February, 1775, the Lodge met in the Bunch of Grapes Tavern. A suspension then occurred, the Lodge holding its next meeting on December 9,

1778. On the 7th of March, 1780, it made a movement for a National G. Lodge, with WASHINGTON at its head. The announcement on the evening of 2d of November, that the Charter was missing, created great excitement; no trace of it could be found; but, on the 2d of December, it re-appeared.' On the 30th of April 1810, the utility of instituting a fund for charity was suggested. A committee was appointed to consider and report a plan, which was adopted July 30. On the 16th of June, 1817, an act of incorporation for the Grand Lodge was obtained. In 1817, the several Lodges procured a lease of apartments in the Exchange Coffee House; these premises were destroyed by fire, November 3, 1818, the Lodge losing much of its regalia. The present arrangements, respecting charity to strangers, were established in 1819. In the spring of 1821, the Lodge took apartments in the Old State House, with other Lodges. On the 29th of March, 1822, a portrait of GENERAL JOSEPH WARREN was obtained. June 17, 1825, the Lodge participated in the ceremonies of laying the corner-stone of Bunker Hill Monument. February 23, 1827, the Lodge took action on the subject of erecting a Masonic Temple; on the 30th of December, 1831, the Lodge met there for the first time. On the 24th of June, 1845, by invitation of King Solomon's Lodge, of Charlestown, the Lodge joined in dedicating the model of the old monument erected by them in 1794, to the memory of WARREN. On the 15th of November, 1858, the Lodge met in Nassau Hall, and on the 10th of January, 1860, in the Winthrop House; on the 5th of April, 1864, this was destroyed by fire, and the Lodge again lost its property, and took temporary quarters in Thorndike Hall. On the 14th of October, 1864, the corner-stone of the new Temple was laid, and the dedication took place on St. John's Day, June 2d, 1867. The first meeting of the Lodge was held the 24th of September following, making the seventeenth place of communication it has known. The whole number of Initiates is 1026, Crafted 1001, Raised 958.

At the close of Bro. Slack's address, M. W. Grand Master, William Sewall Gardner, made an address; this closed the exercises of the afternoon. At half-past six, a reception was held, when the Committee received prominent guests; at half-past seven the company passed to the banquet-hall of the Temple. Floral decorations were abundant, giving the hall a beautiful appearance. Opposite the entrance and against the wall were suspended "G" and the square and compass, formed of red and white pinks, set in roses relieved by smilax. On one side of the hall was "1870," and opposite "1770." Large baskets of flowers hung from the arches of the Gothic windows and over the various arches which divide the hall. The tables presented a tempting appearance, all that was necessary for such an occasion being provided in abundance. The Germania Band occupied the entry adjoining the hall. When the banquet had been partaken of, the W. M. George R. Emerson called the company to order, and introduced M. W. Grand Master, William Sewall Gardner, who called upon R. W. D. G. M. Charles Levi Woodbury, who interested the audience in a humorous manner, by anticipating that Masonry in the future might be composed of women. Mayor Shurtleff was the next speaker, congratulating the Lodge on the success of their first centennial. Bro. Slack closed with a speech. The company now passed to the Gothic Hall, where the Boston Commandery choir gave a musical entertainment. In the meantime the banquet-hall was cleared of its tables, and a well selected order of dances began, to the music of the Germania Band. At Low Twelve the festivities ceased.

Thus closed creditably and graciously, after the manner of Masons, the Third Centennial Observance by a subordinate Lodge in Boston.

The following reflections from the FREEMASONS' MONTHLY MAGAZINE for June, on the "Centennial" observances of the Fraternity are so pertinent to the Celebration, as well as to this Memorial Volume itself, that they are given entire.

The occurrence of the Centennial Anniversary of a Masonic Lodge, wherever located, or under whatever circumstances, is an event eminently worthy of commemoration. The full rounding off of one hundred years of continued existence, is a favor which few voluntary secular associations are permitted to realize. Bound together by no special ties of interest, such societies spring into life, play their allotted part, pass away, and are forgotten. To this general law of mutation, Masonic Lodges, though by no means wholly or even largely exempted, undoubtedly present more exceptions than are to be found in any other class of the community. This may, and probably is, in some measure, attributable to the fact that the Masonic Fraternity, as a secular institution, is more numerous, both in its membership and in its auxiliary aids, than any of the other social divisions. But the true reason is to be found in its peculiar conformation, and adaptation to the social needs and necessities of life. In this respect it is without an equal. Its members, whatever may have been their motive in joining it, soon learn to love it, not from selfish or eleemosynary considerations, but from the harmonizing and softening influences which it exercises over their lives, the sympathetic emotions it awakens in the heart, and the confidence it inspires in each other. And this is the secret of its success and endurance, that which has brought it down along the ages of the past, and will carry it forward in defiance of the prejudices, the opposition, and the persecutions of bigotry and intolerance, for ages to come.

CHRONOLOGY.

IN THE SUCCEEDING PAGES, INTERESTING INCIDENTS FROM RECORDS AND ARCHIVES, — CHRONOLOGICALLY ARRANGED, — ARE PRESENTED, ILLUSTRATIVE OF THE HISTORY OF THE LODGE OF ST. ANDREW.

CHRONOLOGY

1752.	Lodge established under the law of "ancient usage;" meeting at Green Dragon.
1753.	George Bray received as an Entered Apprentice, being the first Initiate.
1754.	Petition sent to Grand Lodge of Scotland for a Charter.
1756. April 10.	Lodge meeting. Seven members present. Three candidates.
Nov. 30.	Petition for Charter of Lodge of St. Andrew granted by the Grand Lodge of Scotland.
1757, March 14.	Seven present; adjourned to 9th of May, at Whateley's Lodge to appear decently clothed.
March 19.	Under this date Grand Secretary of Scotland notifies that the name of St. Andrew has been given to the Lodge.
March 24.	Under this date Lodge notified that the new charter is to be a copy of James IV., charter to Grand Lodge of Scotland.
May 9.	Met at Whateley's Inn. Voted, $1 assessment, part for expenses, the rest to go to Treasurer for aprons.
May 23.	Eight present. Received £3.12s. Reckoning £2.
June 13.	Six present. Expenses 30 shillings.
1758, March 20.	All the members present, excepting I. DeCoster, Master; adj. to 3d April, when four were raised, and one crafted.

1758. April 24.	Adjourned until 4th May.	
July 3.	Reckoning 16 shillings ; adjourned to 6th inst.	
	Next meetings July 24, August 28, August 31. Other dates gone.	
1760, April 4.	James Logan agent of the Lodge instructs Wm. McAlpine in regard to taking the Charter of St. Andrew's over to America, in a letter dated at Falkirk.	
June 24.	St. John's day, celebrated at the Grey Hound Inn, Roxbury.	
Dec. 30.	St. John's day celebrated at British Coffee House, King St.	
July 10.	Lodge vote jewels and a box for the Charter.	
Sept. 4.	Charter laid before the Lodge, first time.	
Sept. 18.	Voted to remove Lodge to Royal Exchange Tavern, King street. Letter of thanks voted to Lord Aberdour and R. W. Bro. James Logan.	
Dec. 18.	One dozen aprons ordered exclusively for visiting Brethren. Letter of thanks to Lodge at Halifax, N. S., No. 2, for copy of By-Laws.	
Dec. 26.	Formal letter of thanks to Lord Aberdour for the Charter, and by same packet 2 buckskins for breeches and gloves sent out to Bro. Logan.	
1761. Feb. 12.	Committee raised to prepare state of the Lodge, to be sent to Scotland. Bro. Moses Deshon thanked for donation of Book of Constitutions. £5. 6s. 8d. voted Bro. Blake " for his loss when Faneuil Hall was burnt."	
Feb. 17.	Bro. James Logan appointed to represent St. Andrew's in Grand Lodge of Scotland. Letter sent to Lord Aberdour, Grand Master, noting the refusal of St. John Grand Lodge to admit St. Andrew's members.	
April 8.	St. John's G. L. pass a vote of " outlawry against a Lodge of Scotch Masons in Boston," — meaning St. Andrew's L'ge.	
May 14.	Wm. McAlpine voted his Initiation fees for bringing over the Charter. Voted to advertise Celebration of Feast of St. John, at Royal Exchange Tavern by St. Andrew's Lodge, holding by authority of Rt. Hon. The Lord Aberdour, Grand Master of Great Britain.	
Sept. 10.	JOSEPH WARREN received as an Entered Apprentice. Lodge held at Bro. Stone's house.	
Nov. 2.	Joseph Warren passed to the degree of Fellow Craft.	
Nov. 26.	Special meetings on the Secretary's answer to summons for mis-behaviour. Joseph Warren admitted to membership.	
1762.	3 gold Johannes voted George Bray for his loss by fire and £26 by subscription.	

1762. June 4.   Date of letter from Earl of Elgin and Kincardin, approving course of St. Andrew's.

Oct. 29.   Letter to Earl of Elgin, Grand Master, appointing A. Mc-Dougal, Proxy for St. Andrew, and soliciting instructions etc., etc., from Grand Lodge of Scotland, also soliciting a Royal Arch Charter, with power to form more Lodges in America.

Nov. 30.   Committee appointed " to write home to Scotland." Voted, "a genteel chair for the R. W. Master." Thanks given to Bro. Samuel Barrett " for donation of two genteel silver ladles." St. Andrew's night, being 30th Nov., voted that it be set apart as Grand Lodge night, to be held annually by this Lodge.

Dec. 10.   Tickets for the Feast voted to Scotch gentlemen, strangers in town. Voted to pay members out of stock for money advanced towards charter.

Dec. 27.   St. John's day celebrated at Royal Exchange.

1763. Feb. 1.   Letter to Grand Lodge of Scotland, calling attention to the un-masonic treatment which St. Andrew's receives from the Provincial Grand Lodge, and requesting Grand Lodge of Scotland not to grant a charter to certain parties in Boston, also acknowledging the appointment of Col. John Young as G. M. for America.

Feb. 3.   Part of a remittance of 7 guineas applied to General Charity Fund of G. L. of Scotland.

Feb. 22.   List of members, occupations etc., sent to G. L. of Scotland.

June 9.   Voted that the Feast of St. John the Baptist, be held at Bro. Col. Ingersoll's, Roxbury.

1764. Jan. 9.   Letter to Grand Lodge, on remittance of seven guineas on account of St. Andrew's.

Jan. 12.   Voted that this Lodge buy five tickets in Faneuil Hall Lottery No. 2. Owing to inconveniences with respect to changes and place, voted to buy a house.

March 31.   Deed of Green Dragon Estate passed to the Lodge from Catherine Kerr, for the consideration of £466. 13s. 4d. and has remained the property of St. Andrew's ever since.

April 13.   Lodge meeting held at Green Dragon Tavern.

June 24.   St. John's day celebrated at Green Dragon for the first time.

Oct. 12.   £6. 13s. 4d. paid Thos. Crafts for painting floor-cloth. £100 paid out of Lodge stock towards Masonic Hall.

Nov. 30.   Voted, that the stewards provide wine, rum, lemons, etc., and take care of the same.

1765, Jan. 7. Bill paid for re-building Green Dragon stable £26. 6s. 11d. lawful money.

Jan. 10. Wm. Lillie thanked "for donation of half a guinea for the good of the Lodge."

Jan. 21. Wm. Hoskiss released his interest, etc., (1764 a wrong date.)

Feb. 14. Committee appointed to receive the Covenant from the House Committee.

April 19. Lodge adjourned to 2d Monday of next month, "and broke up in great confusion."

Nov. 14. Voted unanimously that Doctor Joseph Warren be re-admitted a member of this Lodge.

Nov. 30. Until a certain vote of Grand Lodge be made void, voted not to admit members of any of the Lodges of the town as visitors : — vote of retaliation.

Dec. 2. Thanks to R. W. Bro. Burbeck for past services as Master for many years.

1766. Jan. 9. Committee formed to regulate funeral processions, and also to write to Grand Lodge of Scotland.

Jan. 22. Committee to wait on St. John's Grand Lodge with a complimentary address, and request a " happy coalition."

The Committee reported the answer of St. John's ; the Lodge voted that it was by no means satisfactory, and ordered the same Committee to answer St. John's.

Jan. 24. St. Andrew's officially communicates its desire to St. John's Grand Lodge for a " happy coalition."

Jan. 27. Ed. Quincy, Grand Secretary, sends to St. Andrew's a series of offensive votes by St. John's Grand Lodge in reply to the desire for a " happy coalition."

Feb. 13. Letter acknowledging communication from Grand Lodge of Scotland, and advising of the efforts of St. Andrew's for civilities between St. John's Grand Lodge and St. And'w's.

March 19. Voted, "that there be no stamping with the foot." A committee of five to draw up regulations for charity.

March 27. Thomas Milliken's bill rendered for £95. 14s. 4d. for repairs on Green Dragon after purchase.

April 10. St. Andrew's sent to St. John's Grand Lodge a series of votes in reply to the offensive action of that body. Voted to send copy of all votes to Scotland.

May 2. Report of St. John's Grand Lodge on St. Andrew's Lodge, closing in a vein of mockery.

June 12. Voted to transmit to Scotland all that passed between G. L. and St. Andrew's.

1766. July 10.   Letter for above purpose voted acceptable, and ordered sent first opportunity.

Aug. 14.   Voted, that the charity regulations be shown to Dep'y G. Master Rowe.

Dec. 1.   Thanks to Bro. Jona. Snelling for services as Sec. Thanks to R. W. J. Rowe for generous subscription to charity fund. Voted, that members be expelled, who do not pay Quar'ages by April, if in the Province. Voted, "that R. W. John Rowe be admitted a member of this Lodge."

1767. Jan. 12.   Voted, that the Standing Committee raise the rent of the house to £75, lawful money, or by agreement to secure the hall solely for the use of this Lodge.

June 12.   Committee chosen to write to Scotland. Voted, that James Otis, Esq., be desired to attend to-morrow evening, and a guinea fee be given him.

July 10.   The Sec. to draw up account of members' payment towards the house.

Nov. 30.   Whereas the G. Lodge has forbidden the visits of the members of St. Andrew's, etc., Voted, that this Lodge will not admit the members of any of the Lodges in this town, or persons made therein, until said G. L. make their vote void.

1768. Feb. 11.   Agreement made with Bro. Wm. Burbeck.

Feb. 20.   Estate G. D. conveyed to W. B. for £400 lawful money.

Feb. 22.   Date of Bond from Wm. Burbeck.

March 10.   Thanks to committee for good services in the affairs of the house. Voted, that the Stewards keep the keys of the store closet, and see to drawing all the liquors. Voted, that the Secretary keep the key of the hall.

May 12.   That every member provide himself with an apron, and that the treasurer shall provide 1 doz. aprons and 2 doz. glasses.

Nov. 23.   G'd Mast'r Rowe installed at Concert Hall, sermon at Trinity Church. The band of the British Troops gave the music.

Nov. 30.   Bro. John Webb fined 3 shillings for not attending a committee meeting. JOSEPH WARREN chosen Master. Voted, that a Jewel be provided for the Stewards. Voted, that there shall be no smoking when the Lodge is open, only when called to refreshment. Voted, that a committee of seven be appointed to consider the expediency of applying to G. L. of Scotland, for a Gr'd Master of Ancient Masons. Use of the hall given to Regimental Lodges in the 29th and 64th Regiments.

Dec. 8.   Formal petition sent out for the appointment of Jos. Warren, as G. Master, and nominations for other appointments.

1768. Dec. 8.   Voted, that the Feast of St. John's be kept by St. Andrew's, and "that none vulgarly called modern Masons be admitted." Voted, that the Stewards shall choose two members to assist in providing for the Feast. Voted, that money owing to the G. L. of Scotland be sent by first opportunity, and that there be a committee of three to attend to it. Voted, that Brothers not members of any Lodge, and who have taken the Fellow Craft's obligation in this Lodge, be admitted to the Feast.

Dec. 27.   St. Andrew's advertise St. John's celebration, and say "where the most ancient only are desired to attend."

1769. Jan. 11.   Letter remitting dues to Scotland, and advice in the matter of address of Letters.

Jan. 12.   Officers and Soldiers of the train of Artillery to have the liberty of exercise in the Hall.

May 11.   Voted, that the dispensation granted to the Masons in the 65th Regiment is unconstitutional.

Voted, that huzzaing be omitted for the future except on Feast Days.

May 30.   Joseph Warren, Master of St. A's. made G. Master of Masons in Boston.

Sept.   Paul Revere, Sec., acknowledges the receipt of Grand Master's commission.

Sept. 14.   Voted, that modern Masons not members of a Lodge, may become candidates for the Lodge, they agreeing to stand to the By-Laws.

Sept. 19.   Voted, "that the Lodge adhere to old regulations: that the G. Lodge be provided with Jewels made of any metal under silver: that the Lodge accept Bro. Paul Revere's offer to make the Jewels, and wait for his pay, till the G. Lodge is in cash; that the G. Master be installed Dec. 27 next; that there be a public instalment, but no procession; that this Lodge be at the expense of providing for the G. L. Ribbons, Mallets. Wands." &c., &c., &c.

Oct. 12.   Unanimous thanks given to Bro. Capt. Laurence Frazier for his great care in bringing over M. W. Joseph Warren's commission as Grand Master.

Nov. 30.   14 shillings allowed Bro. Carter for copying letters to and from Scotland.

Dec. 14.   The committee on Instalment report that information be given to the Lodges in the 14th and 29th Regt., that the instalment of a Grand Master will be on Wednesday the 27th, at

1769, Dec. 14.	Masons' Hall. Voted, that the Feast of St. John the Evangelist, be celebrated on the 27th, and that two dozen aprons be provided against the Feast.
1770, Jan. 11.	Voted, a committee of three to buy a quarter cask of wine. Voted unanimously, that this Lodge approve of the Tyler's conduct at the Feast, in taking care of himself.
·May 10.	The consideration of erecting a new Lodge taken up this eve.
Aug. 9.	A committee chosen to provide a Tyler.
Nov. 8.	Voted, that the first paragraph in the letter from G. L. be dismissed till St. Andrew's night. 12 shillings granted quarterly to G. L. in order to defray expenses.
Nov. 30.	Bro. Burbeck's reasons for not att'ding G. L. voted satisfact'y
1771, March 4.	Grand Lodge of Ancient Masons visited in due form. Voted unanimously, that the money advanced by Bro. Burbeck for the Charter, be offered to him.
April 9.	Letters from Lodges 58 and 59 charging this Lodge with admitting Modern Masons, and asking a conference. Voted, that said letters be dismissed.
April 11.	The Master desired to demand the Charter of Bro. Burbeck. Demand made and Bro. Burbeck refused to give it up. Voted, to apply to G. L. of Scotland for a copy of the old Charter. Voted, that a committee be chosen to see how the money for the house can be raised.
May 14.	Above Letters reconsidered, and answer made that this Lodge is accountable only to Grand Lodge.
Dec. 2.	Committee to wait on delinquent members for arrearages.
Dec. 6.	Grand Master Warren notifies his appointment of Jos. Webb as Deputy Grand Master.
Dec. 12.	Grand Lodge thanks St. Andrew's for the use of utensils, and asks for a continuance of their use. Voted, a committee of three to buy a quarter cask of wine, and that two dozen aprons be procured.
1772, March 3.	Joseph Warren appointed Grand Master of North America.
June 11.	Invitation from G. Lodge to St. John's Feast; 6 guineas appropiated for the aforesaid out of stock, and aprons for strange brethren.
July 9.	Bro. Revere "motioned that the new ribbons purchased for the decency of St. John's Day be paid for by the Treasurer." The Master thanked the Brethren for their good behavior on St. John's Day.
Sept. 10.	G. Lodge complained that St. Andrew's was not represented at last meeting; the Master said he was out of town.

1772. Oct. 8.   Lodge adjourned, owing to room being overflowed by water from late storms.

    Oct. 13.   Two members of Lodge 169 refused admittance till that Lodge admit St. A's. members, and withdraw charge of falsehood.

    Nov. 30.   Bro. Burbeck nominated for Master, but declines. $1 paid Bro. S. Webb for bottling quarter cask of wine. Committee chosen to copy letters to and from Scotland into letter book.

    Dec. 10.   M. W. G. Master presented Calcott's Disquisition on Ancient Masonry. and was thanked for the same. Committee chosen to write to Scotland.

1773. Jan. 14.   Masons not made in this Lodge to pay 20 shillings for membership. Mr. Carpenter refused as a visitor, because he was made at Castle William, and is irregular.

    April 22.   Special meeting. Charter demanded of Bro. Burbeck. Master and Wardens report that Bro. B. will give no answer. Application to G. L. for a dispensation to hold a Lodge of St. Andrew, until a copy of Charter comes from Scotland.

    May 13.   Dispensation from G. L. received, and that body thanked for its candor. Voted, that Bro. Wm. Burbeck be suspended, till he gives satisfactory reasons for detaining the Charter. Dispensation ordered to be kept by the Master, and laid on the table each Lodge-night.

    June 10.   Bro. Paul Revere moved a union of two committees, on the Charter matter.

    July 8.   Lodge adjourned on account of the extreme heat.
    Oct. 14.   M. W. Grand Master visited the Lodge.
    Nov. 11.   M. W. Grand Lodge in Due Form visited this evening.
    Nov. 30.   Lodge adjourned on account of the few Brothers present.
                   N. B. Consignees of TEA took the Brethren's time.

    Dec. 2.   Master for this year to be chosen by written vote. A cask of wine ordered.

    Dec. 16.   Present, W. M., S. W., J. W., S. D., and J. D. Lodge closed on account of the few members in attendance, until to-morrow evening.

    Dec. 27.   Jos. Webb commissioned as Deputy G. M. from Jos. Warren.
1774. Feb. 10.   Committee on affairs with Bro. Burbeck chosen.
    March 10.   Voted, that the thanks of the Lodge be given to R. W. Bros. Barrett, Webb and Hoskins. for gift of pillows, arch and platform, also to Bro. A. Newell for two glass lamps.

    Oct. 13.   Bro. Robinson of Antigua presented one guinea.
    Nov. 30.   Bro. McElroy presented jewel and silver lace for the Tyler. The Stewards of St. A's. and Massachusetts Lodge invited

1774. Nov. 30.	to meet in this hall to treat for a dinner on Feast of St. John.
1775. March 3.	Warren's last attendance at Grand Lodge meeting.
1776. Jan. 20.	British army occupy Boston, no record of meeting from April 13, 1775, until this Jan. 20, when the Lodge "clubbed for the bill" and paid all but Tiling.
April 8.	Bro. Perez Morton of St. Andrew's delivered his oration on WARREN. Obsequies of Warren at Granary Burying Ground; services according to the Masonic ritual as perfected by St. Andrew's Lodge.
Aug. 8.	Lodge summoned according to order — no attendance.
Oct. 10.	Bro. Paul Revere motioned that members be waited upon about continuance of their membership and paying Quarterages.
Dec. 2.	R. W. D. G. M. Jos. Webb thanked by vote for care of Lodge jewels, books and furniture.
Dec. 13.	Bro Burbeck's suspension to be reconsidered upon his laying the Charter on the table each night.
1777, Jan. 24.	Bro. Burbeck presented a Book of Constitutions, and was thanked.
March 8.	Jos. Webb elected Grand Master. (This date is claimed to be the true date of the Independence of the G. L. of Mass.)
April 10.	Committee chosen to consider some matters for the benefit of this Lodge and report to the members.
April 18.	Dr. John Warren made a Mason.
May 27.	Col. Peter Faneuil made a Mason. This is not the Peter who gave the Hall.
June 3.	Voted, that members be waited on, and none to be deemed members who have not paid Quarterages since last Nov.; "that the By-Laws be read, and a number be selected to remain as members; that each visiting brother pay his share of expenses each Lodge-night; that Quarterages be raised to 9 shillings, and £5 for Raisings; that no visitors be admitted in any wise on special Lodge-night, but by candidate's invitation.
Nov. 13.	Thanks voted to Bro. Hopkins for 2 glass globes; to others for 6 tapers, for half a chaldron of coal and a cord of wood.
Dec. 2.	At an annual meeting Nat. Pierce says, "God save the Craft."
Dec. 11.	Thanks to Bro. Lazarus Goodwin for his compliments of 1-4 cask of wine.
Dec. 12.	At special meeting thanks to Bro. Robt. Allen for his gift of two decanters.
Dec. 15.	At special meeting, Perez Morton, Paul Revere, Benj. Hitchborn

1777, Dec. 15.	and others, appointed a committee on "Green Dragon" business with Bro. Burbeck. Voted, that sea-faring brothers and brethren of the army in future pay 1 shilling a month. Voted, that Bro. Woart pay £60 rent for the house. Voted, that the Stewards report what is wanting for the "Closets." N. B. This was a large and enthusiastic meeting ; 35 visitors present, and 30 names proposed for membership.
Dec. 26.	Wm. Burbeck's deed to Wm. Bell and others, for £400. etc.
1778, Jan. 8.	Voted to apply to General Court for act of incorporation.
Feb. 12.	Voted lodgings and passage home, to Wallach, a Dutch young gentleman, who had been taken by one of tyrant George's frigates, £18. 15s. collected for him also.
Feb. 17.	£3 given to Sergeant James Andrews, a prisoner in the guard-ship. "in token of the regard for one of the Fraternity though an enemy." Thanks to Bro. McElroy for new Record book, the price of which was $16.
May 12.	For receiving entered apprentices the charge to be £9, and visiting brethren to pay 12s.
Aug. 1	Bro. John Lowell to notify committee on supplies to furnish a quarter cask of wine.
Nov. 30.	£6 a year each, allowed the Stewards for attendance. Tyler. 20 shillings a night. Voted, that £150 be invested in the Loan Office ; thanks to Bro. Webb for gift of 2 chairs.
Dec. 10.	Thanks to Bro. Wallach for a number of elegant Brass Sconces.
1779, Jan. 15.	The hat went round for a British Bro. in distress, £23 collected.
Feb. 11.	Bro. Moses Deshon, presented with $100 out of stock.
June 10.	The "hat passed" for the Tyler and $62 collected.
Sept. 9.	Thanks to Bro. Duval for gift of $60.
Nov. 29.	Treasurer's account settled, showing dealings in Mass. State Lottery, by order of the Lodge.
Nov. 30.	Admission fee to be £100 for those made in other Lodges.
Nov. 30.	£750 put in the Loan Office. Paul Revere thanked for services as Master.
1780, Jan. 13.	Standing Committee confer on purchase of adjoining house.
Feb. 10.	"Petition refering to the Children of late G. Master, Joseph Warren. Voted, to be left with the Standing Committee."
March 9.	Bro. Nathaniel Willis thanked for 500 blank summons.
May 2.	Quarterages fixed at $24. Visitors to pay $40 an evening. Rent of Green Dragon £40, hard money.
July 13.	The hat went round and $293 collected for Mrs. Fadre.
Sept. 19.	The Lodge vote unanimously against General Grand Lodge for America.

Nov. 9.	$513 collected for Bro. Gray ; next meeting. paid £90 for his coffin.
Dec. 25.	Major-General Benj. Lincoln complimented with the degrees this evening.
1781. March 22.	Committee chosen on letting the Green Dragon and locating a new Lodge room.
May 18.	Above committee report a lot near the common, after discussion the matter subsided.
Aug. 31.	Punch bowls ordered and rum and liquors to be laid in, by Col. Fellow's committee.
Dec. 12.	Proclamation for Thanksgiving of the Commonwealth noticed. Perfect Union Lodge granted liberty of Masons' Hall.
1782. Feb. 9.	Committee of nine chosen to petition Grand Lodge for a Charter securing precedency.
March 14.	Petition for act of incorporation, "by the name of St. Andrew's," voted. Hat passed for distressed strange brethren.
Dec. 6.	The name and title of "Massachusetts Grand Lodge" first assumed ; its declaration of independence declared.
Dec. 16.	Lodge of Emergency, vote of 30 to 19 against acknowledging Mass. G. L. independent of all Lodges in the universe.
Dec. 24.	Committee of Mass. G. Lodge appointed to confer with St. Andrew's on their refusal to come in.
1783. Jan. 1.	Committee of Mass. G. Lodge appointed to confer with St. Andrew's, ask to have a special meeting called.
Jan. 29.	Mass. G. L. notified that St. A's consider the step of the G. L. inconsistent with Masonic principles, etc.. but vote 22 to 14 to send up Master and Wardens until peace is declared with Great Britain. A committee from G. L. are admitted to St. Andrew's.
March 9.	Protest of the majority of St. A's Lodge against Mass. G. L. on the ground that Warren's commission died with him. and political changes have nothing to do with Freemasonry.
May 8.	Thos. McGuyer of Bristol admitted to the Degrees on letter of recommendation of Selectmen of said Town.
Dec. 12.	A special meeting called on 4th of Jan. respecting dependence on Grand Lodge of Scotland.
1784. Jan. 8.	Sea-faring Brothers to vote by Proxy.
Jan. 22.	Vote, on continuing under G. Lodge of Scotland,— those in favor to retire to north side of hall, and those who acknowledge the Massachusetts G. Lodge to the south side. 6 majority for Scotland.

1784, Feb. 5. " Massachusetts assumed Grand Lodge," to be informed of vote of 22d of January. No persons acknowledging *assumed* Mass. Grand Lodge to be admitted a member of this. The Secretary to use his discretion in providing for the safety of the papers and jewels, and to be accountable. Letter sent to Mass. G. L. in reference to vote Jan. 29, 1783, by which St. Andrew's consented to be represented in G. L. until peace was declared. After which by a vote of 29 to 23, St. Andrew's decided to remain under G. L. of Scotland. Voted to fill for the balance of the year, all vacant offices.

Feb. 12. Vote to receive back former members, if they will formally disavow the Mass. Grand Lodge claim for independence, and will acknowledge the supremacy of the Grand Lodge of Scotland.

Feb. 12. " Col. P. Revere, Capt. N. Fellows, John Boit, D. Coolidge, and J. Stodder " of the minority of 23 being aggrieved brethren, applied to the door of the Lodge for an interview. A committee sent to inform them if they had anything to say, to do it by writing ; to which answer was made, that Col. Revere, etc., did not wish to write.

March 16. Paul Revere and others offer to divide the property of St. Andrew's according to numbers.

March 25. Set of Resolves passed declaring the attitude of St. Andrew's Lodge in the suit of law by Paul Revere and others, — reviewing the question at issue, — expressing a willingness to submit to referees, and vote to retain as counsel Bro. Hon. Christopher Gore. Letter to G. L. of Scotland read as written by Bro. Burbeck. In this letter, St. Andrew's affirm that they act upon the fundamental principles of masonry in opposing the pretentions of Mass. G. Lodge.

July 20. The 23 members who left St. Andrew's to join " Rising States," relinquish, etc., to the 30 members who remain by St. A's.

Aug. 12. Voted, " that a Circular be sent to all Lodges that have received Charters from Grand Master Warren and Grand Master Webb, while under the jurisdiction of the G. L. of Scotland," — enclosing a copy of St. Andrew's' letter to Scotland for their consideration.

Oct. 7. Grand Lodge of Scotland notified of the continued allegiance of St. Andrew's and the suit at law against it by Rising States Lodge.

Oct. 7. Under this date important letter sent to Grand Lodge of Scotland on the affair between Mass. Lodge and St. Andrew.

1785. March 3. Voted that the matters respecting visits to Rising States Lodge subside for the present.

May 23. The Master and Senior Warden on behalf of St. Andrew's by letter notifies Paul Revere and others in convention at Charlestown that St. Andrew's holds only under the G. L. of Scotland.

July 1. Receipt of Treasurer dated Castle Island, for $300, and £96. 6s. 1d.,—a donation for the "poor and indigent brethren of St. Andrew's and their widows."

July 12. Donation from an unknown friend (Wm. Burbeck), by his will.

Oct. 12. A set of pure brass candlesticks presented by Bro. Dakin.

Nov. 10. Bros. Carter and Sigourney notify that Bro. Burbeck on his death bed handed them the Charter. Voted that Bro. S. keep it till further orders.

Dec. 8. Bro. Harris, Sec. presented alphabetical list of members made in St. Andrew's since A. D. 1760.

1786. Jan. 12. Bro. Moores to be considered a sea-faring Bro. till Charlestown bridge, now building, is done. Documents on the situation of the Lodge ordered to be sent to the Grand Lodge of Scotland. Voted not to celebrate the Feast of St. John this year.

Nov. 30. "Owing to the difficulties of the times," quarterages put at 4 shillings. Stewards to have theirs, and 3 shillings a night.

1787. April 28. By-Laws changed so that Lodge will meet second Thursday of June, July and August.

July 12. Thanks to Bro. Blake for an elegant China bowl imported in an American vessel.

Nov. 30. $2 paid to Bro. Dakin for his offer to supply the Lodge with sea coal for one year. Stewards to be accountable for all utensils. Committee to advertise St. John's Celebration and furnish Bro. Woart a bill of fare.

Dec. 13. Referees on "Rising States" matter in 1784, to have tickets to Feast. Price of tickets to St. John's Feast fixed at 7 shillings and 6 pence.

1788. July 10. Committee report average expense of Lodge meeting £2. 4s. 10d., and that Quarterages be reduced to 3 shillings.

Oct. 9. Bro. Gore presented an elegant "Flooring," and was thanked.

Dec. 1. Landlord of Green Dragon not to let the hall for wire dancing or anything of the kind.

1789. Feb. 28. Correspondence with Lodge "Sister Holy Cross" of St. Croix, W. I., in regard to preventing imposition by clandestine made Masons.

1789, March 16. Subject considered of exempting members of 20 years standing from Quarterages.

Nov. 12. Bro. Sam. Sloan thanked for gift of a sword.

Dec. 9. Charter to be given Sec. and he to lay it on the table each Lodge-night ; notarial copy to be made of it and read " St. Andrew's " night.

1790, Jan. 14. The Treas. to fund the securities in his name, according to act of Congress.

March 11. Voted not to sell the candlesticks presented by the late Bro. Burbeck, out of the Lodge.

Oct. 14. Visitors to acquaint the Lodge, through the Tyler, of their desire to visit, unless made here.

Nov. 11. Royal Arch Lodge indulged with use of St. Andrew's Charter.

1791, May 12. Fifty lists of members with their occupations to be furnished, one to each member.

Aug. 20. Smoking prohibited in Lodge hours.

1792, April 20. Organization of Grand Lodge of Mass. announced by letter, and answered.

Nov. 30. United States 3 per cent's to be taken for all the securities of the Lodge.

1793, April 16. Letter to G. L. of Mass. acknowledging Book of Constitutions, and wishing prosperity. Committee on Charter of St. Andrew's pronounce it valid.

May 19. Letter to G. L. of Scotland asking their advice in regard to St. Andrew's relations with Mass. Grand Lodge.

Aug. 18. Lectures to be given once a week to new Masons.

1794, Nov. 27. Harmonic Lodge forbidden the use of the hall, without permission. Whenever $300 is in hand, it is be invested in 6 per cent. U. S. stock.

Dec. 11. Silver compasses presented by Bro. Sam. Moore.

1795, Dec. 11. Bill for three pair of lambskin drawers costing 31*s.* 6*d.* allowed and paid.

Dec. 18. St. John's Day to be celebrated on the 28th.

1796, July 13. A pair of plated candlesticks presented by Bro. Green.

Oct. 10. Grand Lodge of Connecticut resolve non-intercourse against Lodges holding foreign charters, and who will not join U. S. Grand Lodges (aimed at St. Andrew's).

Nov. 30. H. G. Otis' draft for act of incorporation with petition signed by members.

Nov. 30. Plate for certificate of membership ; " Act of Incorporation " again voted for.

1797, Nov. 25. Members of St. Andrew's constitute themselves a *Proprietary.*

1797. Dec. 26.		The eight survivors of the 1784 transactions, relinquish, etc.
1798. Feb. 8.		Bro. Wm. Harris voted a silver medal, — 11 yrs. as Secretary.
	Feb. 13.	Meeting of Proprietary for organization.
	June 1.	Special meeting on Masonic relations, decided 19 to 8 to write Grand Lodge of Scotland on St. Andrew's passing under Massachusetts Grand Lodge.
	June 12.	Letter to Grand Lodge of Scotland on the expediency of St. Andrew's joining Mass. Grand Lodge.
	Nov. 27.	St. Andrew's subscribes funds towards building "the Frigate."
1799. Dec. 19.		Letter of Grand Lodge of Mass. dated 9th, read, appointing committee of conference.
	Dec. 19.	Letter from Grand Lodge of Scotland dated May 21, was read, and referred to a committee.
1800. Jan. 9.		Voted to clothe the hall in mourning, in memory of our illustrious Brother GEORGE WASHINGTON, — to procure a monument with emblems and a motto.
	Feb. 10.	Committee report on letter from Grand Lodge of Massachusetts. The subject of union (substantially) postponed by vote of 21 to 6. Voted unanimously, to join with the G. L. in paying Funeral Grand Honors on the 11th inst., to Bro. GEORGE WASHINGTON.
	Feb. 10.	Letter to Massachusetts Grand Lodge, courteously saying that St. Andrew's appreciates the advantages of a Parent Grand Lodge at home, but owing to a recent letter from Grand Lodge of Scotland St. Andrew's cannot with honor join Massachusetts Grand Lodge at present.
	Oct. 14.	Full report of the financial state of the Lodge, with recommendations in regard to charity, submitted.
1802. March 11.		Lodge closed early ; members fatigued by the great fire of the 10th inst.
1804. Nov. 8.		Committee of nine to consider the interests of the Lodge.
1807. Nov. 13.		The Burbeck donation invested in Malden bridge. Disposition of its income.
	Nov. 30.	Grand Lodge of Mass. to be notified of conference respecting proposed union. All donations to the Lodge to be put in a separate book.
	Dec. 15.	Committees of Grand Lodge and St. Andrew's this day came to formal agreement in regard to union, contingent on discharge from Grand Lodge of Scotland.
	Dec. 22.	Conference committee on the union unanimously accepted, full remittance ordered of all dues to "Scotland" and an honorable discharge asked.

z

1808, Jan. 12.   Committee of St. Andrew's address letter to Grand Lodge of Scotland asking an honorable discharge of the Lodge for the purpose of enrolment under Grand Lodge of Massachusetts. Account current forwarded to Grand Lodge of Scotland with bill of exchange on London for £90. Number of candidates from 1760 to 1807, 827. Paid for at 2s. 6d. each.

Oct. 13.   Washington Lodge at Roxbury, proposing to confer the higher orders of masonry, condemned, etc.

Dec. 30.   Andrew Sigourney, Treas., by letter asks S. Williams, London, if the £90 has been paid Grand Lodge of Scotland.

1809, March 8.   S. Williams by letter advises St. Andrew's Lodge that the £90 has been paid to Grand Lodge of Scotland.

June 14.   Sword presented by Bro. Andrew Sigourney.

Sept. 7.   The Grand Lodge of Massachusetts notified — that at its next annual communication, Dec. 11, St. Andrew's will take its place as a member, agreeable to the understanding had 15th December 1807.

Sept. 14.   Committee report their visit to Grand Lodge on 11th inst.

Nov. 28.   Voted, that the refreshments for the ensuing year be tongues and bread.

Dec. 14.   Report of St. Andrew's Lodge formally taking its seat as a member of Grand Lodge on the 11th of December, and concerning the Charter.

1811, Jan. 11.   A son of the late Bro. Burbeck relieved. This relief was continued afterwards.

Nov. 27.   Long report with suggestions on the state of the Lodge by Bro. Andrew Sigourney, Treasurer.

1812, Nov. 25.   Bro. Thomas Knox made an honorary member, — the first instance on record.

1815.   Members' committee formed.

Jan. 12.   Committee raised to relieve British prisoners of war, who are Masons.

Jan. 13.   Action on vote of Grand Lodge appropriating $500 for British prisoners of war.

1816, April 24.   The subject of removing Lodge from " Green Dragon " considered.

1817, Feb. 6.   Communication from Boston Lodges on joining in a place or meeting. Lodges meet at Exchange Coffee House.

May 1.   Voted to dispose of articles not wanted in the new hall.

May 8.   A cocked hat to be got for the Master and regalia as needed.

July.   Special meeting at Masons' Hall, Exchange building.

1817, Sept. 11.	First Regular meeting in new hall. Bro. H. Fowle's address.
Nov. 13.	Official visit of Dis. Dep. G. M.; 77 visitors.
Nov. 20.	Lodge to meet at " Green Dragon " next Monday even'g. 25th. Lodge met to choose officers, etc., report in By-Laws.
1818, May 14.	King Solomon's Lodge thanks St. Andrew's for its gift of an altar.
Nov. 3.	Exchange Coffee House burnt while St. John's Lodge were about to receive Dis. Dep. G. M.
Nov. 19.	A lecturer appointed with a salary of $60.
1819, Jan.	Lodges meet at old Hall in Ann Street.
May 13.	Boston Masonic Board of Relief, first considered in St. Andrew's Lodge.
Oct. 14.	Sodality meetings fixed for Monday and Thursday at G. D'n.
1820, Aug. 20.	Andrew Sigourney's death noticed. St. Andrew's vote to express in a public manner their high estimation of his character and eminent services.
1821, Jan. 11.	Old State House apartments. — St. A's assessed $60 for rent. Lease taken by the Lodges for ten years.
1822, Jan. 10.	Bro. Seth Webber who died abroad, left St. Andrew's $500.
1825, May 12.	Bunker Hill Monument, — conference committee on laying corner-stone, June 17.
1826, Sept.	Beginning of Anti-Masonic persecution in New York.
1827, April 2.	New Masonic Temple; purchase of land, etc., $2000 appropriated by St. Andrew's.
Sept. 15.	Death of Bro. Joab Hunt.
Oct.	Retrenchments considered by all Lodges.
Nov. 19.	Special reference to charity fund.
1828, Sept. 6.	Board of Aldermen meet G. D. Proprietors on widening Union St.; 1,368 feet of land taken.
Dec. 13.	Letter of Gen. H. Burbeck in relation to donation of an unknown friend in 1785 (his father).
1830, Oct.	Erection of First Masonic Temple began.
Nov. 18.	Malden Bridge to be sold, and with more added put in Temple [$717.38]. Lodges occupy Washington Hall, opposite Franklin Street.
1831, Dec. 31.	Famous Declaration of the Freemasons published in Boston.
1832, Jan. 31.	Green Dragon Board of Trustees chosen.
Jan. 31.	Bro. Benj. Smith presented at Concert Hall, with silver pitcher for long and valuable services.
Nov. 8.	" Strangers' Charity Fund," — final determination made on report of committee.
Dec. 13.	The Bethel Church presented with the chandelier in Mason's Hall.

1832.   The Lodges occupy the new Masonic Temple.

1833. Jan. 10. Subject of reducing fees considered.

April 13.   Centennial of the introduction of Masonry into this country, celebrated at Masonic Temple.

Nov. 14.   Committee of congratulation to visit the Lodges.

Dec. 12.   Visiting committees came in from St. John's, Mass., Columbian and Mt. Lebanon Lodges. Report of committee to visit Lodges of 1st Masonic District, favorable as to spirit, etc.

1834. Jan.   Memorial surrendering Charter of Grand Lodge to Gen. Court.

Sept. 11.   Death of Bro. Ben. Smith announced.

Nov. 13.   Voted to unite with other Lodges in Sodality meetings.

Nov. 19.   Committee to consider the subject of membership.

1836, April 14. St. John's Portsmouth, N. H., — invitation to celebrate the Centennial of the introduction of Masonry into Portsmouth, N. H. Address by C. W. M. of St. Andrew's. First Masonic centennial address which was printed.

Nov. 17.   Boston Encampment's invitation to St. Andrew's to attend Installation of Officers on 21st Dec. ; unanimously accepted.

1837, Jan. 11. M. W. G. Lodge's invitation to public Installation, 16th inst., accepted.

April 13.   R. W. Bro. Henry Fowle's death announced, — he was an accomplished man and mason.

1840, May 14. Bro. D. Parker moved a committee to consider the subject of abolishing refreshments at stated meetings.

1841, May 13. Invitation to St. John's Day, at Portsmouth, N. H., accepted.

Nov. 9.   50 copies Masonic melodies by Bro. Power, subscribed for. Columbian Lodge communication on the subject of a lot at Mt. Auburn.

Nov. 11.   Bro. Purkitt elected an honorary member.

Dec. 14.   Vote 18 to 12, not to abolish refreshments either at Lodge room or elsewhere.

1844. Feb. 8. Lodge of Instruction formed.

March 11. Eight Past Master Jewels got up for the use of the Lodge.

April 25.   Presented Star of Bethlehem Lodge, Chelsea, a set of collars. New Past Masters' Jewels presented to the Past Masters.

June 14.   Invitation from Portland to St. John's Day. Invitation from Olive Branch Lodge, Grafton ; Voted to attend.

1845, April 10. Voted to pay Lodge's proportion for a new organ ; the old one not to be sold.

May 8.   Voted to accept invitation for 24th of June, of King Solomon's Lodge.

June 12.   Voted to procure a new Banner, and examine regalia.

1845. July 10.	Voted to pay $20 to King Solomon's Lodge towards expenses on last St. John's Day.
Oct. 23.	Ole Bull the distinguished violinist visited the Lodge.
1846. March 12.	Bro. Henry Purkitt's death announced.
March 26.	Bro. Phillips presented a memorial on Bro. Purkitt's death. The Lodge specially convened to hear it.
April 16.	$300 voted towards fitting up the rooms in the Temple.
Dec. 10.	Martin Burr's death at Methuen, on the 19th of Nov., announced ; he was the oldest member of the Lodge.
1847. April 8.	Morning Star Lodge's (Worcester) invitation to St. John's Day accepted.
Sept. 9.	Bro. Wm. Robertson of Celtic Lodge, Edinburgh, Scotland, introduced.
1848. May 11.	Star In The East Lodge's (N. Bedford) invitation to St. John's Day, accepted.
Oct. 12.	M. W. Alexander H. Putney, Grand Master of Maine, introduced in due form.
Oct. 12.	Voted to appear on the occasion of the Water Celebration, Oct. 25, if the Grand Lodge sanction.
1849. Jan. 2.	Unanimously voted to present Bros. J. J. Loring and David Parker, with suitable tokens for long and faithful services.
Jan. 9.	Bro. Hamilton Willis elected a delegate to Grand Lodge Convention ; ordered for the 7th of Feb., "to fix upon a uniform standard of work."
Jan. 11.	Rev. Bro. Leacock, President of the Kentucky Masonic College, introduced and donation made.
March 8.	St. Mark's Lodge's (Newburyport) invitation to St. John's Day accepted.
1850, Jan. 10.	Bro. C. W. Moore resigned as Sec. ; Lodge appoint a committee to procure a suitable token, with vote of thanks.
March 14.	Middlesex Lodge's (Framingham) invitation to St. John's Day accepted.
June 13.	Bro. J. J. Loring announced that he should visit Europe next month.
July 27.	Special meeting at Porter's Hotel, complimentary to Bro. J. J. Loring.
1851, Jan. 19.	Washington Monument Association ask aid of St. Andrew's.
April 10.	Essex Lodge's (Salem) invitation to St. John's Day accepted.
May 8.	New Caledonian Lodge's (Pictou) invitation to St. John's Day. Bro. John B. Hammatt presented a cane which used to belong to Bro. Henry Purkitt ; thanks of the Lodge given.
Nov. 20.	"Washington Monument" communication was taken from

1851. Nov. 20.	committee, and donation made. Bro. George M. Randall (bishop), resigns as chaplain.
Nov.	Sup. Jud. Court, — suit of Jerusha E. King *vs.* D. Parker. decided in favor of the Lodge.
1852. Jan.	New Board of G. D. Trustees chosen.
Feb. 10.	Communication from Clay Monument Association, Kentucky.
April 29.	The death of Bro. John Suter (on the 28th inst.), announced, — aged 70 years.
May 19.	Morning Star Lodge's (Worcester) invitation to St. John's Day.
Sept. 9.	Mount Tom Lodge, Holyoke, presented with a set of collars.
Nov. 18.	Committee appointed to present Bros. Bradford and Phillips, such testimonial for their services "as shall be worthy of this Lodge."
Dec. 9.	M. W. G. M. Randall, Grand Master, visited the Lodge.
1854. Jan. 12.	Committee of Columbian Lodge present, with greetings to St. Andrew's.
1855.	One vacancy filled in Board of Trustees.
March 22.	Grand Lodge Delegation from Pennsylvania, introduced to the Lodge.
May 11.	Invitation from Montgomery Lodge, Milford, to unite in celebrating St. John's Day.
May 11.	Invitation from St. John's Lodge, Portsmouth, to unite in celebrating St. John's Day.
Aug. 1.	R. W. C. W. Moore sailed for Europe, with instructions to invite Grand Lodge of Scotland to "St. Andrew's" Centennial Celebration, Nov. 30, 1856.
Sept. 13.	Death of Bro. Wm. B. Oliver announced.
Sept. 27.	Norfolk and Portsmouth, Va.; $200 donated to inhabitants on account of a great fire there.
Sept. 27.	Centennial Anniversary Committee appointed.
Nov. 8.	Members' Badge voted.
Nov. 8.	Letter of G. Sec. of Grand Lodge of Scotland to St. Andrew's Lodge, under this date, with a copy of G. L. of Scotland, "records and minutes" concerning the grant of the Charter of St. Andrew's in 1756; also a copy of the minutes of that Grand Lodge, Nov. 25, 1855, wherein the invitation to the Centennial of St. Andrew's in 1856, at Boston, is recorded, with the interesting notice of the same, and appointment of Bros. Clark and Taylor, members of "The Lodge Edinburgh Mary's Chapel" to represent G. L. of Scotland at the aforesaid Centennial in Boston, November 29, 1856.
Dec. 27.	Winslow Lewis Lodge, — consent granted to form it.

1856, March 27. History of Columbian Lodge presented to the Lodge, written by R. W. John T. Heard.

Sept. 11. Candlesticks loaned to Wyoming Lodge (Melrose). Death of Bro. Rayner, announced by Bro. Phillips.

Sept. 17. FRANKLIN Statue inaugurated, — the Freemasons in full regalia participate.

Oct. 9. Death of Bro. Loring announced. Born Sept. 23, 1789; died Oct. 6, 1856. Elected Treasurer 1820, and held the office thirty years.

Nov. 29. Centennial Anniversary observed in a distinguished manner. (St. Andrew's Day, 30th. came on Sunday this year.)

Dec. Voted to print the proceedings on above occasion, with interesting historical extracts from records.

1857, March 26. Voted to hold sodality meetings.

April 9. Invitation to participate in the inauguration of the statue of General Warren, on the ensuing 17th of June.

1858, March 11. Gavel presented by Winslow Lewis Lodge.

Oct. 24. Death of Bro. Sampson, Oct. 1, senior member, — made 1805 — announced by Bro. Phillips.

Lodges occupy Nassau Hall, corner of Washington and Nassau Streets.

Nov. 11. $100 donated to the ladies for purchasing Mt. Vernon estate.

1859, May 12. Lodge at Turk's Island ; $50 donated.

June 23. Inhabitants of Fayal, $100 donated. (Famine there.)

Sept. 8. Death of Bro. Phillips announced by Bro. Parker.

Dec. 8. George Bray's diploma — a member in 1756, and named in Charter — presented by Bro. Parker.

Dec. 22. Donation of $400, and vote to pay for the education of a deceased Brother's son.

1860. The Lodges occupy Freemasons' Hall, Winthrop House.

March 22. Monument at Plymouth, $100 donated.

Dec. 13. Aberdour Lodge, formation approved.

1861, Feb. 14. Aberdour Lodge presented with a set of jewels.

April 10. Gloucester, — $100 donated to widows and orphans there, on account of a great fire.

June 26. Sanitary Commission, — $100 donated.

1863, Jan. 8. Sick and wounded soldiers, — $400 donated. (War of the Rebellion.)

Nov. 25. Bros. Wm. W. Tucker and H. A. Whitney present $200.

Dec. 24. Discharged soldiers, — $100 donated. Freedman's Society, $50 donated.

1864, March 31. Centennial Celebration of the purchase of the Green Dragon Estate.

1864. April 5.   Freemasons' Hall burnt, cor. of Tremont and Boylston Sts.
              (Winthrop House.)
    April 14.   Bro. Shurtleff presented a bible to the Lodge.
    June 9.   Bro. Bradford presented 24 inch guage. The Senior and
              Junior Wardens presented batons.
    Oct. 13.   Sailors' National Fair, — $200 donated.
    Oct. 14.   Corner-stone of Free Masons' Hall laid.
    Nov. 30.   Gavel presented by Bro. E. Stearns.
1865. March 2.   Death of Bro. Bradford announced by W. Bro. E. Stearns.
    March 9.   Bro. W. D. Stratton presented a Book of Prayers.
              Eleusis Lodge, — formation approved.
1866, April 11.   Death of Bro. Parker April 7, announced by the Wor. Master.
    May 8.   Death of Bro. Tuttle May 6, announced by the Wor. Master.
    Sept. 9.   Death of Bro. Jordan Sept. 7, announced by the Wor. Master.
1867, Jan. 8.   Death of Bro. Cary Jan. 4th, announced by the Wor. Master.
    March 14.   Five hundred dollars voted to Grand Lodge.
    April 11.   Zetland Lodge, — formation approved.
    June 24.   Masonic Temple dedicated.
              Lodge dined at J. B. Smith's, — first time.
    July 26.   Death of Bro. Baldwin July 24. aged 81, — announced by the
              Wor. Master Bro. W. F. Davis.
    Dec. 12.   Joshua B. Smith made a Mason in St. Andrew's.
1868. Sept. 10.   A piece of the original wall of King Solomon's Temple, pre-
              sented by Bro. Wm. W. Tucker.
    Nov. 30.   Celebration of the CXII. anniversary of St. Andrew's Lodge.
1869. Feb. 24.   Death of Bro. Aaron Leman Feb. 21, announced by the Wor.
              Master Bro. Ezra Palmer.
    Dec. 23.   Celebration of the Centennial of Mass. G. L. by St. Andrew's.
              Voted to unite with Grand Lodge in their celebration.
    Dec. 28.   Grand Lodge Celebration of the " Centennial " of Mass. G. L.
1870. Jan. 13.   The Memorial Committee appointed to examine the records
              and archives, — to prepare a " Centennial Memorial," and
              to report in print.
    Feb. 10.   Committee appointed to arrange records and papers, and to
              provide for their safe-keeping.
    March 10.   Lodge Seal presented to Palatka Lodge, Florida.
    May 12.   " Centennial " of Massachusetts Lodge celebrated.
    May 16.   Mass. Lodge thanks St. Andrew's for relinquishing the Hall
              on their Centennial night.
    June 23.   Regular Quarterly communication, — The Memorial Committee
              report the completion of this volume.

GRAND MASTERS IN MASSACHUSETTS,

FROM 1733 TO 1870.

1733. April 30.	HENRY PRICE appointed Provincial Grand Master, by Grand Master of England, for Boston, etc.
July 30.	Provincial Grand Lodge opened, — denominated "THE ST. JOHN'S GRAND LODGE."
1734.	Henry Price commissioned Provincial Grand Master of North America, by Grand Master of England.
1737–1744.	Robert Tomlinson Grand Master of St. John's Grand Lodge. Appointed by the Earl of Loudon, G. M. of England.
1744–1754.	Thomas Oxnard Grand Master of St. John's Grand Lodge. Appointed by Lord Ward, Baron of Birmingham, Grand Master of England.
1754–1755.	Henry Price P. G. M. *pro tem.*
1755–1767.	Jeremy Gridley Grand Master of St. John's Grand Lodge. Appointed by the Marquis of Caernarvon, Grand Master of England.
1767–1768.	Henry Price P. G. M. *pro tem.*
1768.	John Rowe. This election was confirmed by the Duke of Beaufort, Marquis and Earl of Worcester, etc., G. M. of Britain. Bro. Rowe died in 1786, and no more Grand Masters were chosen for St. John's Grand Lodge.
1769, May 30.	JOSEPH WARREN commissioned Provincial Grand Master by Grand Lodge of Scotland on petition of St. Andrew's Lodge.
Dec. 27.	Second Provincial Grand Lodge, or G. L. of "ancient masons" opened, — denominated "Massachusetts Grand Lodge."
1772, March 3.	Joseph Warren commissioned Provincial Grand Master of Masons for the continent of America.
1775, June 17.	Warren killed in the Battle of Bunker Hill.
1775–1777.	Joseph Webb Deputy Grand Master of "Mass. G. Lodge."
1777, March 8.	Joseph Webb elected Grand Master of Mass. Grand Lodge. This election was an act of Independence, and the earliest independent election of a Grand Master in America.
1777–1782.	Joseph Webb Grand Master of "Mass. Grand Lodge."

1782, Dec. 6.   Declaration of Independence and name of " Massachusetts Grand Lodge " formally assumed.

1782–1784.   John Warren Grand Master of Massachusetts Grand Lodge.

1784–1787.   Joseph Webb Grand Master of Massachusetts Grand Lodge.

1787–1788.   John Warren Grand Master of Massachusetts Grand Lodge.

1788–1792.   Moses Michael Hayes, Grand Master of Mass. G. Lodge.

1792, March   Union of St. John's and Massachusetts Grand Lodges. — denominated The Grand Lodge of Massachusetts.

1792–1794.   JOHN CUTLER Grand Master of The Grand Lodge of Mass.

1794–1797.   Paul Revere   "   "   "   "

1797–1799.   Josiah Bartlett   "   "   "   "

1799–1802.   Samuel Dunn   "   "   "   "

1802–1805.   Isaiah Thomas   "   "   "   "

1805–1808.   Timothy Bigelow   "   "   "   "

1808–1809.   Isaiah Thomas   "   "   "   "

1809–1810.   Josiah Bartlett   "   "   "   "

1810–1813.   Timothy Bigelow   "   "   "   "

1813–1816.   Benjamin Russell   "   "   "   "

1816–1819.   Francis J. Oliver   "   "   "   "

1819–1820.   Samuel P. P. Fay   "   "   "   "

1820–1823   John Dixwell   "   "   "   "

1823–1826.   John Abbott   "   "   "   "

1826–1829.   John Soley   "   "   "   "

1829–1832.   Joseph Jenkins   "   "   "   "

1832–1833.   Elijah Crane   "   "   "   "

1833–1834.   John Abbott   "   "   "   "

1834–1837.   Joshua B. Flint   "   "   "   "

1837–1840.   Paul Dean   "   "   "   "

1840–1842.   Caleb Butler   "   "   "   "

1842–1845.   Augustus Peabody   "   "   "   "

1845–1848.   S. W. Robinson   "   "   "   "

1848–1851.   E. A. Raymond   "   "   "   "

1851–1854.   G. M. Randall   "   "   "   "

1854–1856.   Winslow Lewis   "   "   "   "

1856–1859.   John T. Heard   "   "   "   "

1859–1860.   Winslow Lewis   "   "   "   "

1860–1862.   Wm. D. Coolidge   "   "   "   "

1862–1865.   William Parkman   "   "   "   "

1865–1868.   Charles C. Dame   "   "   "

1868. —   W. S. Gardner   "   "   "

FINIS.

Here is an end, really without a conclusion: The secretary's records and the Treasurer's archives, were only taken in hand a little while by the committee, and are now handed back for further records, from time to time, and for more collections in the archives, — it is to be hoped for as long as time shall last, and the true spirit of Masonry shall quicken the hearts of men. Even this episode upon " St. Andrew's," with its Masonic incidents here and there, which has been called a Centennial Memorial, is, after all, only a waif, a tiny leaflet from the long story of this ancient Order, — the wit of man running not back surely to the time when it began. Besides, nothing near as much has been told, as might have been told, if all had been written out; so that it is not even a history of a single Lodge. Indeed, the sum of the matter is, that a solitary craft christened Saint Andrew, set out in the mighty current of human affairs, more than One Hundred Years ago, with a bold push, where the stream ran through a hemisphere, and has got so far safe and sound, and made a reckoning: that's all! with such circumstance of hap and mishap as these pages have told. Of some things, " St. Andrew's " is proud; there may be other things of which it ought not to be proud, — the Brother members a hundred years hence shall judge. Now, one by one of its good Masters and Mates, its first-class men and all who stood watch, piloting the good craft along the mighty current, have dropped off, and they are still dropping off, and by and by every one who is now left for this sort of holiday memorial-muster will have dropped off too, so that verily the time must come when this pleasant venture, christened as aforesaid, will surely be floated down stream into your hands. — Brethren of 1956! Then will you not pause, — as your Brethren did aforetime, — for another reckoning, in a second Centennial Memorial of the Lodge of St. Andrew?   So Mote It Be.

www.ingramcontent.com/pod-product-compliance
Lightning Source LLC
Chambersburg PA
CBHW021213270326
41929CB00010B/1114